AF445531

Other books by Greg Dorchak:

Of Pigs and Meteorites
Good Shit To Know About Being A Film Actor
How To Pull A Movie Out Of Your Ass
Who Took My Crayons?!
Where Monsters Go When You Grow Up

THREE SCREENPLAYS
by Greg Dorchak

Baba Yaga

The Stone

Apocalypse... WHEN?

Class Clown Publishing
Austin, Texas

Screenplays, by their nature,
are both short stories and novels.
One... on the page,
the other... in the mind.

For my Grandfather,
my first and biggest
influence in this business.

Contents

Three Screenplays
by Greg Dorchak

BABA YAGA
G. DORCHAK '91

BABA YAGA

Baba Yaga will always be one of my favorite scripts, not just because it is an homage to part of my family history, but also because it was the first screenplay I ever wrote.

Back in the winter of 1993, I had gotten my first home computer - an Apple Macintosh - the original box version with the 8 inch square screen. I liberated it from a former employer who was trying to stiff me on pay for the past month work. This guy was a real treat, bi-polar for real, often decided not to take his meds, always ready for a verbal fight, EVERYTHING was a conflict for him. When he announced he wasn't going to pay me (just because apparently he didn't want to) for the month - a month that culminated in Christmas - I got up, grabbed my bag, went into the other room unplugged the computer system, stuck it under one arm, looked him in the eye and said "fuck you."

A month or so later I got a bug up my ass to write a screenplay, and I knew what it was going to be. I was unemployed at the time, so after I would walk the kids to school in the morning, I sat my butt down and started typing. Four days later I had a first draft.

Over the course of the next few months I would polish it up, let it sit for a week or so, come back to it, give it another once-over, tweak it here and there, and repeat. When I finally had it "finished," I had no idea what to do with it.

I should have mentioned, at the time, I had absolutely no training as a screenwriter, and not Clue One about that aspect of the industry. The Austin Film Festival was about to start, and I had missed the submission deadline by months, but as soon as I was able, I submitted the next year.

I still remember getting the letterhead notice in the mail months later saying I had placed as a semi-finalist, and as such, I earned a free pass into the festival. I was ecstatic, I started planning as soon as the lineup was available - what panels I would sit in on, who I would try to get the script to, etc etc.

What blissful ignorance.

Austin Film Festival was a blast, I met a lot of great folks, some famous folks, some nice folks and some absolute dickheads - I got a fantastic introduction into the world... and I was hooked.

I was able to get a meeting with this production company from out in LA, they expressed interest in Baba Yaga, they were very excited about it. Dave gave me his personal phone number and told me to call him the Monday after AFF was over and he was back in the office. I did, we planned meetings, had some phone meetings, Dave's ProdCo was drooling, and it looked like I was on the way.

Until I called him back a week or so later. The new woman on the phone, asked who I wanted to speak to, she informed me that Dave no longer worked there, and she never heard of me.

The education continued, this time it was about hostile take-overs, and what happens when a production company gets obliter-ated from one day to the next by a vengeful former employee. I never heard From Dave again, and Baba Yaga went back onto the market. It won a few first place awards, a few more semi's, and I even got it into the hands of a guy who tried to get it to Terry Gilliam. But clearly - it never saw the light of screen.

It's still my favorite, and I hope you dig the story too.

FADE IN

EXT. WOODS - EVENING

SUPER: VAKYUST, RUSSIA. A LONG TIME AGO.

VLADIMIR BOSHEKOV (8), a thin, frightened young boy
with a shock of blond hair, walks through the trees
nervously glancing over his shoulder.

MOONLIGHT plays on him through the net of leaves and
branches overhead. He hears a NOISE and stops dead.

                         VLAD

          Im...Imya?

An OWL hoots loudly from close by. The loud SNAPPING of
a branch startles the boy. He starts to walk fast.

                         VLAD

          Imya? Is that you?

A mocking, whispering VOICE is heard from the dark.

                         VOICE

          Is that you

The boy starts to walk quicker and quicker, then starts
to run.

                         VLAD

          Sister! Where are you?

Again the menacing voice is heard in echo

> VOICE
>
> Where are you

The boy is running as fast as he can now. The branches whip at him. Moonlit SHADOWS start to move about as if something is criss-crossing the woods around him.

> VLAD
>
> I... I'm not afraid. Hear me? Vladimir Boshekov is not afraid.

He runs a bit farther and stops. He sees LIGHT through the trees and the shadowy shape of a small BUILDING.

The voice whispers again, louder.

> VOICE
>
> Not afraid... You should be.

The boy starts to run toward the light as

A HAND darts out from the shadows and grabs him, pulling him back into the darkness.

A frightened HOWL from the boy melts into an owl's hooting.

EXT. SMITHY - NIGHT

The building Vlad saw has light spilling from the window and open doors. The SOUND of hammer on iron rings out a few times, then stops.

A FIGURE appears at the doorway to the building. It is a large, powerfully built man with a really bad hair cut and a huge hammer in one hand, he is IVOR PETROSHENKO (30's), the blacksmith.

He looks out into the woods as a large OWL glides silently from the top of a tree and lands on something in the field.

> PETROSHENKO
>
> Bah!

He turns and heads back into the smithy out of view.

A second later he peeks back around the doorway out into the night, then draws the DOORS closed.

INT. SMITHY - LATER THAT EVENING

Petroshenko is hard at work as PIOTR FETNIK (30's) enters from a side door and rushes to him.

Fetnik is of a much slighter build, and he looks intelligent. It appears as though he has dressed in a hurry.

> FETNIK

Ivor! Ivor Petroshenko, have you heard?

The smith keeps working and does not adopt his guest's urgency.

> PETROSHENKO

Hear what, Piotr Fetnik? Did you finally win your seat on the Council today?

> FETNIK

I lost by three votes to the well-digger. Again.

> PETROSHENKO

I'm sorry, my friend, maybe next time, eh? What then?

> FETNIK

The Baron's son has been abducted. It's her again.

Fetnik leans on the work table next to the forge, then pulls his hand back quickly.

> FETNIK

Aaah! Blast this shop, Ivor Petroshenko. The Devil himself would burn his hand in here.

> PETROSHENKO

If the Devil were in my smithy, Fetnik, I would smash him with my hammer.

> FETNIK

Why does that not surprise me?

Fetnik watches the blacksmith for a moment, then realizes a response is not coming.

> FETNIK

The Baron is gathering the village to search. We must help.

                    PETROSHENKO

     His son is of no concern to me. The
     spoiled young beast.

                      FETNIK

     That spoiled beast is the third to dis-
     appear in as many months. They had all
     been playing in the woods near her
     shack. We know...

Petroshenko stops pounding and picks up the iron with
tongs and dips it into a bucket of water. A hissing jet
of steam shoots forth.

                    PETROSHENKO

     Let the wealthy Baron buy his way out
     of this problem, Piotr. I have work to
     finish.

                      FETNIK

You'll not help?

                    PETROSHENKO

     If the boy has gotten himself lost and
     into trouble with a wolf, first: I pity
     the wolf. And second: he deserves it. He
     is not my child.

Fetnik backs up and turns slowly to leave.

                      FETNIK

     I pray you never have a child in that
     predicament, Ivor.

He stops and stares up at a hideous IRON MASK with
jagged teeth and chains hanging from it on the wall
behind the bellows.

                      FETNIK

     Perhaps if you put aside your anger at
     the Baron for not giving you his daugh-
     ter's hand, you would have children some
     day. And you would understand.

Fetnik starts to walk away slowly.

Ivor shoves the piece he was working on back into the
coals of the forge and starts to work the bellows, then
stops.

                    PETROSHENKO

       His daughter? Yes. Wait, Fetnik.

He turns abruptly and whacks his forehead with a loud,
hollow "thunk" into some large chuck of metal hanging
from a beam. He doesn't even notice.

                    PETROSHENKO

       I'll help. Where is his daughter?

Fetnik stares at his friend and the wild look in his
eye. He starts to chuckle.

                    FETNIK

       "Son," Ivor, "son."

                    PETROSHENKO

       Right.

Petroshenko and Fetnik hurry out into the night.

EXT. VILLAGE OF VAKYUST - NIGHT

An angry mob of 20-30 villagers with torches,
pitchforks, ropes, etc. congregates behind Petroshenko
and Fetnik, who stand before a seated figure.

GRIGOR BOSHEKOV (70's), the aged leader of the village
sits in an ornate wooden sedan chair. One hand twitches
and trembles.

                    FETNIK

          We are certain now, Lord; Stanislaus'
          dogs have brought back pieces of cloth-
          ing. She no longer just steals our live-
          stock to satisfy her hunger.

                    PETROSHENKO

          I'll put an end to the evil hag, Grigor
          Boshekov, and I'll bring back your son
          before the next dawn is upon me.

Grigor Boshekov glances up at his daughter, IMYA (20).
She stands by her father's side, trying to steady his
palsied his hand in hers.

                    BOSHEKOV

          You go by yourself, blacksmith? You're
          indeed a brave man. I'll send these
          foolish villagers home then, yes?

Petroshenko thinks nervously, he turns and eyes the
villagers.

                    PETROSHENKO

          What I mean, Grigor Boshekov, is that
          I'll lead them, just as I know you
          would, had time not so ravaged you.

Boshekov shifts uneasily in his seat. He makes a face
and his words come out through clenched teeth.

                    BOSHEKOV

          Bring my son back here in one piece,
          blacksmith. And whatever you do...

His voice returns to normal, tired

                    BOSHEKOV

          ...make sure She is dead. If not, I'll
          have your head.

                    PETROSHENKO

          Yes, Grigor Boshekov.

                    BOSHEKOV

          And to make sure the odds are a little
          more even, Petroshenko, I send with you
          Huishka, my loyal friend and sorcerer.

HUISHKA, a robed figure enters from the side. He is a
tall, thin, dark-skinned man who speaks in a cold,
detached manner.

                    HUISHKA

          You send me with a blacksmith who is
          little smarter than a squirrel and a
          small army of loud, angry villagers,
          Grigor? She will hear us from three
          miles away.

                    BOSHEKOV

          (whispering)

          The blacksmith is strong, but not
          bright, Huishka.

Boshekov and Huishka eye Petroshenko.

Petroshenko swats at a FLY buzzing about his head. The
fly lites on his forehead.

Petroshenko swings up his HAMMER hand and whacks the fly
with the hammer.

He goes cross-eyed a moment, then shakes it off.

                         BOSHEKOV

          He will need your help. I beg of you, it
          is my only son.

                         HUISHKA

          (a beat)

          I will go with him, but I will not
          answer to him.

                         BOSHEKOV

          Thank you.

He turns toward Petroshenko

          Now go, blacksmith, brave comrades, be
          stout of heart.

                         PETROSHENKO

          We have the Saucer to help us. We will
          be victorious.

                         HUISHKA

          Sorcerer.

He draws close to Petroshenko

                         HUISHKA

          And if I live not through the night,
          I'll return someday, and I'll find you,
          and I'll make you feel what the iron you
          pound feels in the forge.

Petroshenko flinches, then shakes it off, turning and
heading toward the woods.

                         PETROSHENKO

          To the Hag.

The villagers get into proper angry mob form and head
after the blacksmith.

Imya turns to her father.

                         IMYA

          What if he doesn't return, father?

                    BOSHEKOV

    I care not about the blacksmith, my
    daughter, I only want your brother back.

    (nervously)

    Besides, if he does not return, you...
    will not be obliged... to marry him.

                    IMYA

    Father, how could you? I can not live
    with that man, he... he is so... dumb.

The old man waves dissmissively.

                    BOSHEKOV

    It was either that or have to lead the
    village myself. And as much as I wish I
    could, my dear, he is right.

He holds up his trembling hand and looks at it with
disgust.

                    BOSHEKOV

    I'm too old and frail. Petroshenko is
    strong, the people feel safe behind him.
    Huishka will see to it that the witch
    doesn't harm Vladimir.

They look to the mob, which disappears into the woods.

EXT. THE WOODS - NIGHT

The villagers tramp through woods. They have six dogs,
held by chains, who bark as a man struggles to restrain
them.

EXT. BABA YAGA'S SHACK - NIGHT

Light emanates from the open windows, small pleas of
"help" and "mercy" are heard from inside. There is a
loud crash, a whimper, and muffled cackling.

EXT. WOODS - NIGHT

The blacksmith turns to Huishka.

                    PETROSHENKO

    Are you ready?

                    HUISHKA

    Yes.

PETROSHENKO

Hey, there…

He motions to a man with dogs straining on leashes

PETROSHENKO

…Stanislaus, let them go.

STANISLAUS (40's), a short, heavy man, lets the dogs smell a rag. They bark wildly as he unchains them, and they head off at a tear into the woods.

Petroshenko turns toward the mob and raises his hand.

PETROSHENKO

Remember, free the Baron's son first,
then we can deal with Baba Yaga. She
is ours.

HUISHKA

It is not done until it is done.

PETROSHENKO

Are you scared, wealthy man's lackey?
Are you afraid of real work? Well
I'm not.

HUISHKA

You should be, blacksmith.

Petroshenko looks at Huishka for a moment, then glances back at the mob.

PETROSHENKO

Bah. Onward!

The mob presses on.

EXT. BABA YAGA'S SHACK - NIGHT

Pots and glass crash and break inside. Wicked cackling and cursing is heard.

INT. SHACK - NIGHT

It is a small, dirty, one room dwelling. A large fireplace on the opposite wall from the front door has a fire going in it. A large iron CAULDRON, with ornately carved animal's legs, boils madly.

An old rickety LOOM takes up another wall, with spools of thread and yarn stacked around it. A large iron CAGE hangs from the ceiling in one corner.

BABA YAGA, an old, shaggy woman with bony legs chases
Vladimir Boshekov around the tables and piles of
standard evil witch things.

She stops, winded, and bends over, hands on her knees,
with labored breathing.

>BABA YAGA

You're just prolonging the inevitable,
boy. You can't... outrun me...forever.

Her stomach rumbles loudly.

>BABA YAGA

I hope.

A large, skinny, white FERRET watches from the top of
a bookcase. A bony DOG sits by the fire listening, its
ears prick up and it bays.

Baba Yaga gives a limping chase for a moment more, then
stops and turns her one good eye to the dog.

>BABA YAGA

What is it, Sooka?

Then the mob's barking dogs is heard in the distance,
getting closer.

>BABA YAGA

Eh? Wolves? No, Sooka, you have cousins
coming.

Vladimir crouches behind a barrel in the corner,
beneath the hissing ferret, he is breathing hard and
has cuts and scratches on his face and arms.

Baba Yaga turns, trying to find him with her good eye.

>BABA YAGA

Where are you, boy? Come, let an old
woman eat her last meal, won't you? Boy!

>VLAD

I hope they torture you for seven days,
you old hag. I hope they hang you a hun-
dred times.

>BABA YAGA

I pray they only try to hang me. Anything but the pyre of enchanted wood
will do little more than irritate me.

                    VLAD

    Then I hope they burn you alive.

She again turns toward his voice.

                  BABA YAGA

    They don't hate the lion for eating the
    goat, eh, do they boy? They don't con-
    demn the bear for eating the fish, eh,
    boy?

The barking gets closer, she licks her lips, getting
impatient.

                  BABA YAGA

    I'm no different than that. I need to
    eat. Boy.

EXT. SHACK - NIGHT

The mob closes in on the small clearing where Baba Yaga
lives. Over Petroshenko's shoulder, the lights of the
shack are visible through trees and shrubs.

                 PETROSHENKO

    There it is. She is ahead of us, spread
    out, surround her. Bring her to me.

A small group of men rushes out into the clearing.

INT. SHACK - NIGHT

Baba Yaga inches her way around the big oak table in
the center of the room, her hand rests on a large
wooden spoon. She tightens her hand around it.

She hears the dogs getting closer, voices are becoming
audible now.

                  BABA YAGA

    They come for us, boy? Not for the same
    reasons, though, eh? Where are you, lit-
    tle lamb? Come out, I want to apologize,
    now my time is at hand.

                  VLADIMIR

    You can't trick me, my father has sent
    an army from the village. I'll come out
    after they take your apology.

> BABA YAGA
>
>> (shrugging)
>
>> Well, what can you do, eh? Korosho.
>> Good. I'll go apologize to them.

Baba Yaga turns to the door and starts to chant in a low, guttural voice. Her hands start to glow, she raises them above her head.

EXT. SHACK - NIGHT

The dogs come to a dead halt from their headlong charge. They balk at entering the shack, they whimper and start to turn back.

INT. SHACK - NIGHT

An eerie greenish-yellow ball appears between Baba Yaga's outstretched hands.

> BABA YAGA
>
>> Come, good people, come.

Vladamir becomes nervous behind the barrel, he hesitates a few beats, then runs to an open window.

> BOY
>
>> Help! I'm here. Hurry!

Baba Yaga turns to the boy, an evil grin creeps onto her face, she drools.

> BABA YAGA
>
>> So, there you are, malchick. Stay there until I'm finished, won't you?

> BOY
>
>> No!

He jumps through the window and runs.

Baba Yaga cackles, kicks open the front door. The wooden spoon in her right hand glows red, she raises it and throws it at Vladimir.

> BABA YAGA
>
>> Hold him, Zemeya.

The spoon morphs into a huge ALBINO PYTHON in mid-air. As it reaches Vladimir, it coils around both the boy and a small tree, binding him securely.

Vladimir yelps as the snake's coils slither tighter.

The first group of villagers enters the small clearing, they see the boy and the witch.

PETROSHENKO

Go comrades.

The villagers hesitate at first, then charge.

Fetnik and two others head for the boy, several more head for Baba Yaga.

She now bobs the green-yellow ball in her left hand, she throws it at the approaching group.

BABA YAGA

Catch!

The glowing ball hits the villagers and explodes, most of them fall.

The second wave of the mob bursts through the woods, led by Petroshenko and Huishka.

PETROSHENKO

Now, blast you, Sorcerer. Now!

Huishka raises hands, palms facing down, and mutters. A dark, swirling disc with glowing edges appears at his feet.

HUISHKA

Stand back, do not touch the Ysparatnaya Vortex. When I say, throw Baba Yaga into it. She will vaporize, and the earth will soak her up.

PETROSHENKO

Not before I make sure she eats no more children.

Petroshenko jams his hand into a sack at his hip and pulls out the iron MASK from his smithy.

HUISHKA

Don't be foolish, blacksmith, that is not needed.

PETROSHENKO

(to mob)

Avoid the sorcerer's...

He motions at the portal, can't remember its name.

                    PETROSHENKO

          ..."hole", seize her.

Fetnik tries to pry the snake from around the tree as
the boy groans.

A dozen more attack Baba Yaga, who raises her HANDS
over her head, whirling them about.

The villagers hesitate, eyeing her unsurely.

She meets their gaze a moment, then lowers her hands
and shrugs, grinning sheepishly.

                    BABA YAGA

          You got me, comrades. That fireball and
          the snake are the only good tricks I
          know, curse me.

          (loudly)

          To my side worthless animals. Earn your
          keep.

The villagers move in just as the animals - chickens,
the dog and ferret, a draft horse and two oxen - charge
from behind the shack.

The livestock attacks the mob, scratching, pecking,
biting and stomping.

Petroshenko batters at the beasts aside with his
hammer.

                    HUISHKA

          Hurry, the portal is nearly ready.

                    PETROSHENKO

          Gradiska, Kazmenski, Vaddik! Take care
          of the oxen and horse. The rest of you
          grab her.

The appointed men start to subdue the oxen and draft
horse with ropes and pitchforks. The remaining people
grab at Baba Yaga.

The first ones to touch her are savagely BITTEN. Their
wounds STEAM and HISS, oozing BLOOD and GOO.

Finally, enough villagers grab hold of the witch and
keep her arms, legs and head from moving.

HUISHKA

The portal is at its strongest, she must
be thrown in now!

Petroshenko ignores Huishka, and instead turns to Baba
Yaga.

PETROSHENKO

You'll never again eat our children,
old hag. Let's see how you like iron instead, eh?

HUISHKA

That is not needed, you waste valuable
time.

The blacksmith fastens the iron face-piece around her
head and pounds the bolts shut. Then he fastens the
shackles to her hands and feet.

PETROSHENKO

Pick her up, take her to the hole.

The villagers drag her toward the sorcerer.

Baba Yaga sees the portal and a look of fearful
understanding crosses her face.

Her eyes grow wide with terror and she starts to
struggle harder, whipping the chains wildly at her
captors.

PETROSHENKO

Hold fast, you fools.

Beads of sweat appear on Huishka's brow from trying to
maintain the portal.

HUISHKA

You are the fool, blacksmith. I cannot
keep this power under control for much
longer, throw her in before it takes
us all.

PETROSHENKO

Yes!
(motions to mob)
Throw her in.

Baba Yaga thrashes about, knocking many villagers down.

The group of them dances around the edge of the portal,
which is glowing stronger now and starting to pull at
its surroundings with a powerful vacuum.

                         HUISHKA

          Make haste.

A funnel appears in the center of the portal and
electricity crackles throughout it.

Baba Yaga wrenches free from her final captor and turns
to run, but she comes face-to-face with Huishka.

Her eyes grow wider yet, a muffled scream emits from the
mask she wears. Her clawed hands grab at the ROBES of
Huishka.

                         HUISHKA

          Blacksmith!

Petroshenko whirls from one of his fallen comrades and
runs up behind Baba Yaga. He raises his hammer with
both hands.

                        PETROSHENKO

          Basta! Your time is now.

He brings the hammer down full force on the back of
Baba Yaga's head, there is a loud clang of hammer
on iron.

Baba Yaga pitches forward into Huishka, and they get
tangled in the iron chains and robes.

                         HUISHKA

          No! She takes me with her.

The two stumble and fall onto the edge of the portal
and start to slowly dissolve into it.

The portal has started to suck in unconscious villagers
and any loose debris. Their bodies start to swirl with
the darkness.

                        PETROSHENKO

          Small price to pay to rid the land of
          Baba Yaga, magic-man.

Baba Yaga spins to face the blacksmith, as he raises
his hammer again, she claws at his face, SCRATCHING her
fingers into his CHEEK.

                    PETROSHENKO

          Do-sfidanya.

His hammer smashes her forehead.

As strong as he is, her head splits open only very
little, emitting a green OOZE as she pitches back into
the sucking portal and disappears into its depths.

Huishka claws frantically at the edge of the portal.

                     HUISHKA

          Help me, I have to reverse the portal's
          powers.

Petroshenko looks back toward the villagers who
are still trying to free the boy. He sneers at the
magician.

                    PETROSHENKO

          As Boshekov said. I must save his son
          first.

                     HUISHKA

          If I don't reverse the portal's affects,
          there will be no son to save.

                    PETROSHENKO

          If you are still here, I will come back
          for you.

Petroshenko drives a PITCHFORK into the ground near
the sorcerer, who grabs the tines as the portal draws
him in.

One of Huishka's hands grabs Petroshenko's sleeve.

                     HUISHKA

          (snarling)

          No - I'll be back for you, Blacksmith.

Their eyes lock onto each other, then Petroshenko yanks
free, slapping away Huiska's hand. He runs to help with
Vladimir.

The snake's coils grab Petroshenko and Fetnik as the
portal sucks the other two men into it from across
the clearing.

Huishka tries to chant the reverse spell and the portal
starts to sporadically heave.

Petroshenko, Vladimir, and Fetnik struggle. They watch as the animals and the house are sucked toward the portal.

Huishka's fingers slip from the tines.

The portal HEAVES with one last great effort. The sorcerer screams as he is finally whisked in.

                    HUISHKA

          I... will... be... ba...

His voice fluctuates as the portal SWELLS outward momentarily, then is sucked back into the earth.

The house and everything else loose in the clearing, loudly crashes into it as it collapses with a great WHOOSH of air and crackling of electricity.

Soon, all that shows is a blackened CIRCLE on the ground.

Seconds later Baba Yaga's huge iron CAULDRON lands opening down to cover the spot.

As the smoke clears from around the cauldron, the python crackles with electrical energy and returns to a wooden spoon and falls.

The three captives drop to the ground. Nothing loose remains in the clearing except the cauldron, the spoon and them.

                    PETROSHENKO

          Bozhe Moye.

                    FETNIK

          She is gone? Yes? No? Eh, did we pre-
          vail?

                    PETROSHENKO

          (unsure)

          Yes. She is gone, we have defeated her.
          I've saved the Baron's son, and all of
          our children for years to come.

                    FETNIK

          You? You have killed almost half the
          village because you did not listen to
          the sorcerer.

Fetnik looks at the boy, who has fainted.

And Boshekov's son is now dead.

Petroshenko grabs Fetnik and pulls him close.

                    PETROSHENKO

        No, comrade. I'm a hero. Imya will now
        be my wife.

He thinks a little, then relaxes his grip on the man.

        You, too, Fetnik. You and I will be
        showered with thanks, and wealth. Eh?
        Eh? WE...

He points himself and Fetnik.

        ...are heroes.

He lets go of Fetnik and drops him.

                    PETROSHENKO

        Or WE killed half the village.

Fetnik thinks, and decides being a hero beats the hell
out of being tortured and having your head removed.

                    FETNIK

        Yes. Yes, Petroshenko, we are heroes.

He looks nervously toward the cauldron.

        I really hope we are.

Petroshenko looks to cauldron also, waves his hand in a
dismissive manner.

                    PETROSHENKO

        Bah! She is gone, and so is anyone who
        can denounce us. And look, the boy
        lives.

Vladimir coughs and stirs, Fetnik and Petroshenko help
him to his feet. He looks up at the two with tired eyes
and sobs.

The three walk through the trees as the sun comes up
and light streams into the small clearing and touches
the cauldron.

EXT. VAKYUST - DAY

SUPER: TWENTY-ONE YEARS LATER

The village is busy, people going about their daily
chores and jobs.

The hammering of the blacksmith's shop can be heard in the background.

Children run here and there.

INT. SMITHY - DAY

Petroshenko, hair now graying, tries to teach his young son IVOR (8), messy hair and friendly face, the finer points of being a blacksmith. Ivor does not care and is not particularly adept.

> PETROSHENKO
>
> No, no, Ivor. Strait up and down. Hard, like this.
>
> (he pounds)
>
> You must work quickly, or the iron will cool while it waits for you to make up your mind to kiss it or hammer it. BAH, you'll never be like you older brothers.

> IVOR
>
> Father, I don't like this work. I want to be an explorer, like Dedooshka Boshekov.

> PETROSHENKO
>
> Bah! Your head is too filled with idiotic dreams to work iron, son. Perhaps I could find you a nice piece of sack-cloth, eh?

Petroshenko sticks the iron back into the forge, pumps the bellows, then turns back to his son.

> PETROSHENKO
>
> Ivor, where is there to explore, eh? Everywhere is found already.

> IVOR
>
> What do you mean, papa? Look...

Ivor points out of barn and gestures.

> IVOR
>
> Everywhere is to explore. Like Dedooshka Boshekov, and Dyadya Vlad.

                    PETROSHENKO

        Grandpa Boshekov is exploring only his
        grave in the meadow, Ivor.

        (his mood changes)

        And Uncle Vlad is a Cossack.

A man's VOICE comes from doorway of barn.

                    MAN O.S.

        And what's wrong with that, dear
        brother?

Ivor and his father turn to see a tall, burly man,
well-dressed for the road, dismounting a horse just
outside the smithy.

It is Vladimir Boshekov, now into his thirties. He
enters with a swagger.

                    VLADIMIR

        Perhaps my nephew would like to ride
        with me today, yes, Ivor?

                    IVOR

        Oh, Papa, could I? Please?

                    PETROSHENKO

        No, Ivor. Go and play.

Ivor grumbles and leaves. Vladimir pats his head as he
shuffles out.

Vlad turns to Petroshenko.

                    VLADIMIR

        Do not push him so hard to follow you in
        life, my brother. My father pushed me,
        and now look.

He gestures to himself in a grand manner.

        I'm an evil Land Baron. The
        villagers hate me, yet they all look
        up to you, eh?

He picks up an ornate DOORKNOB and fumbles with it.

        The hero who still gives his work away
        because he cannot do simple math to
        charge them properly.

                    PETROSHENKO

      Do not call me your brother, Boshekov.
      I'm old enough to be your father.

                    VLADIMIR

      No, dear brother. In another twenty
      years you'll be old enough to have been
      my aged, twisted father. You marry my
      sister,

      (he shrugs)

      ...you're my brother.

                    PETROSHENKO

      Had I known what you would turn out
      like, Vladimir Grigorovich, I would not
      have rescued you.

                    VLADIMIR

      Had I known what you were like, I'd have
      let Baba Yaga eat me.

At the name of the witch, Petroshenko becomes agitated.

                    PETROSHENKO

      Do not call it back from its grave,
      foolish boy. I'll not save you again.

                    VLADIMIR

      What is to fear, dear brother? You and
      Council Fetnik destroyed the beast, did
      you not? We may yet find out the truth,
      eh?

                    PETROSHENKO

      Shut up!

Petroshenko tries to slap him, but Vlad grabs the arm
and holds it. It is difficult, but his face barely shows
it. His other hand grabs his sword hilt.

                    VLADIMIR

      You may be the smith, dear brother, and
      you may have my sister's hand. But if
      you ever try that again, I'll take your
      whole arm.

      (he lets go)

> Enough idle chat. I've come for Katkha's
> shoeing. I'll be back in a few hours.
> Good day, brother.

Vladimir exits.

Petroshenko looks to Katkha, Vlad's horse, then warily
looks about the barn.

He shakes off a chill down his spine and starts to
gather his shoeing tools.

EXT. BEHIND SMITHY - DAY

Ivor is playing with his best friend ILYA FETNIK.
Ilya is Ivor's age and height, and does not seem too
concerned about how he dresses.

They balance on a log at the edge of the woods.
Ivor sits.

> ILYA

> What is the matter, Ivor? Lessons
> again today?

> IVOR

Yes. Always with the hammering and bending and heating
and cooling. I hate my father.

> ILYA

> No you don't Ivor.

> IVOR

> No, I don't. But he is as dumb as the
> iron he pounds on, Ilya.

Ilya laughs and sits next to his friend

> ILYA

> I'll agree with you there, Sputnik. As
> will everyone in three counties.

Ilya laughs a little too much. Ivor punches his arm.

> IVOR

> Hey, that's my father.

> (he laughs)

> Ilya... he is so rigid. Why won't he let
> me do what I want?

                              ILYA

          Because maybe, he's been a blacksmith
          all his life, and his father, and his
          father. And maybe, my friend, he's
          afraid you won't be one.

                              IVOR

          That is as stupid as it is true, Ilya. I
          wish he was more like your father.

                              ILYA

          The honorable Piotr Fetnik, Acting Head
          Council? Bog save us all.

He does an exaggerated salute, laughs, and runs away
toward street.

          Come on, Sputnik, I'm in school and
          you're being trained for a boring trade
          - we'll run away, travel and explore
          the world.

He grabs up a stick and fences with an imaginary foe.

          Slay dragons, capture exotic animals,
          raid villages. We will come back as
          Tsars.

Ivor thinks a bit, shakes his head, then gets up and
runs after him.

                              IVOR

          And we'll sleep tonight with switch
          marks on our backsides.

                              ILYA

          Whatever.

They run off toward the woods.

EXT. STOREFRONT - SAME TIME

Vladimir exits a shop with a BUNDLE. He looks after the
boys as they run, and he smiles.

He turns away, but then turns back with a look of
concern on his face.

INT. PETROSHENKO'S HOUSE - DAY

IMYA, older, still confident, and MARUSIA (18), her
daughter, wash vegetables and prepare them for storage.

Marusia is a bright girl with a kind, intelligent face.

                    MARUSIA

     Mother, Ivor and Young Fetnik have been
     skipping classes and playing in the
     woods again.

                    IMYA

     Don't be a tattle-tale, Marusia.

                    MARUSIA

     They've been playing in those woods.
     Where Baba Yaga lives.

She turns and goes to the table and starts to tinker
with a CONTRAPTION. She loads a BEET, turns a crank,
and the machine PEELS the vegetable.

                    IMYA

     You know your father doesn't like that
     name spoken in this house.

She looks at the contraption in amazement, forgets what
she was saying for a minute.

     It works? You're such a clever girl,
     Marusia. You should make those and sell
     them in town.

                    MARUSIA

     Father won't let me. He says no man will
     marry a smart woman.

                    IMYA

     Your father forgets whom he married.

                    MARUSIA

     He is not bright, mother.

                    IMYA

     Hush. He is strong and a good provider.

     (a beat)

     And is easily confused by inanimate
     objects.

They laugh a bit, then get back to their work.

                    IMYA

     Anyway, I already know your Uncle is
     selling them for you in the city.

MARUSIA

Please don't tell father. He and Dyadya
already despise each other.

IMYA

Vladimir Grigorovich does not despise
your father. They simply don't get
along.

There is a knock at the door, Vlad's voice comes from
the other side

VLADIMIR

Imya, dear sister, are you home?

IMYA

Yes, come in.

Vlad enters and sweeps Marusia up in a great hug. She
kisses him on both cheeks. He then goes to Imya and
they hug and kiss.

MARUSIA

Uncle, are you home to stay?

VLADIMIR

No, Dyevooshka, just to rest a while. I
need to be in Moscow in a few weeks.

He spies the contraption on the table.

Oho! You've modified it. It looks more
compact. Good Job, Marusia.

He hands her the bundle.

VLADIMIR

Here, a new dress and beautiful scarves,
for the smartest, most beautiful girl in
all of Russia.

MARUSIA

Thank you.

Marusia smiles and takes the bundle to her room; Vlad
fiddles with the peeler.

IMYA

Don't let her father find out about you
helping her.

                    VLADIMIR

He doesn't frighten me. Your daughter
has a great gift.

                    IMYA

I know, she takes after you.

                    VLADIMIR

No, sister. She mirrors you.
As does Ivor.

(a beat)

He and his friend are off to no good
again, by the way.

                    IMYA

I know. Fetch them later, won't you?

                    VLADIMIR

Certainly, I'll have some fun with them
first, though, eh?

Marusia re-enters from her room wearing a new red scarf
on her head.

                    MARUSIA

Yes. Scare some hair onto their bare,
sunken chests.

                    IMYA

Marusia.

(turns to Vlad)

First you have some tea and crullers. It
has been months since we've seen you.
Tell us what you've been up to.

                    VLADIMIR

Very well, I'll stay a while.

He sits, looks at Marusia wearing her scarf.

        Ah, that kerchief's beauty in the store
        pales in comparison to you when you wear
        it, niece.

                    MARUSIA

Thank you, Uncle. But I would give up
both the kerchief and beauty to spend
time with you and hear your stories.

                         VLADIMIR

          And so kind. Anyway, when I left last
          Fall, I was out on that hunting trip,
          the one where tigers ate our guides.

                         MARUSIA

          Really. What happened?

Vladimir's voice trails off as he tells the tale.

EXT. WOODS - DAY

Ivor and Ilya climb on rocks and over fallen trees.
They spy a DEER, it has a jagged SCAR on its face, and
start to sneak up on it.

                          ILYA

          Look Ivor, a dragon. Let's capture it
          and ride it back to town, eh?

                          IVOR

          Why?

                          ILYA

          'Cause no one has yet.

                          IVOR

          And how do we do that?

                          ILYA

          I'll think of something.

                          IVOR

          Ah. Your father taxes the villagers, and
          you tax your brain.

                          ILYA

          Whatever.

Ilya heads in the direction of the deer. Ivor follows,
they make tactical gestures to each other and sneak
closer.

INT. BLACKSMITH SHOP - DAY

Petroshenko is working on Katkha. A heavier, bearded
Piotr Fetnik enters.

                         FETNIK

          Petroshenko, don't you ever leave this
          oven? Stop... we must talk.

PETROSHENKO

Piotr, what is it? I'm just finishing.

Fetnik eyes the available sitting areas, covered with spiky, iron objects.

FETNIK

No, I'll stand, thank you.

PETROSHENKO

As you wish.

He hammers a shoe while Fetnik speaks.

FETNIK

Francis Bartok lost another ox today in the woods. That is the fourth one this month, Ivor.

PETROSHENKO

So? I'm a blacksmith, Fetnik, not a oxen grower. Let Bartok mind his own animals.

He picks up the shoe in tongs, steps to the water.

FETNIK

He found it at the edge of the woods. It's throat ripped out.

PETROSHENKO

Wolf.

FETNIK

No. It would take a pack of them to bring a healthy ox down.

PETROSHENKO

Bear?

FETNIK

Very large one?

(shrugs)

Perhaps. Unlikely, though.

PETROSHENKO

I have neither the time nor the youth for games, dear friend. What was it then?

A beat

> FETNIK

Her.

Petroshenko dips the hot shoe in the water, a cloud of
steam spews forth. He shoots Fetnik a nervous glance.

> PETROSHENKO

You're getting forgetful in your old
age, Fetnik, she has been dead these
twenty years, twenty one almost.

> FETNIK

No, blacksmith. I think she has been
sleeping.

Petroshenko starts putting the last shoe on Katkha.
The discussion, a twenty-year-old one, escalates

> FETNIK

Listen to me. We never found out
for sure.

> PETROSHENKO

I saved the boy.

> FETNIK

You took too much time showing off your
handiwork that night; remember the mask?

He picks up chains from next to the forge and waves
them, they are hot, and he drops them. He puts his
fingers in his mouth.

> FETNIK

Ahhh! Cursed iron.

> PETROSHENKO

My work has burned you. It doesn't like
being spoken ill of.

> FETNIK

Your work may well have burned us all,
Petroshenko. I tell you, I do not like
the smell of the air these days.

> PETROSHENKO

Perhaps your mother-in-law comes
to visit?

FETNIK

>No, thank Bog, she is dead this
>last year.

He quickly makes the sign of the cross on his chest and
casts a glance skyward.

FETNIK

>(smiles, softens)

>Listen friend, I hope I only imagine,
>but I fear I do not. We did not do such
>a good job years ago, I think. And I
>think it comes back to plague us.

The blacksmith finishes on the hoof, straitens up.

PETROSHENKO

>I'm not afraid. You worry too much,
>think too much - that is the plague
>of smart people. You should be more
>like me.

Fetnik sighs in resignation. He leans against a beam.

FETNIK

>Perhaps I should.

>(a beat)

>Where is Ilya, he is with Ivor, no?

PETROSHENKO

>That is a wager you would make money on,
>Piotr. Those two stick together like
>good friends should, eh?

He looks at Fetnik with a sideways grin, sees the look
on his friend's face, and finally nods in contrition.

PETROSHENKO

>I'll go look at dead ox with you later.
>I finish here first.

He puts out his large, dirty hand. They shake.

FETNIK

>Yes, we'll go look at the ox.
>You'll see.

Fetnik turns to leave, stopping a moment as he exits
the smithy. He looks to the sky, sniffs, pulls his cloak
closer and hurries away into the street.

EXT. FOREST - DAY

The grazing deer doesn't notice, or is ignoring Ivor
and Ilya as they get closer.

                         ILYA

          Ready, Sputnik?

                         IVOR

          Yes.

                         ILYA

          One... two... three.

The two leap at the deer.

                     IVOR/ILYA

          Haha! Gotcha.

A FIGURE drops from out of a tree, landing between the
deer and boys. Spooked, the deer runs off.

The boys see the figure, large and shaggy, waving its
arms and cackling, they scream and head off deeper into
the woods.

The figure lingers for a second, cackling. The cackling
turns into the deep laughter of Vladimir. He pulls off
the MASK and FURS and laughs louder.

He takes his bow and sword from behind a tree and
follows after the boys.

EXT. WOODS - DAY

Ivor and Ilya are running, looking back occasionally.
They stumble through brush into a clearing.

EXT. WOODS - DAY

Vladimir runs, trying to keep up with the boys.

                       VLADIMIR

          Ivor! Fetnik! It's just me. Come back,
          you fearless adventurers. Give me an act
          of bravery to tell your families.

EXT. WOODS CLEARING - DAY

It is very quiet. Ivor and Ilya stand back-to-back and
look around.

The clearing is overgrown with coarse weeds everywhere
except for a blackened RING covered by Baba Yaga's

CAULDRON, now a little rusty and mossy, almost in the center.

EXT. WOODS - DAY

Vladimir starts to get uneasy, talking to himself.

> VLADIMIR
>
> Captain Boshekov, you are a lot more frightening than you thought.
>
> (aloud)
>
> Boys? Where are you?

He picks through the trees and brush.

EXT. WOODS CLEARING - DAY

Ivor and Ilya hesitantly spread out and explore the clearing, gravitating toward the cauldron.

Ilya spots something near a tree and goes to it. It is the huge wooden SPOON, matted down by old grass.

> ILYA
>
> Ivor Petroshenko. Look here. Treasure!

Ilya holds the spoon overhead.

> IVOR
>
> What is it, Fetnik?

He sees the spoon, looks back to the cauldron, then back to Ilya.

> IVOR
>
> Bozhe Moye. Fetnik, come here.

Ilya bounds to Ivor's side.

> ILYA
>
> What is it, Sputnik?

> IVOR
>
> This huge pot, that spoon. This is where it happened.

> ILYA
>
> Eh? What?

He looks at the cauldron then at the spoon. His eyes widen.

                    ILYA

          You're right, Ivor. Baba Yaga's grave.
          It was not just a story. It all really
          happened.

                    IVOR

          We shouldn't be here.

                    ILYA

          Whatever. She's dead.

Both boys freeze dead in their tracks and listen
intently at a far-off CALLING.

They sigh in relief as they realize it's Vladimir
shouting for them.

They look to the cauldron, then to each other and grin
mischievously.

EXT. WOODS - DAY

Vladimir hears a scream tear through the trees from the
clearing.

He unsheathes his sword and charges forward, crashing
through to the clearing.

It is empty save for the cauldron.

Vlad carefully walks forward, then, realizing where he
is, he gasps.

                    VLADIMIR

          No...it can not be.

A dull CLANG emanates from the cauldron,

Vladimir's head snaps in that direction.

He gasps again as another clang is heard.

He turns to leave as another clang is followed by a
spooky VOICE.

                    SPOOKY VOICE

          Vladimir Grigorovich. I've come back for
          you. Come here, boy. Come to me.

                    VLADIMIR

          B...b...but how? I saw y... y... you...

                    SPOOKY VOICE

          And I've been watching you, Vladimir
          Grigorovich,

(louder)

and now I'm going to finish you.

Ilya jumps up from behind the cauldron and SNARLS.

                    ILYA

Yaaaargh!

Vlad reels in terror, turns to run, Ivor jumps out from behind a bush.

                    IVOR

Yeearg!

Vladimir cringes, near tears as he seeks to escape. The two boys laugh, as Vladimir eventually realizes what has happened and calms down.

                    VLADIMIR

Why, you little Cossacks, you've ambushed me. I shall have your heads.

He grabs at them, they all laugh and fall to the ground.

                    ILYA

Oy! We got you good, Vladimir Grigorovich. You're as white as a winter in Minsk.

                    VLADIMIR

I guess I am, Ilya Fetnik. I should have expected such treachery from the son of a council member.

                    IVOR

We are even now, eh, Dyadya?

                    VLADIMIR

Yes, yes, we are even, I won't tell on you cowards, if you don't tell on me.

They each NOD a solemn deal to each other. Vladimir looks back at the cauldron.

                    VLADIMIR

But we must not stay here, this is a bad place.

> ILYA

What? You mean that old chunk of iron?
It's worthless.

> VLADIMIR

Not the iron, boy, but she who sleeps
under the iron. We dare not wake her.

> ILYA

Bah! I'm not afraid of her.

He jumps up and runs to cauldron, picks up the spoon
and raises it to strike.

> IVOR

Stop, you shouldn't play with such
things.

> ILYA

Wake up, old witch.

He BANGS on the cauldron with the spoon.

> Ha! Are you deaf?

> VLADIMIR

Basta! Stop that. Do not mock that
Devil.

> ILYA

Rise and shine, grandmother. You'll be
late for breakfast.

> IVOR

Stop it, Ilya. Stop it.

Ilya pounds for a moment longer.

Vlad grabs the spoon from him, Ilya shrieks and looks
off toward another noise.

> ILYA

> (pointing)

Bozhe Moye, it's her.

Ivor and Vlad snap in that direction, there is a
squirrel.

Ilya laughs.

> ILYA

Got you both.

Ivor and Vlad look at each other.

                    VLADIMIR

          (irritated)

          Yes. You did.

                      IVOR

          I guess some things skip a generation in
          the Fetnik home. Come on, Ilya, lets go.

                    VLADIMIR

          Ah, the son of the blacksmith is the
          voice of reason. It is a sad day for
          us all.

          (laughs)

          Come, Ilya, your parents will eat
          without you.

He puts his arm around the boys and they turn to leave.

Vlad's face is struck by a bony HAND and he falls
backward.

Ilya and Ivor look up from him and gasp.

                   ILYA/IVOR

          What...

Baba Yaga looms over them, much taller than before,
more menacing.

Her eye GLOWS green, her smile shows off jagged iron
TEETH. Her arms and legs have CHAINS coiled about them
that seem to be part of her.

She snarls, dripping thick green GOO.

                   BABA YAGA

          It seems I've missed breakfast already.
          Anyone for brunch?

The boys turn to run, but Baba Yaga grabs both into one
hand. They struggle, but she slaps them down to the
ground.

They stare up at her, terrified.

                   BABA YAGA

          So, little malchiks, I'll bet right
          about now you're wishing you had lis-
          tened to your parents, hmmm?

She smiles a toothy, evil smile as she glares down at them.

> BABA YAGA
>
> Now all I need is my fireplace and we're cookin'. Can't survive too much longer with only raw deer and oxen. House.

She calls out seemingly to no one in particular, then gestures with one hand, beckoning with her claw.

Soon a low RUMBLING can be heard, the whole clearing shakes.

From under the cauldron, the point of a ROOF emerges up from the earth. The two boys look on with terror and amazement.

Baba Yaga cackles.

Soon the entire SHACK pushes up through the ground and climbs out of the earth on huge CHICKEN LEGS.

> BABA YAGA
>
> Find a spot you like, I need my stove.

The shack CIRCLES around itself like a dog, then settles. It's DOORS and WINDOWS fly open and emit a dusty COUGH, a fire LIGHTS in the fireplace.

Baba Yaga grins at the two boys.

> BABA YAGA
>
> Two for dinner?

She cackles evilly, throwing her head back like a true villain in triumph.

INT. PETROSHENKO'S HOUSE - EARLY EVENING

Petroshenko washes his hands in a basin, Imya looks out window, she has a loaf of fresh-baked bread in a pan.

She turns from the window to Ivor.

Marusia is at the table, adjusting another contraption.

> IMYA
>
> Ivor and Young Fetnik are not back yet, and neither is Vlad.

Marusia takes the bread and puts the loaf in the contraption, which SLICES it up.

Petroshenko frowns in her direction.

PETROSHENKO

They are fine, they just lose themselves
in their idleness.

IMYA

But what of the bear that is killing
oxen? What if they meet up with it?

PETROSHENKO

A bear is not interested in two scrawny
boys, especially one who talks as much
as young Fetnik.

IMYA

What about Vlad?

PETROSHENKO

A bear is not interested in two scrawny
boys.

IMYA

Ivor Petroshenko, why do you hate
him so?

PETROSHENKO

Because he is bold and proud, and has no
respect.

He becomes angry while watching Marusia use her
invention.

PETROSHENKO

Stop that, Marusia. Use a knife.

Marusia looks up from her invention, then takes out the
sliced bread.

MARUSIA

Yes father.

She puts the bread on a plate, Imya pats her shoulder
and silently acknowledges the machine.

MARUSIA

Should I set the table for Dyadya Vlad,
mother?

IMYA

Yes, dear, he should be here any minute.

They start to set the table when the door flies open;
Vlad staggers in, bleeding.

He drops to the floor. Imya and Marusia rush to him.

> IMYA

Vladimir. What happened? Where are the
boys?

> MARUSIA

Dyadya Vlad. You're bleeding.

She runs to get a rag and water from the basin.
Petroshenko steps over him to get to table

> PETROSHENKO

You're late picking up your horse,
Vladimir Grigorovich. I do not run
a... a...

He motions in the air with his hand, searching for
the word.

> PETROSHENKO

Horse place.

> IMYA

Ivor! He is wounded.

> PETROSHENKO

He is faking. He tries to play with us.
I do not play, I...

> VLADIMIR

Shut up you stupid old man. It is Baba
Yaga. She has Ivor and Young Fetnik.

> PETROSHENKO

Bah! She is dead.

> VLAD

Could a dead woman do this?

Vlad pulls out the HILT of his sword, all but six
inches of the blade is gone, and it is TWISTED and
SCORED with teeth marks.

Petroshenko grabs it and examines it angrily. He
realizes the damage is real.

                    PETROSHENKO

Boshe Moye! Daughter, go and fetch Piotr
Fetnik, now.

                     MARUSIA

Yes, father.

She exits quickly. Imya watches after her.

                    PETROSHENKO

Boshekov, how did this happen. Where are
the children?

Imya helps Vladimir to his feet and into a chair.

                      VLAD

In the same clearing we last saw
twenty-one years ago.

Petroshenko realizes the weight of the situation.

                    PETROSHENKO

Huishka failed us.

                      VLAD

It does not matter. We must act
quickly now.

                    PETROSHENKO

We'll wait for Fetnik. He and I will go.
Imya, you must get a group of villagers
together to follow us.

He crosses to a CABINET and throws open the door. The
shelves inside are lined with all manner of HAMMERS,
like a gun rack. He picks a large one.

                    PETROSHENKO

We have no magic this time, but I'll
wager she can still be smashed with a
hammer.

                      IMYA

Not every problem can be solved by
smashing with a hammer. We need to
think.

                    PETROSHENKO

You and Marusia think, woman, you're
good at it. I'll go smash.

> VLADIMIR

You haven't listened to me, Ivor. She is
stronger than you remember her.

He tries to rally, but falters and slumps into the
chair. Imya cleans the blood off his face.

The door flies open, Fetnik and Marusia enter.

> FETNIK

Where is my son, Blacksmith?

> PETROSHENKO

Baba Yaga has Ilya and Ivor. There is no
time to explain, we must go.

> MARUSIA

Papa, will they be okay? What do we do?

> PETROSHENKO

Fetnik and I have done this before, we
will get the boys and take care of her
properly this time.

> FETNIK

You idiot, your stupidity has cost us
our sons. I wish it were you instead.

> PETROSHENKO

You may tear me apart with your words
later, friend. We must go. Now!

> FETNIK

If anything happens to Ilya, I'll tear
you apart with more than my words.

> IMYA

Ivor, I'll come with you.

> PETROSHENKO

No, wife. We go alone. Fetnik, take an
ax from the forge.

They exit, Marusia gets water and cloth and goes to
Vlad. Imya pulls on her cloak.

> MARUSIA

Mother...

                    IMYA

     I know, daughter. Your father is rash
     and does not think. You're smart, help
     me think of a plan while your father and
     Council Fetnik buy us some time. I'll go
     tell Esmeralda Loblinka, the whole town
     will know in minutes.

                   MARUSIA

     Okay, mother. Be careful

                    IMYA

     Bar the door, Marusia.

She exits, Marusia bars the door. She stares at Vlad as
he stares at the floor.

EXT. WOODS - NIGHT

Petroshenko and Fetnik steal through the woods. Fetnik
has a heavy ax, Petroshenko has his hammer.

They get close to Baba Yaga's clearing, and can see the
shack just ahead.

As they sneak closer, the shack TURNS to watch them
with it's windows.

                   FETNIK

     What sorcery is this? The house.
     It's back... and it watches us.

                 PETROSHENKO

     Our eyes play tricks on us, Fetnik.

EXT. SHACK - NIGHT

Petroshenko and Fetnik sneak up to the front GATE,
flanking it.

Inside the shack can be heard CLATTERING and CACKLING,
and the two boys' CRYING.

                   FETNIK

     Thank Bog, we are not too late.

                 PETROSHENKO

     Quickly now, before she can prepare.

He raises hammer and moves to enter. Fetnik puts a hand
on his shoulder.

> **FETNIK**
>
> No, comrade. We must plan.
>
> **PETROSHENKO**
>
> Okay, we plan.
>
> **FETNIK**
>
> Korosho. Here is what...

Petroshenko stands abruptly and charges through
the front gate, which creaks noisily, and up onto
the porch.

INT. SHACK - IMMEDIATELY FOLLOWING

Petroshenko bursts into the shack and bangs his head
into a hanging cage in which the boys sit.

Baba Yaga whirls from her cauldron at the fire to
face him.

> **IVOR**
>
> Papa!
>
> **ILYA**
>
> Ivor Petroshenko.
>
> (a beat)
>
> Why do I not feel so safe?

Ivor jabs him with his elbow.

> **IVOR**
>
> Shut up, Ilya.
>
> **PETROSHENKO**
>
> Prepare to be sent back to your sleep,
> Hag.

Baba Yaga trains her good eye on her attacker, her gaze
wanders to the scar on his face.

> **BABA YAGA**
>
> Blacksmith? Yes, my sight is bad, but
> I see you.

Fetnik runs up behind Petroshenko, flustered.

> **BABA YAGA**
>
> You only bring one friend this time? Not
> too popular back in town, are we?

                    FETNIK

      We didn't want to endanger the lives of
      my constituents, we can handle you.

                   BABA YAGA

      An election year, is it dearie?

                  PETROSHENKO

      Enough talk, now is to die.

He charges at Baba Yaga, hammer raised.

She grabs his weapon-hand with one of hers and BITES
the head of his hammer in half with a loud metal-on-
metal rasp. She then bats Petroshenko across the room
with her other hand.

Fetnik's eyes grow wide and his jaw drops, but he
charges with the ax.

She raises a HAND, not touching him. Fetnik stops,
drops the ax and COLLAPSES to the floor in pain.

                    FETNIK

      Aah, my chest. Let go.

Fetnik passes out; Ivor gets to his feet and staggers
back at Baba Yaga.

Through his blurred vision, Baba Yaga's FACE seems to
shift and CHANGE from hers to Huishka's.

                   BABA YAGA

      (in Huishka's voice)

      "If I live not to see this morning,
      Blacksmith, I'll come back, I'll find
      you, and I'll make you feel what the
      iron you pound feels in the forge."

Petroshenko blinks and tries to focus. Baba Yaga's face
changes back again.

                  PETROSHENKO

      Hui... Huishka..?

                   BABA YAGA

      (as Baba Yaga)

      We got well-acquainted in the
      portal, blacksmith. All of us. We all
      were sucked in; I could feel the very

fiber of my soul being ripped from me.
Huishka started to reverse the spell
and we all started to come back
together. Only all the pieces got mixed
up, squished together.

She cocks her head to one side.

Am I being too technical for you?
Anyway, it makes for some very
interesting conversation, huh?

The big skinny ferret appears on a shelf above them,
it has a rooster's COMB on its head.

FERRET

Blacksmith! I'll get even with you.
Look at me. Not even a dog at... a lousy
ferret.

PETROSHENKO

Stanislaus? Is that you? I did not mean
for this to...

FERRET

I'll bet my cart's axle still isn't
finished yet, either. You're the slowest
blacksmith in three counties.

PETROSHENKO

Don't mock me, hunter. It was I who kept
your family safe from this beast for
twenty years now.

BABA YAGA

You like to crow so much about yourself,
eh, blacksmith?

She waves a hand at Petroshenko, he starts to glow and
shrink and change until he is a rather large ROOSTER.

PETROSHENKO

What are you doing to me witch? Aargh!
I'm a duck.

FERRET

You are not bright. I thought it was
an act.

                    BABA YAGA

    And your friend the councilman thinks
    he is so sharp.

She waves at Fetnik on the floor. He, too, glows,
shrinks and changes until he is a large HEDGEHOG.
He stirs.

                      IVOR

    Papa! Oh, no, Papa.
                      ILYA

    My father is a hedgehog.

    (a beat)

    That is so neat.
                    BABA YAGA

    Now watch, blacksmith, and be helpless
    as I prepare your kids for dinner. Sorry
    there are no h'oers doevres, I was kind
    of rushed.

She cackles and starts to gather spices and things from
her shelves and brings them to the table. She whistles
as she prepares her stew stock.

ROOSTERSHENKO and HEDGEHOGNIK scurry underneath the
cage and look up.

                  HEDGEHOGNIK

    How are you Ilya, my son?
                      ILYA

    I'm scared father. How are you?

                  HEDGEHOGNIK

    How am I? I'm a hedgehog, but I guess
    I'm all right.

                  ROOSTERSHENKO

    Ivor, you're well?
                      IVOR

    We're doomed. Ilya and I can't open
    the door, and these bars are too strong
    for us.

ROOSTERSHENKO

You should have paid attention when I
taught you how to open simple locks,
son. Blast! If we were men we could
smash the bars and lock.

HEDGEHOGNIK

Well, we aren't, but we can do something
as the animals we are. Ivor, let me get
on your back.

ROOSTERSHENKO

You're a strange, prickly creature,
Fetnik. What is your plan?

Fetnik shoots a glance to Baba Yaga who is doing
a sassy little DANCE as she prepares the cauldron
seasonings in a bowl, oblivious to anything else for
the moment.

HEDGEHOGNIK

I'll pick the lock. Pull a quill from
my side.

Roostershenko plucks a QUILL with his beak and hands it
to Hedgehognik, who climbs up on the rooster's back and
starts to work at the lock.

HEDGEHOGNIK

Boys, keep an eye on the hag. As soon as
the lock is open, run.

BABA YAGA

(sees them)

Oho!

Hedgehognik grabs the cage DOOR with both paws and
swings it open, dangling from it.

HEDGEHOGNIK

Run boys.

Ilya drops to the floor and runs like mad for the front
door. Ivor is slower getting out.

BABA YAGA

I've lost my lunch! No matter what you
change them into, politicians are
trouble. Where's my kitchen help? Boy!

She heads for the cage.

Ilya ducks under Baba's grabbing hands and sprints out the door and into the woods.

The rooster starts flapping, crowing, pecking and goring the witch with it's beak and spurs. The hedgehog pokes with his quills.

ROOSTERSHENKO

Run Ivor.

BABA YAGA

Ouch. Stop that. Oh, what a poor choice of doppelgangers.

She flails about with her arms trying to block the attacks as her SERVANT BOY enters. He is young, shy and has long hair. A scar across his face does little to hide his good looks.

The boy tries to help Baba Yaga. She slams the cage door shut on Ivor, knocking him out.

HEDGEHOGNIK

Go, blacksmith, run.

He heads toward the door, Roostershenko balks at first, then follows.

ROOSTERSHENKO

We can not leave my son.

FETNIK

We can't help him or your daughter if we get caught. Run.

Roostershenko scurries toward the door, as he does, Hedgehognik swings onto his back and they try to charge out of the shack.

Baba Yaga reaches the door first and slams it shut, and they run into it full-steam, then fall backward, dazed.

She looks down at them with an evil grin.

BABA YAGA

Daughter? He has a daughter, too, eh? What a delicious perk.

She grins at the servant boy.

I'll throw her in the stew as well. Put those two to work.

She gestures to the rooster and hedgehog and then to
the servant. He picks them up, one under each arm.

                    SERVANT BOY

         Yes, Baba Yaga. Doing what?

                    BABA YAGA

         I don't care, slave stuff. Mopping,
         cleaning the pool, use your imagination,
         stupid boy.

                    SERVANT BOY

         Y... yes, Baba Yaga.

He turns and tries to find a direction to leave before
he finally exits.

                    BABA YAGA

         It's a pity adult flesh is so stringy
         and tasteless, or I would eat your wife,
         blacksmith.

She pulls some nasty, pointy IMPLEMENT from a shelf.

                    BABA YAGA

         But I'm sure we can find something
         for her.

She STABS the pointy thing hard into the tabletop.

                    BABA YAGA

         Ivor Petroshenko will know pain and
         despair.

She looks out the window at Ilya running away through
the creaking gate. The house lurches to give chase.

                    BABA-YAGA

         Let him go, house. I still have the
         blacksmith's boy, and soon his daughter
         and wife. Oh, just think, the whole fam-
         ily together for dinner.

She laughs to herself and returns to preparing
vegetables for the stew.

INT. PETROSHENKO'S HOUSE - NIGHT

Vladimir, Marusia and Imya work frantically at the
table.

Imya packs some FOOD and things into one of her new red
KERCHIEFS.

Imya and Vladimir are in a heated discussion.

                         VLADIMIR

     That is foolish, sister. You can not go
     alone. Baba Yaga will kill you before
     you can enter her house.

                           IMYA

     Ivor thinks he can solve with force.
     Sometimes a simple, unassuming plan will
     work better.

                         VLADIMIR

     Tell me your plan, I'll go alone.

                           IMYA

     No, dear brother. You're wounded
     already, and she knows you. I'll go.
     You wait and go with the rest of the
     village.

                          MARUSIA

     I'll go, mother, Dyadya always said
     Baba Yaga is only interested in
     children. I have a better chance.

                         VLADIMIR

     She is interested in children to eat
     them, Marusia.

                          MARUSIA

     But It would be easy for me to get into
     her house.

                         VLADIMIR

     ... and not out again.

He slams his fist on table.

     No!

                           IMYA

     Marusia may be right, brother. And she
     is very smart, she could...

The door is thrown open, Ilya, torn clothing, scratched
arms and face enters.

                    ILYA

Imya Petroshenko. I've escaped.
                VLADIMIR/IMYA/MARUSIA

Ilya!

                    IMYA

Where are Ivor and Fetnik and my husband.

                    ILYA

Baba Yaga has enchanted my father and
your husband and she holds them. Ivor
could not escape in time.

Vladimir pulls out a chair for the boy.

                  VLADIMIR

Sit boy, tell us everything.

Ilya sits and gulps down water from a cup on the table.

                    ILYA

I got out of the cage just before she
saw us. Papa and Ivor Petroshenko held
her off while we ran. But she grabbed
Young Ivor...

                    IMYA

So when last you looked, they were all
alive?

                    ILYA

Yes. Young Ivor was unconscious, Papa
was curled in a ball with his quills
sticking up and Ivor Petroshenko was
pecking madly at the hag.

Vlad and Imya look dumbly at each other and then look
back to Ilya, who gulps more water.

                  VLADIMIR

Have you been struck in the head, Boy?
What did you say?

                    ILYA

I said I escaped from the...

IMYA

No, Ilya. I think he means the "curled
in a ball; pecking madly" part.

ILYA

I told you, she had enchanted them.
My father is a hedgehog, and Ivor
Petroshenko is a rooster.

VLADIMIR

The child is in shock. Marusia, you talk
to him. You're closer to his age, eh?
Marusia?

They all look around the room. Marusia is gone, as is
the bundle Imya was preparing, the door is still open.

VLADIMIR

Bozhe Moye! She has gone on herself.
Stop her.

IMYA

No. She knows what she is doing,
she is very smart and very strong.
I would rather it was me, but better
just one goes.

EXT. WOODS NEAR THE SHACK - NIGHT

Marusia is in view of Baba Yaga's shack. As she
approaches, the shack waddles around to watch her.

Marusia approaches and opens the front gate, which
CREAKS noisily.

MARUSIA

Oh, my, what rusty hinges.

She takes from her kerchief BREAD that has butter on
it. She takes butter and OILS the hinges. The gate no
longer creaks.

As she walks through the gate, a DOG, thin and mangy
looking, trots up to her.

DOG

Moooo. Moooooo.

MARUSIA

Hello. My, what a strange little dog
you're. You look hungry, yes? Here, hun-

> gry little dog, I have something
> for you.

She reaches in and takes out the bread and gives it to
the dog, who gobbles it down. Marusia pets it while it
eats, it licks her hand, moos, and then trots off.

As she watches the dog go around the house, the servant
boy touches her arm and she jumps.

> MARUSIA
>
> You startled me. Who are you, boy?
>
> SERVANT BOY
>
> You should not be here. Don't you know
> who lives here?
>
> MARUSIA
>
> Oh, yes, I know who she is, she is my
> Tetka, my Aunt. My mother has sent me to
> fetch some sewing things from her.

Marusia notices that the boy's long hair keeps getting
in his face, and he has a hard time keeping it out, it
bothers him.

> MARUSIA
>
> Here, would you like this kerchief?
>
> SERVANT BOY
>
> It is very nice. I couldn't take it. She
> would not approve.
>
> MARUSIA
>
> Nonsense, here, take it.

She empties the bundle into her apron pockets, then
ties the kerchief around his head.

> MARUSIA
>
> Now you can see, and I can see you.
> You're very handsome, why do you look so
> sad, though?
>
> SERVANT BOY
>
> I want to leave. I was frightened in the
> woods and almost ran into a bear, she
> saved me. But now she makes me work as
> her slave.

Just then Baba Yaga appears behind them on the porch.

60

                    BABA YAGA

Boy! Who is that? Why do you waste your
time talking to her?

                   SERVANT BOY

Now it is too late.

(to Baba Yaga)

It...it is your niece from the next village, mistress. Her mother has sent her
to fetch sewing things.

Baba Yaga peers at Marusia with a flaming eye for a
few seconds.

                    BABA YAGA

My niece, eh? Didn't know I had one.
But, if you say so, come my child, I'll
get your mother her things. You can stay
for a snack, yes?

                    MARUSIA

Oh, thank you, Tetka, that would be
lovely, I've had a long trip, and am
very hungry.

                   SERVANT BOY

(under his breath)

Be very careful.

Baba Yaga shows Marusia into the shack and cackles.

                    BABA YAGA

There you go, child, make yourself at
home, I shall be in directly to get
you... a snack.

She whirls on the boy.

                    BABA YAGA

How many times have I told you not to
talk to strangers, Boy?

                   SERVANT BOY

She said she was your niece. I thought
you would want...

BABA YAGA

(smacks him hard)

Dumb animals should not try to think.
What is this?

She sees the kerchief and rips it angrily off his head.

BABA YAGA

Pretty little piece of cloth she gives
you to tie up your antlers and make you
forget who you are?

SERVANT BOY

It was just a gift. To keep my hair out
of...

BABA YAGA

I like your hair long, boy. It makes you
look like you could be named "Lars" or
something, and do my landscaping. Oooh,
trim the hedges with no shirt on...

She gets a distant look in her face, then comes back.

BABA YAGA

Now go finish fetching water for my stew.
I'll be going after the blacksmith's
daughter soon. Perhaps this girl can
help me.

SERVANT BOY

But... but...

BABA YAGA

Bah! You'll listen to me, boy.

She smacks him again, breaking his lip.

BABA YAGA

This revenge is too long in coming. Fill
the cauldron, call me when it is ready.

He wipes his bloody mouth and casts his gaze downward.

SERVANT BOY

Y... yes, Baba Yaga.

Baba Yaga blows her NOSE long and hard into the
kerchief, coughs up a nasty loogie and SPITS it in.

                    BABA YAGA

          Here, boy, I'm sorry. You can have this
          back now.

She snorts and heads back into the shack.

The boy takes the kerchief by a corner, the mucous
SMOKES. He sobs quietly, drops it as it catches flame,
then turns to do her bidding.

INT. SHACK - NIGHT

Marusia stands in the house. She looks around the
room, she sees the cage hanging from the ceiling,

Ivor spots her and starts to speak, she places a
FINGER to her lips and he slumps back down, eyes wide
and waiting.

A noise startles her. She turns to see the ferret
playing in the loom against the wall.

                     FERRET

          Ho ho! This never gets old. Who would
          have thought a piece of string could be
          such fun.

He spies Marusia, stops his frolicking, and bounds over
to her.

                     FERRET

          What are you doing here, child? Don't
          you know where you are?

                    MARUSIA

          Oh, yes, nice little ferret, I'm at my
          Tetka's house.

She notices the rooster comb on his head.

                    MARUSIA

          You look as strange and hungry as that
          poor little dog outside. Would you like
          something to eat?

                     FERRET

          Would I? Baba Yaga doesn't feed us but
          once a year, and then it is little more
          than crumbs.

Marusia looks through her pockets for something to feed
the ferret, but finds only a small piece of thick bacon

                    MARUSIA

    I gave my bread to the dog outside.
    Would you like this bacon?

                    FERRET

    Dog? I should have been a dog. I raised
    dogs all my life, my father raised
    dogs... but NO, a ferret.

    (sniffs the bacon)

    Thank you.

He snatches the bacon in his mouth, takes it away,
mumbling about being a ferret.

Baba Yaga enters the room and slams the door behind
her, hobbles over to Marusia and waves a gnarled fist
toward the ferret.

                    BABA YAGA

    I saw that, ferret. You'll have no
    dinner this year.

The ferret blows a raspberry at her and lifts a hind
leg in her direction before jumping behind the loom.

                    FERRET

    Korosho. Now I don't feel as bad about
    peeing in your shoes.

                    BABA YAGA

    Heh heh, I try not to spoil the animals.
    Come, my child, sit by the fire. The boy
    is filling a basin for you to wash up in.
    I'll prepare you.

                    MARUSIA

    Excuse me?

                    BABA YAGA

    I'll prepare you... a meal, that's it.
    Then while you eat, I'll fetch what my
    dear sister needs. How is the old girl
    these days?

                    MARUSIA

    She is very old, dear Tetka, and very
    weak, or she would have come herself.
    But she gave me directions and sent her
    love to you, her older sister.

BABA YAGA

Older sister?

MARUSIA

But I must say, you look very young and
healthy.

BABA YAGA

... heh heh; well, I'm glad you didn't
get lost in the woods, there are many
terrible dangers for young children
here.

MARUSIA

Oh, I just stayed on the path to the
west, like mama said.

BABA YAGA

West? But I'm east of the nearest
village.

MARUSIA

Oh my! Are you sure?

BABA YAGA

I may be older than your mother,
sweetie, but I know which way is up.

MARUSIA

I've come upon the wrong house. A
thousand apologies, Tetka, I mean...

BABA YAGA

No no, dearie, that is perfectly all
right, you didn't know. Prastiti, please
- call me grandmother.

MARUSIA

Oh, now I'll never get to my Tetka's
house tonight, it's a whole day's walk
from my village. What shall I do?

BABA YAGA

Try eating more protein for that tiny
brain of yours.

MARUSIA

What?

                      BABA YAGA

    It, um, it looks like it's going to rain
    for sure. You may as well stay here the
    night, sweet child. I'll send you off in
    the morning rested, and with food and
    water, Yes?

                      MARUSIA

    Oh, you're too kind. Thank you. I'll
    work for my keep, though. Have you any
    chores that need doing? Sewing perhaps?

She motions toward the loom.

                      MARUSIA

    Weaving?

                      BABA YAGA

    Do I look like I need help sewing or
    weaving?

Baba Yaga stands and spreads her arms out to show off
her clothing. She takes a look at herself as a large
piece of tattered clothing falls away.

She sighs.

                      BABA YAGA

    Okay, maybe just a nice house dress or
    something.

She shuffles over to busy herself by the stove.

                      MARUSIA

    Oh, thank you again, I'll make you a
    lovely dress.

Marusia gets up and walks to the loom and sits. She
starts to dust it off, figuring it out and fixing it as
she goes.

The ferret jumps out from behind it and perches near
Marusia.

                      FERRET

    Hey, watch it.

                      MARUSIA

    Excuse me, Mr. Ferret, I'm sorry. I'm
    going to make this nice woman a dress.

                    FERRET

     (makes a face)

     Why?

                    MARUSIA

     Because she is nice enough to let me
     stay here tonight even though she isn't
     my Aunt.

The ferret looks over to Baba Yaga, who is sniffing at a
covered bowl at the table. Something gooey spits at her
from inside.

                    FERRET

     You're either very kind, or else as dumb
     as the blacksmith.

                    MARUSIA

     (whispers, excited)

     You have seen my father?

                    FERRET

     He's your father? Oy.

                    MARUSIA

     Please, good ferret, I've come to find
     my father and brother and Councilman
     Fetnik.

                    FERRET

     Then you must be a very smart and brave
     girl indeed.

He looks at her sideways and narrows is eyes.

                    FERRET

     Are you sure you're the blacksmith's
     daughter?

                    MARUSIA

     Where are they?

In the window flies the rooster with the hedgehog on
its back, they perch on window sill. Hedgehognik holds
a handful of HERBS.

Neither notices Marusia or the ferret in the corner.

                    HEDGEHOGNIK

        Here are your herbs, hag, I hope you
        choke on them.

Baba Yaga, obviously leaning and listening in on
Marusia and the ferret, turns her attention toward
the window.

                    BABA YAGA

        Eh? Oh, hand them here, you spiky little
        rodent.

Hedgehognik holds the herbs out to Baba Yaga, then just
as she grabs for them, he drops them on the floor.

She angrily swipes at Hedgehognik and Roostershenko,
who scramble out of her way.

When she bends over with a loud creak to pick up the
herbs, the rooster PECKS at her butt.

                    BABA YAGA

        Aaaarg! You black-hearted little
        hen-chaser. If I didn't need you around
        for my own filthy plans, I'd rotisserize
        you.

                    MARUSIA

        (whispering)

        Father! Councilman Fetnik.

Roostershenko and Hedgehognik fly out the window.

                    BABA YAGA

        Remember - you do as I say, or I'll eat
        them right now.

                    MARUSIA

        They are well.

                    FERRET

        That's your idea of "well?"

                    MARUSIA

        Now I must get a plan working.

                    FERRET

        Can I help?

                    MARUSIA

     Oh, no, I couldn't ask you to endanger
     yourself for me.

                    FERRET

     Hah! Many years ago I tried to help
     your father - he is not bright - and I
     paid for it. But maybe I get rewarded
     this time.

Ferret starts to bound away, then he turns back to
Marusia.

                    FERRET

     Besides, you were kinder to me the first
     time ever you saw me than that old hag
     has been in a hundred years.

                    MARUSIA

     Spaceba. Thank you.

                    FERRET

     Keep doing what you're doing, I'll be
     back. There are others who feel the
     same way.

He leaps away, Baba Yaga hobbles near to Marusia.

                    BABA YAGA

     (pleasantly)

     How are you doing young one?

                    MARUSIA

     Very well, grandmother, I think I've
     this old loom working.

                    BABA YAGA

     Oh goodie. Now I must attend to some
     business outside, I shall be back in
     a minute. Help yourself to some yummy
     snacks.

Before leaving, she motions to the table, where nasty
LUMPS of food and bubbling oozing TEA sit.

Marusia looks after the ferret, who is climbing up to
Ivor in the cage, then she turns back to her weaving.

EXT. SHACK, BY THE WELL - NIGHT

The servant boy is filling a wooden BUCKET with water from the well. Baba Yaga hobbles over to him.

BABA YAGA

Go fill the basin with clean water, make sure the girl scrubs plenty. She has saved me a trip to town. Oh gastric pleasure. I'll boil and eat her and her brother while her father watches.

She cackles and farts.

The boy stammers but can say nothing. He stares stupidly at Baba Yaga who claps her hands and dances a jig.

Baba Yaga stops when she sees the boy staring.

BABA YAGA

(Mocking)

Duh duh duh.

(smacks him)

Did you hear me, boy? Do as I say.

SERVANT BOY

Yes, Baba Yaga.

She cackles and hobbles back toward the house singing "I feel like chicken tonight."

The boy lowers his head and sighs, then he raises his head and smiles.

He picks up a hatchet from a nearby chopping block and chops small holes in the bucket's bottom.

He fills it up, then lifts it to carry toward the house, it leaks as he walks.

INT. STABLE - SAME TIME

Hedgehognik and Roostershenko watch the boy from the stable's hay loft.

ROOSTERSHENKO

What is this? He chops holes to make room for more water? You can't do that, I've tried.

HEDGEHOGNIK

I think something's up.

                    ROOSTERSHENKO

    Bah. Nothing is up. I think he is loose
    with the brain... or maybe he has figured
    out the secret to getting more water in
    a bucket?

                    HEDGEHOGNIK

    I think you are loose with the brain.

                    ROOSTERSHENKO

    Clever boy...

EXT. STABLE - OXCART - SAME TIME

Baba Yaga starts to unharness the oxen, who pant with
their tongues hanging out.

                    BABA YAGA

    Fortune has smiled on us, my stupid
    beasts, you need not work tonight, the
    blacksmith's daughter is here already.
    No need to give you that drink of water
    now, eh? What luck.

The oxen whine like dogs that have just been tied to
the porch, Baba Yaga cackles.

                    BABA YAGA

    Come, let me lock you back in the
    stable.

The oxen snarl and growl, one snaps at her hand,
she slaps it on the nose with a rolled up paper
from her apron.

                    BABA YAGA

    Mangy animals. When my powers grow, the
    first thing I'm going to do is change
    you all back. All this infernal business
    of animals not making proper sounds.
    Freaking irritating.

She walks them to the stables.

INT. SHACK - NIGHT

Marusia sits at the loom and works. The loom clacks
noisily away. The ferret sits on the floor next to her.

> FERRET
>
> It's all set, do you have anything else
> for me to do?
>
> MARUSIA
>
> No, you have done your part well, Mr.
> Ferret, thank you.

She turns toward the cage, where Ivor sits holding the
bars with his face pressed against them.

> MARUSIA
>
> Do you remember what to do, Ivor?

Ivor's voice is not very convincing.

> IVOR
>
> Yes.
>
> MARUSIA
>
> Don't be afraid, little brother. We
> will prevail, we can't lose if we work
> together.
>
> IVOR
>
> I trust you, sister. I'll be brave.
>
> FERRET
>
> Here she comes, back to your weaving.

He perches next to Marusia as Baba Yaga enters,
whistling some cheesy, happy tune, and goes to the
table. She sees the cauldron hanging on a swing-arm
near the window.

The servant boy empties water into the cauldron from
outside.

> BABA YAGA
>
> Hurry up, stupid boy. What takes you so
> long?
>
> SERVANT BOY
>
> Al... almost done. It seems to take for-
> ever with this small bucket.
>
> BABA YAGA
>
> Then use this one.

She picks up a bigger bucket and throws it at the boy.
The bucket hits the boy and knocks him down.

He takes the new bucket and heads toward the well.

EXT. SHACK - NIGHT

The boy picks up the hatchet and chops holes in the
bigger bucket as before, then starts to fill it.

INT. STABLE - SAME TIME

Roostershenko and Hedgehognik watch as before.

                    ROOSTERSHENKO

        Bozhe Moye. He does it again. His ax
        must be magic.

                    HEDGEHOGNIK

        Come, Petroshenko, let us investigate.

He hops onto the rooster's back and they head toward
the shack.

INT. SHACK - NIGHT

Marusia works at the loom, the ferret sits off in one
corner with the dog, watching unnoticed.

Baba Yaga sees that all the crullers and tea are gone.

                    BABA YAGA

        Ah! You had quite an appetite, eh? I'm
        glad you're eating, it's good for your
        muscles.

        (under breath)

        and saves me the hassle of preparing
        stuffing.

                    IVOR

        She didn't get to eat them, you old hag.

                    FERRET

        Shut up, stupid boy.

Baba Yaga glares at Ivor, shoots a glance at Marusia,
then turns slowly to see

The ferret chewing at his tail. He looks up nonplussed,
CRUMBS all over his whiskers.

                    BABA YAGA

        So! Eating pretty well at my expense,
        eh, ferret?

                         MARUSIA

         Oh, please don't be angry with them,
         grandmother. I let the ferret and the dog
         eat most of them. They're so hungry.

                         BABA YAGA

         (feigning exasperation)

         I work and work all day to put food on the
         table and all you animals do is gobble it
         up in one sitting.

         (angrily)

         I'll show you.

She grabs up a frying PAN and chases the ferret, who
lazily hops up to the mantle.

                         FERRET

         (flatly)

         No, please don't. Ouch. Stop that. Help.
         Mercy.

Baba Yaga swings at him, he easily leaps clear and
the iron pan CLANGS loudly on the oak. The vibrations
shudder up Baba Yaga's arm.

The dog races past her and nips at her legs before
heading out the door.

                         BABA YAGA

         Rotten little poop-making, butt-sniffing bag
         of bones.

She chases the ferret and dog toward the door, then
turns quickly to Marusia.

                         BABA YAGA

         I had better hear that loom working while
         I'm outside, blacksmith's daughter, or
         I'll eat your brother first. Yes, I know who
         you are.

Marusia's eyes widen and she stops her work for
a moment.

                         BABA YAGA

         I was gonna say "got your nose," but I
         think that was more attention-grabbing, eh?

Marusia is flustered, and turns away to the loom, hiding
her face from Baba Yaga.

Baba laughs, then turns back toward the door.

The ferret scratches and bites her bony legs,
she screams.

                         FERRET

          Pick on someone your own girth, hag.

Baba Yaga chases him out the door.

EXT. SHACK'S FRONT PORCH - IMMEDIATELY FOLLOWING

Baba Yaga sees the dog licking his lips on the porch,
crumbs all around his mouth.

                       BABA YAGA

          Aha! There you are, you biscuit-stealing
          cur.

She swings at him, but barely misses, the dog moos. The
dog and the ferret run off, she chases.

                       BABA YAGA

          Get back here.

She sees that her oxen are loose and running around
barking at the chickens and a winged BIRDBATH that is
flying around the yard.

                       BABA YAGA

          What! Who let you out? Where the hell
          did that come from?

She throws up her hands, then spots the servant boy
walking toward the window with the leaking bucket.

The boy stops, looks down at the leak, then back up
to Baba Yaga.

He smiles, then drops the bucket and runs.

                       BABA YAGA

          Oh, that's really aggravating.

She snarls, makes a small FIREBALL in her hand and
throws it at the boy.

The fireball hits him from behind and his hair and
clothes BURST into FLAMES. The force of the explosion
throws him headlong into the bushes.

                    BABA YAGA

     Guess you'll have to try the clean
     shaven look for a while, Boy.

One of the oxen narrowly misses her with its horns,
but knocks her down as it tramples by barking and
chasing the birdbath.

                    BABA YAGA

     Yaaa! My sciatica.

The dog, snorting like an angry bull, leaps at her
as she tries to get up, she throws it off and gets to
her feet.

Angry animals surround her and they stare each other
down for a few seconds

                    BABA YAGA

     Wait a second, wait a second, shhhh!

The animals stop their noises for a second, Baba Yaga
cranes her head toward the house, she still hears the
CLACKING of the loom.

                    BABA YAGA

     Okay. Now, where were we?

She jumps at the animals and a manic brawl ensues.

EXT. SHACK - SAME TIME

The ferret slips around the back of the house
unnoticed.

EXT. BACKYARD - NIGHT

The ferret sees Roostershenko and Hedgehognik at the
wall under the window.

                  HEDGEHOGNIK

     What's going on, Stanislaus? The animals
     are rebelling?

                    FERRET

     We buy time for your daughter, black-
     smith, she has come to free your
     worthless hide.

                  ROOSTERSHENKO

Marusia! Where?

                         FERRET

        She is as bright and brave as you are
        stupid, but she needs our help. You both
        help the creatures out front.

                       ROOSTERSHENKO

        Right, as you go sleep by the fire,
        Ferret?

                        HEDGEHOGNIK

        Shut your beak, Petroshenko.

                         FERRET

        I go to help Marusia. Hurry, we haven't
        much time.

The ferret leaps through the window. Roostershenko flaps
his wings and CLUCKS wildly.

                       ROOSTERSHENKO

        Marusia? Marusia! My daughter is in
        danger. Marus... Ouch!

He stops his ranting as Hedgehognik jams a QUILL into
his butt.

                        HEDGEHOGNIK

        Basta! The only danger she is in right
        now is of you helping her. Listen to
        Stanislaus. Let's do our part.

The two of them race around the corner to the front
yard.

EXT. SHACK FRONT YARD - NIGHT

Roostershenko and Hedgehognik join in with the fracas
in the front yard.

Every now and again, Baba Yaga LISTENS to make sure
Marusia is still working.

INT. SHACK - NIGHT

Marusia works at the loom craning her neck to see
outside. The ferret lands next to her and drops a KEY
on the floor.

                         FERRET

        Now. Go!

Marusia jumps up, taking the key, and the ferret takes
her place making the loom work. It is difficult and
awkward work for a ferret.

                    FERRET

     And away we go.

Marusia runs to the cage and opens it, Ivor climbs down
and they hug.

                     IVOR

     Oh Marusia. I was so scared.

                    MARUSIA

     All brave people are scared, dear Ivor.
     They merely do what they must in spite
     of the fear.

Ferret is laughing while he gets tangled in the loom.

                    FERRET

     Wait! Ivor! In the crone's cupboard. The
     brush and kerchief. Take them.

                     IVOR

     Right.

He runs to the CABINET across the room as Marusia peeks
out the window.

                    FERRET

     Marusia, when Baba Yaga comes after you,
     the first time she gets near you, throw
     the kerchief over your right shoulder.
     The next time, throw down the brush and
     run as fast as you can.

Ivor runs back from the cabinet with the wooden hair
BRUSH and a plain blue KERCHIEF in his hands. He gives
them to his sister and then they leave through the
back door.

EXT. SHACK - IMMEDIATELY FOLLOWING

Marusia and Ivor turn around from closing the door,
they start to run, but stop dead and scream.

A blackened figure is standing before them, hands
outstretched.

They realize it is the servant boy, singed and smoking.

                    SERVANT BOY

        Leave through the gate, if you don't,
        the house will chase you down before you
        reach the woods.

                      MARUSIA

        Oh, poor boy. I should bandage you.

She takes another colorful neckerchief from her pocket
and goes to him.

                        BOY

        No, brave Marusia, you have already
        showed me great kindness. I'll help you
        escape. Do-sfidanya Ivor, good luck.

                      MARUSIA

        You have such courage. Here, take this,
        for your hair.

She takes off her neckerchief and ties it around his
neck and kisses him softly on his cheek. They look at
each other for a moment, Ivor pulls her away.

                       IVOR

        Marusia. Let's go. (to boy) Thank you.
        Do-sfidanya.

They run to the gate and look back. The boy joins the
fray, which the animals are losing.

Baba Yaga bats them down to the ground. She still
listens for the loom, then cackles as she bashes the
rooster.

INT. SHACK - SAME TIME

The ferret is beside himself giggling hysterically as
he seriously messes up the loom.

EXT. SHACK - SAME TIME

Marusia swings the gate open, it does not squeak, Ivor
runs through, Marusia turns.

                      MARUSIA

        Wait! I can not leave father and Fetnik.

                       IVOR

        We have to go. They are losing ground,
        Marusia. If we do not go, then this is
        all for nothing.

                    MARUSIA

        But...

Hedgehognik comes flying through the air and hits a
tree. His quills make him stick to the bark a few feet
up off the ground.

                  HEDGEHOGNIK

        Run, children. Warn the village, they
        will send help. Save yourselves.

He tries to wriggle free from the tree but can not
manage it.

                  HEDGEHOGNIK

        But first... could you...

He makes a gesture at himself

Ivor hurriedly grabs him and pulls him free and drops
him to the ground. Hedgehognik gets up and scurries
back toward the melee.

                     IVOR

        Run!

They run off into the woods.

EXT. SHACK - LATER THAT NIGHT

Baba Yaga ties the flying birdbath to the porch, it
strains at the cord, occasionally banging Baba Yaga on
the noggin with a loud clank.

She absentmindedly swats at it as if shooing a fly.

                   BABA YAGA

        Oh, lay off already.

The animals lay about the yard breathing hard, the loom
can be heard clacking away from inside the shack.

                   BABA YAGA

        That ought to teach you ungrateful
        beasts how to behave. Bite the hand that
        feeds you, eh? Mooing dog, barking cows,
        eh? Well that's gonna change...

She looks at all the beaten animals and something
clicks in her mind. She starts to count all of them.

                   BABA YAGA

        Eh? Ferret? Ferret!

Insane laughter comes from the shack.

Baba Yaga's eye glows nuclear-meltdown white and she hobbles as fast as her bony legs can take her inside.

INT. SHACK - IMMEDIATELY FOLLOWING

The ferret has made an incredible MESS of the place. YARN is woven all over, under and through everything. He is badly TANGLED and suspended in the air in front of the loom laughing.

                    BABA YAGA

          I'll make you wish you'd never been
          born, ferret

                    FERRET

          I already wish that, hag. Right now
          I wish that I could get a portrait of
          your face.

Baba Yaga clears the room in one leap, grabs up the ferret in her claw and pulls his face close to hers.

                    BABA YAGA

          Where... are... they?

The ferret LICKS Baba Yaga's NOSE and belches right in her face.

Baba Yaga winces.

                    FERRET

          I just cleaned myself.

Baba Yaga flies into a rage. She tries to throw the ferret across the room, but he just goes out a few feet, straining the yarn that binds him and then bungees back to his web and bounces a bit

                    FERRET

          Don't be getting too worked up, Baba
          Yaga. Remember, you're not quite all
          there yet.

                    BABA YAGA

          (to herself)

          House. House didn't chase them, so they
          must have left through the gate.

She runs to the front porch and searches the woods with her eyes.

                    BABA YAGA

     Then why didn't Gate warn me? She proba-
     bly buttered the gate up like she did my
     servants, eh? HOUSE!

Baba Yaga's shack lurches to it's feet and stands at attention.

                    BABA YAGA

     Find her, now.

The house turns one way, then another. It chooses a direction and takes off at a loping plod. Baba Yaga holds onto a porch rail as the building approaches the tree line at a breakneck pace.

House lumbers into the woods three steps and is immediately JAMMED between two immense OAKS. The impact sends baba yaga hurtling into the woods.

Incoherent SWEARING makes House sag between the oaks.

EXT. SHACK - LATER

Baba Yaga scratches her head as she pulls thorny branches from her butt.

                    BABA YAGA

     So, House has gained too much weight to
     make it through the trees,eh?

House sighs, and hangs its head in shame.

Baba Yaga snaps her fingers.

                    BABA YAGA

     Oxen.

Baba Yaga races around the shack, the oxen are sleeping and doing that "Doggy-dream" thing.

                    BABA YAGA

     Curses, I'll never catch up to them with
     you.

She spies a bony HORSE standing behind the oxcart eating grass.

                    BABA YAGA

     Horse!

The horse looks to her and whinnies, shaking its matted
mane.

                    BABA YAGA

     At last. An animal that isn't something
     totally gloopy.

She limps over to it quickly.

                    BABA YAGA

     Good horse. Take me after those chil-
     dren. Fly like the...

When she comes around the cart, she sees that the
horse's body is on a stone base and birds are splashing
in the WATER in a hollow BASIN of skin on its back.

                    BABA YAGA

     Didn't see that one coming.

     (turns toward house)

     House would never make it very far into
     these thick woods.

     (a beat)

     Cauldron.

She throws her hands up over her head and starts to
CHANT.

A clanking and crashing NOISE emits from the house,
then two large BUMPS.

On the third bump the Cauldron, running on its own
legs, CRASHES through the wall and runs next to Baba
Yaga.

                    BABA YAGA

     There is a door. Spoon.

The spoon flies through the window and she catches it,
then climbs into the cauldron and points toward the
village.

                    BABA YAGA

     Forward!

The cauldron takes off at a gallop in the opposite
direction of Baba's pointing finger, clearing out
of view.

A few seconds later there is a crash, then the cauldron runs back across view with Baba Yaga leaning on her elbow facing behind it.

EXT. WOODS - NIGHT

Marusia and Ivor run through the woods, crazy MOONLIGHT flashes through the trees.

Ivor slows down and leans against a tree.

> IVOR
>
> Wait, Marusia, I must rest, I cannot run... any farther.

> MARUSIA
>
> Ivor, we have to get home before Baba Yaga finds out we are missing and comes after us.

> IVOR
>
> But I'm so tired.

> MARUSIA
>
> If you don't come with me, you'll be dead. Mother should have the village ready to go. We must let them know.

She pulls him to his feet and they run on.

INT. PETROSHENKO'S HOUSE - NIGHT

Imya, Vladimir and villagers ready themselves with torches and weapons, hastily spilling out the door into the yard.

Vladimir limps around checking supplies and weapons.

> IMYA
>
> Vlad, You should stay here.

> VLADIMIR
>
> My niece and nephew are in the hands of that creature. I'm well enough to go until the day they shovel dirt on my face. Tantikov, you have dogs?

> TANTIKOV
>
> Yes, Vladimir Grigorovich, I've got a dozen of the toughest dogs in all of Russia, they wait my orders.

VLADIMIR

Good, good. They may distract Baba Yaga
long enough to let us take her.

IMYA

Just make sure they wait until the
children are safe, Tantikov.

TANTIKOV

They wait for me.

VLADIMIR

Good citizens of Vakyust. We go to do
battle with Baba Yaga. Are you ready?

The small group cheers as they brandish weapons, tools
and torches.

IMYA

Then let's go. We break up into three
groups. Tantikov, Droblu and Miraputnik,
you have your people?

The three named nod and point, two of the teams have
half a dozen dogs each.

IMYA

Vladimir, dear brother, you stay with me
in Droblu's group.

VLADIMIR

Yes, sister, as long as I get to help
destroy that devil.

They charge toward the woods.

Three smaller bands break off from the main gathering
and head into the forest.

Vladimir scans the mob with his eyes.

VLADIMIR

I hope this goes better than last time.
I would hate for her to come back again.

IMYA

It will work, brother. Have faith.

VLADIMIR

I have faith, Imya. But faith has it's
bounds.

                         IMYA

          No, brother. It does not.

EXT. SWAMPY AREA - NIGHT

The cauldron is STUCK in some swampy ground.

Baba Yaga climbs out, cursing and flailing her arms. She
tries to lever the heavy iron pot out with her spoon,
but falls into the muck.

After much muddy work, she is on her way again.

EXT. WOODS - SAME TIME

Marusia and Ivor are running. Ivor trips, his leg
caught between two logs.

                         IVOR

          Marusia, I'm stuck.

Marusia turns, she runs to his side and starts to pull
him out.

They hear dull thudding coming from behind them,
getting louder, until finally

The bushes CRASH open and Baba Yaga and the cauldron
bear down on them. The cauldron stops a few yards from
the children, Baba Yaga throws up her hands in an evil
villain attack stance.

                       BABA YAGA

          Haha! I've got you now, you cringing
          little waifs. I'll eat you both right
          here, to the devil with that "cooking-
          you-and-making-your-father-watch" plan.

Quickly Marusia reaches into her apron and takes out
the blue kerchief.

                       BABA YAGA

          And after I've eaten, my powers will be
          returned to their fullest, and with the
          Sorcerer Huishka's knowledge, I'll soon
          destroy your whole village, and then the
          world will be mine.

There is a long moment where nothing happens.
Baba Yaga slumps a little then SLAPS the side of the
cauldron hard.

BABA YAGA

(To cauldron)

That would be your cue.

The cauldron springs to life, revs itself up on its short legs, then charges forward.

Marusia quickly tosses the blue kerchief over her right shoulder.

As soon as the kerchief touches the ground, it grows and spreads fluidly, becoming a huge, rushing river.

Baba Yaga charges straight into it headlong and her heavy cauldron sinks.

BABA YAGA

Now that was a neat trick. Was that mine?

Marusia and Ivor sprint away as fast as their legs will allow.

Baba Yaga drags herself and the cauldron out of the river and snarls and shakes her fist at Marusia and Ivor on the other side.

BABA YAGA

You'll never get away from me, you little brats. I'll get you yet, so why run?

MARUSIA

Mr. Ferret has given us more time, let's not waste it.

The children disappear in the trees.

Baba Yaga turns toward her cauldron.

BABA YAGA

Like anybody ever expects them to stop just because you tell 'em to. Why do I bother?

The cauldron shrugs. Baba Yaga stares at the river.

BABA YAGA

You're too heavy to cross it, and I can't swim.

(snaps her fingers)

>   I've got it. Come, back to the house.
>   Quickly, forward.

She hesitates, turns to face behind her, but the cauldron goes in the proper direction.

EXT. WOODS - SAME TIME

Imya and Vladimir's party, they have stopped and are peering into the darkness of the woods.

>   DROBLU

>   What is it?

>   VLADIMIR

>   It is very large from the sound of it,
>   we need more light. Mirta, bring a
>   torch.

A WOMAN brings a torch, Vladimir and another villager wrap cloth around their arrow tips, light them, and fire toward the noise. They stand tense and frightened.

The arrows hit a tree and soon the light shows a huge GRIZZLY rearing up at them.

>   VLADIMIR

>   Whew. I thought it was the witch.

They quickly realize they now have to deal with a large angry bear and they ready weapons.

The bear charges in as Vladimir hastily readies another arrow.

EXT. BABA YAGA'S SHACK - SAME TIME

Baba Yaga pulls at her oxen, who bark and growl.

>   BABA YAGA

>   Come, stupid beasts. You're so thirsty,
>   eh? Drink all you want.

The oxen start to wag their tails and prance about her, baying. She hops into her cauldron and leads the way.

Roostershenko and Hedgehognik sit on the porch and spot them leaving.

>   HEDGEHOGNIK

>   Something happens toward Vakyust. Let's
>   follow, we may yet be able to help.

                    ROOSTERSHENKO

    Bah! What is the use. We have failed.
    We have unleashed an evil spawned in
    Hell and now the end of the world waits
    in line.

                    HEDGEHOGNIK

    OK, you stay here with hungry dog. I
    choose to go and finish what we started
    years ago.

Roostershenko looks over at the dog, who has
chicken feathers in its mouth and leers hungrily at
Roostershenko, who

Turns and runs after Hedgehognik.

                    ROOSTERSHENKO

    Just kidding.

Hedgehognik jumps on his back and they head out after
the oxen.

EXT. WOODS - NIGHT

The villagers pull the dead bear off of Vladimir.

                    IMYA

    Are you alright brother? I thought it
    would eat you for certain.

                    VLADIMIR

    It was only a bear, sister. Droblu, we
    come back and get this later, eh? It is
    a fine one.

                    DROBLU

    Yes, good shot, Vladimir Grigorovich.

EXT. WOODS, MAGIC RIVER - NIGHT

Baba Yaga and oxen come through the woods to the magic
river.

As the oxen smell the water, they go into a frenzy and
run headlong into the river and lower their heads and
drink.

                    BABA YAGA

    Drink thirsty animals. Drink!

The river starts to subside, and soon is gone.

The oxen belch happily, their BULGING bellies full of water. They go to lift their legs on a tree.

Baba Yaga cackles, and charges across the mud.

EXT. WOODS - night

Marusia and Ivor halt, and crane their heads to listen. They can hear barking but can't quite tell which direction it comes from.

> IVOR
>
> Oxen?

> MARUSIA
>
> No, Ivor. I think it is Mama and Dyadya Vlad! Over that way.

They both resume running with renewed vigor and shout as they go.

> IVOR
>
> Mama! Over here.

> MARUSIA
>
> Mama, it is us.

EXT. WOODS - SAME TIME

Tantikov's party stops and tries to hush the dogs.

> TANTIKOV
>
> Quiet. Listen!

The sound of the children gets louder.

> VILLAGER
>
> Over there. They are coming toward us.

Soon the shadows of the children can be seen coming through the denser trees toward them, the party gives a small cheer and rushes to meet them.

They hug the children and put warm cloaks on them.

> MARUSIA
>
> Where is mother and Dyadya Vlad?

> IVOR
>
> Where is Fetnik?

> TANTIKOV
>
> They are just North of us, we are in

separate parties to surround Baba Yaga.
Where is she?

> IVOR

She stopped at the river, she couldn't
cross.

> VILLAGER

River? There is no river in these woods?
It is back...

> MARUSIA

It is a long story, one I'll gladly tell
when this is over. For now, we have to
move. Her powers are still fairly weak,
if we..

Before she can finish, a rapid, heavy thudding can be
heard coming from the denser wood. The party looks in
that direction.

> IVOR

Marusia. She's here.

> MARUSIA

Let the dogs go, they will slow her
down. Where are the others?

> TANTIKOV

Wadislav. Get word to the others.
Children, behind us, we stand until
they arrive.

WADISLAV raises a hunting horn and gives a signal.

EXT. WOODS - SAME TIME

Miraputnik's party reacts to the signal.

EXT. WOODS - SAME TIME

Droblu's party reacts to the sound.

> DROBLU

They have found the children.

> IMYA

Marusia, Ivor.

> VLADIMIR

Baba Yaga.

They hear the horn again and then charge off in the direction of the horn blast.

EXT. WOODS - SAME TIME

The thudding gets louder and deeper until the ground shakes.

> TANTIKOV
>
> Ready everyone. Let her know who we are.

They raise their weapons to the ready, a few seconds later

The cauldron CRASHES through a thick TREE in a headlong charge, pieces of wood fly everywhere

> TANTIKOV
>
> Boshe moye!

As the wood, leaves, and dust clear, the villagers look up again and see the cauldron, empty, plow into their ranks. It stomps about, knocking people aside.

> IVOR
>
> Where is she, Marusia?

> BABA YAGA
>
> (From above)
>
> Looking for me? You remembered. My heart is full.

She floats down from a tall tree and lands softly in front of them, then raises herself up to her full height and bares her teeth in a dripping snarl.

Her eye glows ultra green.

> BABA YAGA
>
> The children are mine.

> TANTIKOV
>
> No, hag. You'll have to kill us all first.

> BABA YAGA
>
> Procedures, procedures. Very well, then. First things first.

Tantikov motions to the dog holders who unleash the animals, who charge at Baba Yaga.

Tantikov motions to the other side and three villagers
aim and fire arrows.

Baba Yaga faces the archers. ARROWS speed toward her,
she opens her mouth and BITES the arrows in half as
they reach her.

She quickly makes and throws fireballs at the dogs,
stopping all but two, who turn and run.

                    BABA YAGA

        My turn?

Another volley of arrows is fired and one catches her in
the shoulder. She tries to throw another fireball, but
it sputters and dissipates when she is struck.

                    BABA YAGA

        Every time I really need it. It's magic
        for crying out loud, not some government
        program.

She clutches her spoon and chants, the spoon glows red
and she raises her hand to throw it.

                    BABA YAGA

        This is gonna hurt someone.

The cauldron, which has been going in a straight line,
slows down and turns, then charges back toward her.

It plows through the party again, then slams into Baba
Yaga.

The spoon goes up and comes down on her as the albino
python, entangling her and the cauldron.

                    TANTIKOV

        Now!

                    BABA YAGA

        No, no, you stupid snake.

        (she chants)

        Zemeya begone. Zemeya away. Zemeya,
        you're crushing my bladder.

The townsfolk rush at her, but the hopping cauldron and
her flailing snake make it hard to land blows. Many of
the mob still take wounds and drop away from the melee.

The python's coils grab some of the villagers and
untangle the cauldron and Baba Yaga.

MARUSIA

Ivor. She is getting free. We must hurry
to the others.

IVOR

But we can't outrun her, what do we do?

As the mass of people and witch tussle and fight, they
move away from the cauldron, Marusia spies this.

MARUSIA

Quickly, brother, follow me.

She races toward the fray.

IVOR

Are you crazy? We will be killed.

MARUSIA

Look, Ivor, we can't outrun her, but
this can.

She climbs into the cauldron and shouts "Forward". The
cauldron starts to plod toward Ivor, then she commands
"Halt" and it does so near him.

MARUSIA

Get in, hurry.

He clambers in and once again she commands it forward.

BABA YAGA

My own steed turns against me. Cauldron.

MARUSIA

No, don't stop. Faster, faster!

The cauldron takes off at an awkward gallop.

Baba Yaga throws the few remaining villagers aside
and runs after them. The cauldron quickly moves away
from her.

She summons her last remaining strength and creates a
huge ball of fire and throws it.

BABA YAGA

Catch, Kiddies.

The ball explodes just short of the two children and
sends the pot of them spinning through the brush.

Baba Yaga then cackles and starts after them, but stops short, and collapses to her knees.

EXT. WOODS - SAME TIME

Miraputnik's and Droblu's parties meet in the wood, they all quickly confer and then head off in a new direction, over their shoulders from behind them the huge fireball explodes through the trees and brush.

                    IMYA

     NO!

                  VLADIMIR

     Be brave, my sister, press on. We don't
     know for sure.

                 MIRAPUTNIK

     Something's coming this way.

Toward them from out of the woods hurtles the cauldron, smoking and whistling.

It breaks through some smaller trees, sails over the heads of the crouching villagers, and hits a large oak and falls, opening down.

                  VLADIMIR

     Get her.

Some of the villagers rush to the cauldron and attempt to right it, others stand ready with dogs and weapons.

Finally the pot is turned over and we see the two children, scorched and smoldering sitting under it.

                  MARUSIA

     Bozhe Moye!

                    IVOR

     That was fun.

Imya rushes toward the children.

                    IMYA

     My children. You're safe now.

                  VLADIMIR

     Marusia. You have done it. You're
     a hero.

> MARUSIA

Father, councilman Fetnik, I think they
are...

> VLADIMIR

Time for that later.

> IVOR

Baba Yaga, she was behind us.

From behind them a loud din is heard, Vladimir sends
part of the group to investigate

> VLADIMIR

Imya, you must get them to safety, we
will stay and fight to the death. Go
South to the river and take the ferry as
far as you can.

He directs some of the villagers standing around.

You go with her, get all the children to safety, we
will make time.

From behind them, in the direction of the din.

> BABA YAGA

There's not time enough to keep me from
my revenge.

Torn, tattered and bleeding green ooze, she holds the
disembodied arm of some unfortunate person. As others
approach her, she takes huge noisy bites out of them,
eventually, she is surrounded, but they keep their
distance.

> IMYA

Give it up, witch. You can not win now.

> BABA YAGA

(shrugging, nodding)

Oh, okay, sure.

> VLADIMIR

You... you surrender?

> BABA YAGA

Do I look like a moron? No self-respect-
ing evil terror ever gives up.

She throws back her head and shouts as loud as she can
muster.

                    BABA YAGA

        Give me the Blacksmith's family and I'll
        leave here. Refuse me, and I'll take as
        many of you with me as I can.

        (she staggers, breathing hard)

        I'll give you... five minutes... to
        decide.

She looks at her wrist, as if timing with a watch,
glancing up from under her stringy hair to see what
the villagers do.

They shift uneasily and look to Imya and Vladimir and
the children. Imya stands forward.

                    IMYA

        No, Crone. We don't make deals with the
        devil. I'll not barter with my family's
        life.

                    BABA YAGA

        Okay. Just one child. And two dogs.

                    VLADIMIR

        You're wasting your breath, Baba Yaga,
        we will never stop until you're dead
        once and for all.

The villagers that surround Baba Yaga shuffle their feet
and some lower their weapons.

                    VILLAGER 1

        Why don't we trade the few to save the
        many?

                    VILLAGER 2

        Yes! Why not? How many more of us must
        die. She only wants the blacksmith's
        family. And where is Ivor Petroshenko?

                    VILLAGER 3

        He and Council Fetnik run off and leave
        us to die for them. I say, trade them.

A few others second the motion and Imya, Vladimir and
the children look on horrified.

All attention is turned toward debate and argument,
Baba Yaga is forgotten for the moment.

                    MARUSIA

     Dyadya Vlad...

She notices some cuts and scrapes on Baba Yaga are
healing themselves, and her heavy breathing has
stopped.

Marusia pulls at Vladimir's cloak.

                    VLADIMIR

     Not now, niece.

                    MARUSIA

     (quietly)

     Uncle Vlad, look, she's healing herself.
     She's just stalling us until she can
     attack again.

Vladimir looks hard at the witch and sees it is true

                    VLADIMIR

     Our weapons have only been slowing her
     down.

The villagers are still arguing amongst themselves
about the trade. He steps forward, hands raised.

                    VLADIMIR

     She plays with us. She whittles away at
     us a little at a time as she regains her
     strength. She'll kill us all. Look.

The villagers stop their arguing and stare at her. Baba
Yaga shifts her eyes back and forth at them. Then looks
down at herself, then back up.

                    BABA YAGA

     No. I'm nearly done in, see? I bleed,
     see. Ooooh, my head.

She makes pathetic attempts at staggering and groaning,
more to mock and mess with the villagers than to
convince them.

                    BABA YAGA

     Fools!

She throws her arms out to her sides and the

surrounding townsfolk are knocked back and to the ground.

Smoke and electricity come from her hands as she brings them in front of her. Even she looks surprised.

> BABA YAGA
>
> Shto etah? That was a rush. Eh? I may not need those children as much as I thought. My powers are awakening on their own.
>
> (Staring into space)
>
> I see Huishka's thoughts in my head.

Vladimir and Imya and the children look on in terror.

> VLADIMIR
>
> We are in deep boorak.

> MARUSIA
>
> Mother, what do we do? She never stops.

> IVOR
>
> Marusia. The brush.

Ivor pulls the brush out of Marusia's pocket and brandishes it.

> VLADIMIR
>
> Sure, why not. Might as well look good for our ancestors.

Marusia grabs the wood-handled brush from Ivor.

> MARUSIA
>
> No, Dyadya, this is an enchanted brush, we took it from the Baba Yaga's house.

Baba Yaga spies the brush and her eye glows white hot.

> BABA YAGA
>
> Eh? Little thieves. I know that one's mine. Give it.

She reaches out a claw and pulls at the air, the brush starts to slip from Marusia's hand, but she holds on tight.

Soon Marusia starts to be dragged toward the witch, Vladimir, Ivor and Imya grab her, but they all start to move.

                              IVOR

          The ferret said throw it down, sister.

                            MARUSIA

          NO! If I let it go, she will have it, we
          must keep it.

Some villagers make it to their feet and attack Baba
Yaga, but she bats them back or bites them as they
close in.

Soon the brush, as well as those attached to it, is
within an arm's length of Baba Yaga.

                          BABA YAGA

          Let go! It's just a plain old ordinary
          brush, for crying out loud.

She reaches for it, just as a loud crowing is heard
from above. She shoots a glance upward as Roostershenko
dives at her face clawing and pecking at her eyes.

                       ROOSTERSHENKO

          Run children, run wife.

                            MARUSIA

          Papa.

                             IMYA

          Ivor!

Baba Yaga's hold on them dissipates and they fall
backward, Hedgehognik lands next to Ivor.

                         HEDGEHOGNIK

          This may be our last chance, children.
          Bog be with you.

Baba Yaga grabs the rooster by the legs and holds him,
then wheels on the small party, her good eye scratched
badly.

Sizzling green GOO sputters from her jagged teeth.

                          BABA YAGA

          (really pissed)

          No more Mrs. Nice Witch.

She snarls, and green goo gushes from her iron teeth.

Marusia and Ivor scream. Ivor grabs Hedgehognik by the
belly and

WHACKS Baba Yaga hard in the EYE with the spiny back.

Baba Yaga reels back in pain and rage.

                         BABA YAGA

          Argh! I meant him to be a harmless
          little burrowing rodent, not a weapon.

She swears and complains incoherently as she flails
about trying to grab Hedgehognik.

Marusia jumps to her feet and helps her mother up, Ivor
helps up Vladimir.

                         IVOR

          Now, Marusia. Throw it!

Marusia THROWS the brush at Baba Yaga's feet. As soon
as the brush touches the ground, thin ROOTS grow out
of the HANDLE and the BRISTLES stretch and grow upward
quickly, soon sprouting leaves.

The thin saplings entwine Baba Yaga's legs and hold
her fast.

She pulls the bloody hedgehog out of her eye and
looks down.

                         BABA YAGA

          Well, this is not a good day. Now I'm
          legally blind.

She looks at Hedgehognik in her hand.

I can't see you, spiny creature, but I'm going to pick
my teeth with you, from the inside.

Baba Yaga tries to toss Hedgehognik into her gaping
maw, but saplings wrap her arm and instead she drops
him.

She snarls and chews at the thin trees forming around
her, biting half a dozen at a time, but for each
chewed, TWO grow in their place, twice as fast.

                         BABA YAGA

          Enchanted trees. What was I thinking?

The party watches in amazement as the enchanted forest
springs up around her in seconds, getting denser and
denser as they watch.

She can be seen chewing frantically and snarling for
a few seconds, but soon there is nothing but thickly
twisted trees spreading to fill the small clearing.

                    VLADIMIR

     Bozhe Moye!

                    MARUSIA

     Is... is she gone?

                     IVOR

     Look!

He points to the base of the new forest. Out from
the thick trees scrambles Roostershenko, dragging
Hedgehognik in his beak. They come to the feet of the
group and collapse.

Marusia drops to her knees beside them and cradles the
rooster.

                   MARUSIA

     Papa. Oh, Papa.

Roostershenko looks up with half-opened eyes.

                 ROOSTERSHENKO

     I'm sorry, my children. I've nearly lost
     you because I... I...

                  HEDGEHOGNIK

     ...are as stupid as a box of iron
     scraps?

                 ROOSTERSHENKO

     Yes.

The magic forest, forgotten temporarily, still creeps
closer to them. Soon it is only about a foot away.

                 ROOSTERSHENKO

     I was too proud, too ignorant to see
     that my actions would affect my family
     later. I should have listened.

A claw shoots out from the trees and grabs Marusia's
arm, then a huge SWATH of the thick trees is bitten
away and Baba Yaga's head appears in the hole.

                   BABA YAGA

     ...should have listened to me, eh,
     blacksmith.

Baba Yaga's FACE is starting to resemble Huishka's more
now, as is her voice, only deeper and more evil.

                    IMYA

          Marusia!

Ivor runs and grabs his sister.

Vladimir draws his sword, and with a mighty, blade-
breaking WHACK, severs Baba's claw from her arm.

Marusia drops to the ground. Vines quickly wrap around
the claw and drag it back into the swelling thicket.

                  MARUSIA

          The plants are growing faster now, soon
          she will be trapped forever.

Baba Huishka's VOICE is heard as she starts to CHANT.
As the chant grows louder, the trees start to wither
and dry up, when she bites at them, they no longer grow
back.

                  MARUSIA

          No! What is happening?

                HEDGEHOGNIK

          Oy.

There is a general cry of dismay from those still
standing in the clearing. Villagers cling to one
another and point at the drying branches.

Vladimir picks up one of the dry branches and snaps it
in half, staring at the thicket of magical trees.

He HEARS Baba Yaga's words from years ago.

              BABA YAGA (VO)

          I pray they try to hang me. Anything but
          the inferno of enchanted wood will do
          little more than irritate me.

Vladimir comes out of his trance and shoots a look
around the clearing, spies a LANTERN by a fallen
comrade and runs to it.

                 VLADIMIR

          Everyone get back, go.

They back away quickly, Roostershenko is taken in
Marusia's arms, Ivor picks up Hedgehognik.

Vladimir gets out an arrow with CLOTH wrapped at the
tip, he soaks the cloth with OIL from the lantern,

lights it in one of the failing fallen TORCHES and aims
at Baba Huishka.

Before he can fire, the PYTHON drops from a tree and
coils around his arm, making his shot go off into the
real woods.

                         VLADIMIR

     Aagh!

                          IVOR

     Dyadya Vlad.

Imya runs to Vladimir's side, picks up his broken SWORD
and hacks at the python with half a blade.

Baba Huishka is breaking free quicker now,
Roostershenko looks at Vladimir.

                      ROOSTERSHENKO

     What is that boy doing now. He burns
     perfectly good arrows while...

                         MARUSIA

     Papa. The lantern. Vladimir was…

She snatches up a lit lantern and moves toward the
trees, careful to avoid Baba Huishka's eyeline.

Roostershenko watches as his daughter struggles through
the flying branches and snake coils. Then he looks to
Vladimir and the lantern.

Something clicks in his small brain.

With a final burst of effort, Roostershenko darts to
Marusia and snatches the lantern from her.

                      ROOSTERSHENKO

     No! I have hurt too many people already,
     daughter. I go.

                         MARUSIA

     Papa. No!

Roostershenko charges headlong into the thicket
underneath Baba Huishka. She stops chewing, the sound
of glass BREAKING is heard, then SMOKE is seen, and
soon FLAMES are spewing up at her face.

Roostershenko does NOT EMERGE from the spreading flames.

BABA HUISHKA

Oh great... no matter where I stand the
smoke is in my eye. Well, I guess this
is as good a time as any to panic, so...

Baba Huishka spastically wiggles and thrashes about,
trying to free herself, to no avail. She looks down
into the branches.

BABA HUISHKA

Ow! Stop that scratching and pecking,
blacksmith; can't you see I'm about to
become Baba-Cue? Ouch!

The flames quickly engulf the witch, and as she
disappears into the inferno, she howls at the sky.

BABA HUISHKA

Never. NEVER tell your enemies how to
destroy you.

MARUSIA/IVOR

Papa! Council Fetnik, help him!

Hedgehognik stares into the flames sadly.

HEDGEHOGNIK

A very noble gesture, blacksmith, you
will be missed. I'm sorry Marusia.

Imya still hacks at the python, until suddenly the
snake disappears as her sword comes down. Vladimir
looks up in terror as it nears his groin.

VLADIMIR

Sister, stop!

Imya stops just short of trimming Vladimir's legs off;
she drops to his side, letting go of the sword, and
helps him up.

They look at the bonfire, sparks fly as it burns.

VLADIMIR

It is finally over.

IMYA

She is gone?

VLADIMIR

Yes, I remembered what she said when

> I was a boy. She is gone. Marusia has
> saved us all.

Marusia runs up to her mother and hugs her.

MARUSIA

> It was Papa. Papa saved us.

She sobs and hides her face in her mother's dress. As
the flames start to recede,

The MANACLES Petroshenko fashioned twenty-one years ago
fall noisily to the ground, glowing red hot.

VLADIMIR

> So, his work has merit after all, eh?

Hedgehognik stretches and grows, and soon is council
Fetnik again, he staggers to the ground.

FETNIK

> Bozhe! My head feels like one of Petros-
> henko's anvils. Help me up, young Ivor.

Ivor helps him to his feet

IVOR

> Council Fetnik. You're back.

FETNIK

> Yes, dear boy, and I'm sorry that your
> father is gone, he was a good man. A
> little gloopy, but a good man.

Fetnik scans the cluttered clearing.

FETNIK

> Let us see who else lives. We've work
> yet to do.

They check on the villagers in the light of the dying
fire, some get up when shaken, others do not.

FETNIK

> We must send a party to burn her shack
> and all her belongings. Then we can
> rest.

The villagers all mill about, gathering belongings and
wounded neighbors as they hobble off toward the village.

Marusia helps gather things, then something catches her
attention.

> IMYA

Marusia, let's go.

Marusia looks up and makes eye contact with a young deer off in the forest. She sees a colorful NECKERCHIEF around one antler.

She smiles as the deer leaps away into the woods.

EXT. VAKYUST - DAY

SUPER: YEARS LATER

Children play in the street, people carry packages, food. Some horses stand at a hitching post.

In the foreground, JAN, 20s, a serious young man, rushes across the street and into the smithy. WE HEAR the hammering of the blacksmith's hammer.

INT. SMITHY - IMMEDIATELY FOLLOWING

A grown Ivor Ivorovich Petroshenko pounds some iron on his anvil. He is bigger than his father, very handsome.

The smithy is full of ORNATE IRONWORK stacked about the room. A CHART on the wall shows neatly labeled columns for new orders and completed orders.

Jan enters, out of breath.

> JAN

Ivor Petroshenko, the council is at a standstill.

> IVOR

How is this my problem, Jan? I don't sit on the council.

> JAN

We were voting on the proposal to finally erect the monument to your father. They don't like it.

> IVOR

And why is that?

> JAN

They - well, really Head Council Fetnik - does not approve of the design. He keeps vetoing it.

                    IVOR

     Let me guess. He wants me to come to the
     council and explain again, yes?

                    JAN

     Yes.

     (a beat)

     He is your brother-in-law, Ivor; you're
     smart, make him understand.

                    IVOR

     (he sighs)

     Okay, I go.

INT. COUNCIL ROOM - MINUTES LATER

A dozen angry COUNCIL MEMBERS argue across the tables.
A grown Ilya Fetnik sits at the head of the council
table trying to calm the members down.

                    ILYA

     Please, please, all I ask is for black-
     smith Petroshenko to explain why...

He looks up as Ivor enters shaking his head.

                    ILYA

     Yes! Here he is now. Ivor Ivorovich,
     will you be so kind as to...

                    IVOR

     Explain the design again?

                    ILYA

     Well, yes.

                    IVOR

     Ilya Piotrovich Fetnik, I've told you a
     dozen times. That is the design I came
     up with, it is fitting.

                    ILYA

     Yes.

                    IVOR

     It is honorable.

                    ILYA

     Yes.

                         IVOR

     It is what my father would have wanted.
     And most importantly...

                         ILYA

     Yes?

                         IVOR

     I'll use my hammer to make sure you
     never reproduce with my sister if you do
     not okay it. Now!

The room goes quiet as the two men stare at each other
across the table. Then Ilya shrugs.

                         ILYA

     Whatever. Make statue.

He STAMPS the paper. The council cheers and wipe at
their brows with handkerchiefs; some shake Ivor's hand.

EXT. VILLAGE SQUARE - SOMETIME LATER

Ilya, Ivor, Marusia and a few other villagers look up
at the STATUE honoring Ivor's father.

                         ILYA

     Ahh! Is a good likeness, Ivor, you did
     well.

                         MARUSIA

     Yes, brother, father would have indeed
     liked it. Your skill is incredible.

                         IVOR

     It is easy when you love your work. And
     I also had a good teacher.

The statue is now seen: A seven foot tall ROOSTER with
a lantern in its beak and a hammer in its claw stands
atop a prostrate witch on a pedestal.

A large HEDGEHOG stands by his side, quill at the
ready.

Baba Yaga's cauldron, filled with earth, is bolted to
the side of the base.

A GARDENER plants FLOWERS in the cauldron.

A plaque on the base dedicates it to Ivor Ivorovich
Petroshenko "As strong as the iron he pounded on".

> ILYA

Do you ever regret not going off on adventures, Ivor?

> IVOR

I've had adventure enough for now, my friend. Perhaps later.

> ILYA

You know, I'm glad you used my idea, Ivor, it will flatter this village for years to come.

> MARUSIA

Oy, please, husband.

> ILYA

Let me speak, wife. I also feel a holiday coming on in my father's honor, Bog rest his soul, Ooh, and a breakfast sausage, too. "FetLinks". Hey! How about little hammer-shaped keychains? Or… or…

He trails off and they walk away and the gathering breaks up. Some people lay flowers at the base of the statue, others point and nod or make other appreciate gestures as they make their departure.

After the last villagers exit, the gardener finishes the planting of some healthy, LUSH plants, he cleans up and puts his tools in a wheel barrow, then slowly moves away.

After a beat, the flowers BLACKEN, wither and CRUMPLE.

FADE OUT

THE END

THE STONE

114

The first time I ever read (or had read to me) the story of Stone Soup was in second grade. I distinctly remember sitting in Story Circle as Mrs. Durkin read the book and showed us the illustrations. I loved it, on the base level that most kids love a good story.

As with Animal Farm and many other stories I was introduced to at a young age, and then subsequently re-read every few years, I found more and more that I liked about Stone Soup the older I got. I never really knew what I was going to do with the different levels of understanding about the story, it seemed I was just going to appreciate it more and more as the years went by.

Then, as luck would have it, I started to work in the entertainment industry, and wound up in a place where I was writing screenplays; at first with an eye on selling them, and then with an eye on producing them myself. One night as I lay there staring at the ceiling, the story of the magic stone that fed a village came back to me, for no apparent reason.

I got up and started to write out a basic story-line, and the next day started to work on the script. And soon, like the villagers contributions to the soldier's meager meal, new ideas came to me as I wrote. I even found a place, and an outlet, to pay homage to one of my favorite Poets, Yevgeny Yevtushenko.

The pieces came together pretty neatly, and when I finished the final draft of this tale, I was pretty happy with the outcome. Some screenplay competitions were happy with it too, as it placed in and won a handful or awards over the next few years.

Soon after, I got some traction with some producers here and there, and damn near got into production on it one summer. An hour north of Austin we found a fantastic location to film 90% of the action, we got permission from the owners of the loca-tion, I had some financing in the chute - the stew was cooking to perfection.

And then somebody kicked the pot over and we were back to square one.

Ahhh, Show Bi'ness.

I have never given up on it though; the story is still good and the location is still there. Most of all, I still have what the soldier brought in the form of a simple stone: hope.

FADE IN

EXT. - COUNTRY ROAD, DAY

Three MEN walk on a dirt road. They are dressed poorly
for the spring chill. Their pace suggests no urgency.

In the far distance of the background, wisps of
dark SMOKE waft towards the clouds. VULTURES circle
ominously.

The men all wear some kind of military uniform. Two
have old, weathered rifles. The insignias and styles of
their uniforms are not recognizable, but they all wear
the same. Their faces and uniforms are dirty and they
all have scraggly beards.

The trio are MIKAH, PASHE and TEODORO. Mikah, 30's, is
confident and calm. His face suggests a good nature, but
there are scars that show the wear he has endured.

Pashe is older and taller than Mikah, a strong build
and harsh facial features accented by a pair of
spectacles with cracked lenses.

Teodoro is young, heavy-set, dopey and smiling. He has
no weapon, and his uniform doesn't fit well.

EXT. MOUNTAIN STREAM - DAY

The trio crosses on large STONES jutting out of the
water.

Teodoro stops and sees a FISH resting in a small eddy. He stares as his friends walk on.

Pashe stops when he notices Teodoro is not keeping up. He turns.

> PASHE
>
> Teodoro, no time for games. Let's go.

Teodoro licks his lips, looks up to see where Pashe and Mikah are, then back down at the fish.

> MIKAH
>
> Leave him be, he'll catch up.

Pashe gives Mikah a quick look.

> PASHE
>
> We stick together, remember? I won't
> leave him behind, not even for a minute.

Mikah shrugs slightly as Pashe heads back toward Teodoro, whose gaze is still attached to the fish.

> TEODORO
>
> I could catch you.

EXT. ROLLING HILLS — DAY

Pashe and Mikah look off into the distance as they walk. Teodoro is dripping wet just behind them, his bottom lip sticking out in a huge POUT.

> TEODORO
>
> Stupid fish.

> PASHE
>
> We've told you Teodoro, don't try to be
> clever; you're not good at it.

> TEODORO
>
> I would have caught it, Pashe. If the
> rocks weren't so slippery. And if the
> water wasn't so deep. And if...

Pashe and Mikah stop dead and stare ahead. Teodoro has his head DOWN and doesn't see them stop; he RUNS INTO Pashe. He looks up to see what they are staring at.

Tendrils of SMOKE come into view over a low hill. The three climb the small hill toward the haze.

Upon reaching the top of the rise, they see the REMAINS

of a small village at the bottom of the other side of
the hill, burned to the ground.

                         TEODORO

          Have they left any village untouched?

The scene seems to affect Pashe somewhat more than his
companions. Mikah steals a sideways peak at Pashe, then
gently PATS his shoulder.

They stare for a moment longer at the charred remnants
of buildings, wagons and tools, then start walking
again. Pashe tears his eyes from the scene and spots
SOMETHING on the ground a step or so away.

                         PASHE

          Look.

Pashe steps over, kneels and picks up something SHINY
and shows it to Mikah.

INSERT — METAL BUCKLE

A square, heavy BUCKLE with a black DRAGON etched into
it. A shred of purple material hangs from it.

Mikah squints at the buckle, then the three exchange
glances.

                         PASHE

          Yes. The same ones.

                         MIKAH

          Hmm.

                         PASHE

          Over there.

Pashe points at the ground a few yards away and walks
over, then kneels. Mikah and Teodoro follow. Pashe
examines the disturbed earth.

                         PASHE

          These are not the same tracks. Looks
          like many more, but lighter, moving
          faster.

                         MIKAH

          Dangerous?

                          PASHE

          Hard to say. I would have to guess no.
          They don't move the same.

                         TEODORO

          Well, some good news anyway.

Mikah and Pashe look at him quizzically.

                         TEODORO

          At least we know one of them can't keep
          his pants up anymore.

                          PASHE

          Teodoro, what would we do without you?

Mikah and Pashe smile and pat Teodoro on the shoulder.
They turn and slowly start on again, walking out of
sight.

EXT. DIRT ROAD - LATE AFTERNOON

At the edge of a small village, a young girl, Rifka —
10, shaggy hair, torn clothing - watches the trio of
Mikah, Pashe and Teodoro as they approach.

Her sister, Antolina — 13, similar clothing - comes up
from behind her and pulls her away.

                         Antolina

          Rifka, come, father wants...

She notices the three men, then shoots a frightened
glance behind her. She hurries off with Rifka.

EXT. VILLAGE STREET — DAY

Mikah, Pashe and Teodoro walk into the village,
glancing around at the modest, practical buildings.
This village has not been cared for in recent years.

PEOPLE - men, women, children - rush into their houses.
A few MEN stay outside, trying not to act afraid, but
not really looking very brave, either.

Mikah, Pashe and Teodoro stop in the middle of the
street and look around them.

It is a small village, little bigger than the one that
was burned from the look of it. Trash piles dot the
area, broken equipment sits unattended in a smithy; the
well is boarded up.

Their eyes stop for a moment on a small sward where
GRAVE MARKERS stand as a grim reminder of the recent
war. Mikah scans the names on the markers; his gaze
rests on one particular marker that has a SYMBOL above
the name.

Insert: grave marker: "Elana - Faith Keeper"

Mikah looks up to the villagers.

> MIKAH

Hello. Hello!

The villagers who remain in the street shuffle
nervously.

> MIKAH

Hello?

One observer starts to SAY something, he is NUDGED by
HENRIK (50s) — a sturdy, fussy lump of a man - and
shuts up.

> MIKAH

We mean you no harm. We just need a
place to rest for the night.

> PASHE

It would help us out greatly, friends,
if we could camp...

Henrik hesitantly speaks.

> HENRIK

You are not welcome here. Leave.

> PASHE

That is not very friendly.

> TEODORO

We will be gone by morning.

> HENRIK

Better you are gone now.

The three look at each other in mock surprise.

> PASHE

You hear that, Teodoro? How these sheep
do speak.

>   (to Henrik)
>
> We are going home from the war.

Henrik gets agitated, waving his hand absent-mindedly.

>   HENRIK
>
> If you are going to burn us out, do it
> now. Get it over with.

>   TEODORO
>
> You want us to burn you out?

>   VILLAGER 2
>
>   (indicating Henrik)
>
> I don't know him.

Villager 2 hurries away from the other man, finds his
house and disappears inside.

>   HENRIK
>
> We saw smoke from over the hill, that
> village was destroyed. Now you are here.
> Just coincidence?

Teodor, Pashe and Mikah look at themselves again, all
nod.

>   TEODORO/PASHE
>
> Yes.

>   VILLAGER 3
>
> You have guns, you look like all the
> others.

>   HENRIK
>
> So get it over with already.

>   MIKAH
>
> They've got us.

>   PASHE
>
> Yes, they must have had spies in that
> other village. Now we'll have to proceed
> with our plan.

>   TEODORO
>
> And they won't even fight back. How easy.

Mikah pulls an old LIGHTER from his pocket, stares
right at Henrik. He raises it, flips it open.

Teodoro and Pashe laugh evilly and start to un-sling their gear.

Henrik and the other mens' faces show surprise and fear, they back off, bump into each other, and finally RUN for their houses and SLAM doors behind them.

EXT. VILLAGE SQUARE - DAY

Mikah, Pashe and Teodoro continue into the village square. Mikah points to a spot and they start to set up a camp. Pashe gathers up fluffy MOSS clumps to make bedding for their blankets.

> PASHE
>
> I have never seen so much of this. It
> grows well here.

They continue to set up camp, oblivious to the village around them.

INT. RIFKA'S HOUSE - SAME

Antolina peers through a CRACK in the window shutter. She watches the three men work.

> Antolina
>
> They are setting up camp.

> Rifka
>
> I thought they were going to burn us
> out?

> Antolina
>
> They are.

> Rifka
>
> Who would sleep where they plan to burn?

Antolina makes a face and turns from the window.

> Antolina
>
> You don't know anything. Bar the door,
> they will be gone by morning.

INT. RIFKA'S HOUSE - DAY

Antolina is asleep at the window, Rifka sleeps on a cot in the corner. Antolina raises her head with a start. The sun is up and shining through the window. She opens the shutter a crack and peers out at Mikah's camp.

Mikah sets up a COOKING AREA with fire ring and tripod.

Teodoro and Pashe move lazily, one scrubs CLOTHING in a basin of water, the other hangs them on a LINE to dry. They show no signs of leaving.

Henrik is behind her now, peering over her shoulder at the soldiers. He licks his lips, vexed.

> HENRIK
>
> Looks like bad weather, we should stay inside today.

> Antolina
>
> You should do something.

> HENRIK
>
> I am...

> Antolina
>
> Hiding in your house is not doing something.

> HENRIK
>
> I'm not hiding. And it is not my place...

> Antolina
>
> Do you want this to end up like the last? How many times must...

> HENRIK
>
> It is not my place.

Antolina harrumps and pulls away, She throws the bar from the door and rushes outside.

EXT. RIFKA'S HOUSE - FOLLOWING

Antolina stands at the doorway and GLARES defiantly at the soldiers. They take no notice of her.

She scans the ground by the house, spots a BRICK, stoops to pick it up.

Henrik is behind her again.

> HENRIK
>
> What are you doing?

> Antolina
>
> Your job.

She HEAVES the brick toward the soldiers, then stoops to grab another. Henrik wrestles the second brick from her hands.

                    HENRIK

          Are you insane? What if…

The first brick CRASHES nosily through the soldiers
camp, upsetting the wash basin.

Pashe and Teodoro look up toward RIFKA'S HOUSE. Mikah
spots Henrik standing there, holding another brick.

                    HENRIK

          Get inside, Antolina. Now.

Mikah stands. He grabs a short thick piece of WOOD from
the firewood pile and brandishes it.

                    Antolina

          No, I'm not afraid of them.

                    HENRIK

          Now.

Antolina fumes, goes into the house. Mikah starts to
march toward Henrik menacingly, cudgel in hand.

Henrik panics, he looks around for support. CURTAINS
and SHUTTERS close in nearby houses. Sounds of bars
going on doors, and latches being thrown.

He looks back toward Mikah, who is getting close.

Henrik starts to freak, he looks at the brick in his
hand, then up at Mikah, quickly closing in. He drops
the brick, turns to run

Bam

He runs into the side of his house and falls.

Henrik opens his eyes, Mikah is over him, brandishing
the cudgel.

                    HENRIK

          Sorry… I… I was trying to

Antolina's voice breaks in from inside house

                    Antolina (VO)

          He was trying to get rid of you thieves.

                    HENRIK

          Yes, I was… NO! No... that's not it at
          all, I…

Mikah GRABS Henrik by the front of his shirt and yanks him to his feet — they are face to face now. Mikah holds the stick up for Henrik to see.

> MIKAH
>
> This is very good firewood. Do you know where can we find some more of it? We just want to dry our clothes, then we'll be leaving.

INT. RIFKA'S HOUSE - LATER

Henrik argues with Antolina.

> Antolina
>
> Liars. Three days now. We should have run them off when they first arrived.

> HENRIK
>
> They were almost gone, they'll probably just stay longer now after what you did.

> Antolina
>
> You were doing nothing, father! Somebody needs to do act. Look at how they have us trapped in our own homes, terrified to leave.

> HENRIK
>
> I like spending time with you and Rifka.

> Antolina
>
> Oh father, please!

> HENRIK
>
> T do — in fact I hope we have a few more days so that Rifka and I can...

Hew looks around the room.

> HENRIK
>
> Rifka? Rifka? Antolina, where is your sister?

She spies about the small dwelling for her sister, but does not find her.

She glances back out the WINDOW, and sees Rifka approaching the soldiers unafraid.

EXT. CAMPSITE - DAY

Mikah looks up from his work and sees Rifka approaching
cautiously. Mikah SMILES faintly.

EXT. COUNTRY ROAD — DAY

A half dozen HORSEMEN and about a dozen more men on
foot are stopped in the middle of the road. On a
shield is visible the black dragon emblem from the
belt buckle.

GURKIN, a fat, dumpy walrus of a soldier in black
leather and thick glasses, seems to hold his PURPLE
BELT SASH proudly as he stares into the distance.

The VOICE of Drakko booms behind Gurkin OC.

                        DRAKKO

          Well, Gurkin?

                        GURKIN

          The prisoners have come this way,
          Oh Biceptuous One. But the trail is
          muddled here.

                        DRAKKO

          They have covered their tracks?

                        GURKIN

          I think they split up. No matter. I am
          wily, fearless, and untiring. They will
          be found.

He abruptly turns and thrusts his clenched fists over
his head.

                        GURKIN

          Our vengeance will be swift and
          terrible.

His belt sash FALLS apart where he was holding it and
his pants DROP around his ankles, showing dingy, lacy
BOXERS.

His fellow soldiers laugh out loud. Gurkin quickly
tries to pull his trousers up.

A tall, hulking man in black chain armor steps past
Gurkin to observe the countryside. His back to us.

This is DRAKKO, 50's, a cruel and hateful behemoth.
He has slung on his back a huge sturdy CLUB with the
pointy end of a spike protruding from it.

He turns, and a large, fresh SCAR/WOUND is revealed on
his face, diagonally bisecting his visage.

                    DRAKKO

          Forgive me if I am less than confident.
          Find the man who did this to me.

                    GURKIN

          WHOA! That looks like it might be
          getting a bit puss-y...

Drakko glares at Gurkin.

                    GURKIN

          ...Which only improves your darn-near
          perfect looks anyway. A Regal Nastiness
          to be sure, my Elephant-Sized Warlord.

A BIRD alights on a small downed TREE near the roadside
and chirps happily.

In one motion, Drakko whips the club off his back and
smashes the tree into kindling. Bird FEATHERS float up
from the road.

                    DRAKKO

          Find the trail, Gurkin, before I feel
          like hitting something again.

                    GURKIN

          Yes, Most Offensive One.

EXT. VILLAGE SQUARE - DAY

Rifka stops and stares at Mikah, who takes out a small
POT to hang on a cooking TRIPOD - made from the rifles
and a sturdy stick - and sets it over a small pile of
sticks.

Mikah pats the stump next to him. Rifka accepts the
invitation and sits, smiling.

Teodoro and Pashe see what is happening and smile to
each other.

                    PASHE

          It starts already.

                    TEODORO

          He gets better every day. He should be
          king.

                         PASHE

       Bah. He would be wasted as king.

They watch for a few moments as Mikah talks quietly
with Rifka while readying his cooking area. He shows
Rifka the different utensils he has.

Suddenly, Antolina appears behind Rifka. She brandishes
a piece of FIREWOOD.

                       Antolina

       What are you doing with my sister?

Rifka is startled.

                        Rifka

       Antolina! This man is showing me how to
       cook a great feast.

                       Antolina

       He is, is he? Planning to steal what
       little food we have to gorge themselves?

Antolina yanks Rifka to her feet, shielding her younger
sister, holding the cudgel at the ready.

Mikah rises slowly to a standing position.

                        MIKAH

       I did not mean to upset you. I was just
       showing your sister here...

                       Antolina

       ...How to bully your way through life,
       taking what you want, no matter how you
       harm others?

                        MIKAH

       Have I taken anything I shouldn't have,
       other than your sister's attention for a
       few minutes?

                       Antolina

       N... no.

                        MIKAH

       I do not plan to take any of your food.
       We have more than what we need, anyway.

                    Antolina

          Good, because there isn't any. You said
          you would go. Go.

                    TEODORO

          Why are you so hostile?

Antolina thinks a moment.

                    Antolina

          Soldiers come and take and take and
          take. We have nothing left.

                    PASHE

          How do you feed yourselves, then?

                    Antolina

          We do not eat.

Pashe and Teodoro laugh.

                    PASHE

          You do not eat? Did you hear that,
          Teodoro? This must be a special village
          indeed. No need for food.

They laugh some more.

                    MIKAH

          We will use only what we have. You and
          your sister are welcome to share.

He motions for them to sit, Antolina ignores him and
backs up.

                    Antolina

          So, you plan to torture us by making us
          watch you stuff your fat faces with goods
          taken from others? Is that it?

                    MIKAH

          If that is what you want.

He shrugs and bends to his work again, shifting his
bulging pack closer to the pot.

Antolina and Rifka watch as he pours the last water
from his CANTEEN into the pot. It is not much.

He puts out his hand without looking as Teodoro and
Pashe drape their canteen straps across his palm.

Mikah empties the little bit of water from these
canteens into the pot as well.

PASHE

It is not much, Mikah, will it work?

MIKAH

Probably better.

TEODORO

(Smiling)

He makes the best soup.

Antolina and Rifka lick their lips and stare at the
pot, almost willing it to fill with delicious soup.

Rifka

What kind of soup, Antolina? Lentil?
Beef?

Antolina

Don't waste your time dreaming, Rifka.
In the end, they will not share. They
never do.

PASHE

You could always share with your neighbors instead.

Antolina

Ha. No one shares.

TEODORO

No one? Why?

Antolina

There is nothing left to share. We keep
what little we have for ourselves.

MIKAH

I said you are welcome, you are. Sit.
When it is ready, eat.

TEODORO

Yes, join us. You two will eat way
better than the rest of your village
tonight.

Antolina eyes the three warily, then greedily sits, rubbing her hands and nearly drooling.

Rifka does not sit, she glances back toward her house.

> MIKAH
>
> What's the matter, girl? You're not hungry?

> Rifka
>
> No, not now. Thank you, though.

> Antolina
>
> Sit, Rifka! We will have a meal fit for kings and queens tonight.

> Rifka
>
> I would rather have what father is eating, Antolina.

The three men look quickly to each other. Mikah eyes the girl, his face reflects a bemused admiration.

> Antolina
>
> Sit. It is better a few of us feed off of these who have been leaching off of us for so long, than for all of us to starve.

> MIKAH
>
> They may all join us.

> Antolina
>
> What? Who?

> MIKAH
>
> The village. Go and tell your family, Rifka, they may all join us for a meal.

> Antolina
>
> You have barely enough water for broth for the two of us.

> PASHE
>
> Five of us.

> Antolina
>
> Whatever... and now you want the whole village to join in? What kind of soup are you making?

Mikah rummages in his backpack and finally finds what he
is looking for.

                    MIKAH

     Ahh, here it is.

He unceremoniously drops a large STONE into the pot of
water with a dull CLUNK and smiles up at Antolina.

Antolina's face twists in anger and frustration.

                 Antolina

     You lying...

                  TEODORO

     (Smiling)

     He makes the BEST soup.

A thin wisp of steam rises from the pot into the air. A
very faint smiling FACE can be seen in the wisp for a
second, then is gone.

INT. RIFKA'S HOUSE — DAY

Antolina and Henrik argue; it's hard to tell who is
the parent and who the child. Rifka stands by, eagerly
waiting to jump into the discussion.

                  HENRIK

     What? He makes soup with rocks?

                 Antolina

     Yes! And then he invites the entire
     village to eat with them.

                  HENRIK

     You are crazy, daughter. Men do not eat
     rocks. It must have been a large turnip
     or something.

                   Rifka

     It was a stone, father. He said it was
     magic!

                 Antolina

     Hush, Rifka!

Henrik steals a furtive peek out the window.

                  HENRIK

     Is he the Devil?

                              Rifka

          No, father. He told me an old man gave
          it to him years ago. It is magic and it
          makes any kind of food you like, as much
          as you like!

                             HENRIK

          Bah! You know I do not believe in magic.

Henrik peers out through the crack in the shutters at
the men who laugh and joke around the cooking fire.

EXT. VILLAGE - DAY

Eyes peer out through cracks in shutters or from behind
curtains in half a dozen houses.

TRESLYN — 30ish, a confident young woman — does not hide
herself. She stands and peers out through an open door.

EXT. COOKING FIRE - DAY

Pashe spies Treslyn as he warms his hands over the fire.
Treslyn closes the door slowly. Pashe smiles as he
steals a glance toward RIFKA'S house and the shutter
SLAPS closed.

                             MIKAH

          They'll be out soon.

                             PASHE

          This village is not like the others.
          These people have been through much.

                             MIKAH

          All villages are alike, Pashe. Big or
          small. East or west.

                             PASHE

          This one is different.

Mikah looks up at his friend, who looks about uneasily,
nervously.

                             MIKAH

          It reminds you of yours, yes?

                             PASHE

          They have nothing to give, Mikah.

                    MIKAH

        You never know what you have, my friend,
        until you have what you know.

Pashe relaxes a bit, nods in agreement. The three sit a
moment or two, then Teodoro turns to Pashe; he motions
with his hands.

                    TEODORO

        Is that one of those... thinking things?

Pashe nods. Mikah smiles and stirs the pot with a
wooden spoon.

Henrik approaches abruptly and the four stare at each
other for a beat. Pashe MOTIONS toward the pot, and
Henrik leans over and peers into it.

                    HENRIK

        My daughter tells me you cook magic
        rocks to eat.

                    MIKAH

        It's a stone.

Henrik looks suspiciously at the three, peers into the
pot again and sees a hot, wet stone at the bottom of
roiling water.

                    HENRIK

        How can that little bit feed so many? If
        it were edible.

                    PASHE

        My friend here is the magic man. Treat
        him right and he can do a world of good.

                    HENRIK

        Magic. Hah!

                    MIKAH

        No magic, eh? You must be the Faith
        Keeper for this village then.

Henrik looks to the ground, then makes a brief motion
toward the graveyard, before looking back at the
ground.

                    HENRIK

        Our Faith Keeper died years ago.
        She was...

                    MIKAH

     We understand. (a beat) They do usually
     work in pairs.

Henrik glares at the men briefly.

                    HENRIK

     He is buried with her.

There is silence between the four men. Then Henrik
looks back in the pot.

                    HENRIK

     And what if I treat this Magic Man
     wrong?

                    TEODORO

     Then you do yourself a world of bad.

                    HENRIK

     Ha. If you can do, I can do better.

Henrik looks around, picks up a ROCK and brandishes it
threateningly.

                    HENRIK

     Hah! I will make my own stone soup.

                    MIKAH

     No.

                    HENRIK

     Why? I have a stone. I will make soup
     too.

                    MIKAH

     That's not a stone. That's a rock.

                    HENRIK

     Eh? No matter.

Henrik tosses it aside and grabs up another.

                    PASHE

     That's a rock too.

Henrik throws it aside and picks up another.

                    TEODOR

     Rock.

Mikah shakes his head.

                    MIKAH

You have a lot of rocks around here.

Henrik picks up a number of rocks, to which they all
shake their heads.

              MIKAH/PASHE/TEODORO

    Rock.

                   TEODORO

    Ooh, over there. That is a stone.
    Right there.

Henrik scurries over and picks it up.

                   TEODORO

    Oops, sorry. That's also a rock.

Henrik angrily HURLS the rock toward the woods. Pashe
and Teodoro chuckle.

                   HENRIK

    Bah!

                    MIKAH

    My friends play a joke on you,

Mikah waves his hand, waits for an answer.

                   HENRIK

    Henrik.

                    MIKAH

    Henrik. Sit. I'll tell you about this
    stone here.

                   HENRIK

    I do not need stories from you. Where is
    the food you promised my children?

                    MIKAH

    It's here in the pot.

                   HENRIK

    Bah! I have cared for my children for
    years and have never had to eat rocks.

                    PASHE

    I think you will be happy with his soup,
    Henrik. Give him a chance.

Henrik wheels on Pashe, all at once very angry.

> HENRIK
>
> Give him a chance? The mother of my
> children gave soldiers a chance five
> years ago, and where did it get her?
> Where did it get us? Don't speak to me
> of chances, you thieving liar...

Pashe stands up slowly in front of Henrik, a good head
or so taller, and much wider than the short, round man.
He looks ready to fight.

Henrik's eyes bulge, he swallows nervously but does not
back away.

Teodoro looks between Mikah and Pashe, he does not
move. Mikah motions discreetly to Pashe, who then
relaxes his stance.

> MIKAH
>
> What can a short tale hurt, my friend.
> If, when I am done, you still want us to
> leave, we will. Agreed?

Henrik fidgets and stares at Pashe, like a deer in
headlights.

Pashe smiles and gestures with both hands.

> PASHE
>
> I'm sorry, sir; it has been a long
> journey, and my manners are hidden by
> my fatigue.

Henrik, visibly relieved, turns as he sits next to
Mikah.

> HENRIK
>
> Very well, what of your rock?

Mikah taps the pot with his wooden spoon, then FROWNS
at the water.

> MIKAH
>
> You see, a long time ago, hmm...

> HENRIK
>
> What?

> MIKAH
>
> Oh, nothing. Maybe.

                    HENRIK

What's wrong?

                    MIKAH

Just looks like the water is a little
low, probably won't matter, but

                    HENRIK

But what? What?

                    MIKAH

Might have to give just a tiny bit less
to everyone. No great matter. Now,
Henrik, this stone was given to me by...

                    HENRIK

If you had more water, could we have
more soup?

                    MIKAH

Excellent reasoning there, sir; but
again, I think it should maybe be
enough.

                    HENRIK

I... may have some water in my house.
Just a little, mind you.

                    MIKAH

No, we couldn't. We said we'd take
nothing from you good people.

                    HENRIK

I don't mind. I shall get it.

He stands to leave.

                    PASHE

Well then, friend, you shall have an
extra little bit then.

Henrik heads toward his house; thinks a moment, then
looks back toward Mikah.

                    HENRIK

It... it is all of us. My family and me.
WE have a little water to spare.

Mikah and his friends look to each other.

                    TEODORO

     Then you all shall have a little extra.
     Thank you.

                    HENRIK

     No problem.

He hurries off toward his house, stealing suspicious
glances at the other houses.

EXT. DRAKKO'S ENCAMPMENT - DAY

Drakko's men engage in all manner of foolish GAMES of
strength - cheating at every turn. Many get severely
injured, to the amusement of the rest.

Drakko sits on his throne, watching the games. Gurkin
fusses about him, trying to clean and touch-up the
wound on Drakko's face. He has to keep shooing a large
FLY away from the wound.

Drakko's face travels back and forth from stupid
amusement, to pained anger as Gurkin dabs at the gash.

                    GURKIN

       Please hold still, my Larger-than-
       is-necessary Master, I can't clean
       your... uh... Handsomeness Accent.

                    DRAKKO

       My men grow restless to raid, Gurkin. We
       can't stay here for too long.

Gurkin motions OS to the men and games.

                    GURKIN

       As you wish, Sire. After this round of
       "Poke My Eye With A Stick," we will be
       on our way.

A loud, sickening SQUISH is heard. Gurkin and Drakko
flinch.

                    GURKIN

       I believe we have a winner.

Gurkin addresses the camp, still trying to shoo the fly.

                    GURKIN

       Make ready to ride, men. We must find the
       prisoner before nightfall.

The FLY alights on Drakko's nose, Gurkin double-takes, then smashes the fly (and so Drakko's face) with a backhand.

Drakko screams and lunges to his feet, holding his face. Gurkin cringes.

                    DRAKKO

        Aaaah! When I find him, I will destroy
        him and every living thing nearby!

                    GURKIN

        Your destruction will be legendary, Most
        Wide and Thick Antagonist. (to the men)
        You heard Drakko - get ready NOW.

The men quickly start to pack up.

INT. RIFKA'S HOUSE — DAY

Henrik pulls small BASINS from hiding places in the house - under floorboards, behind the woodpile, etc.

                    Antolina

        Father, what are you doing? He mocks
        us and taunts us and you give him our
        water? We will die.

                    HENRIK

        No, Antolina. We will eat well for a day
        or two.

                    Antolina

        No stranger has ever given us anything
        but pain; why do you do this?

                    HENRIK

        Do not question me, child. It is my
        duty to take care of you and your
        sister. I'm doing that. If we give him
        our water, he will give us a little
        extra soup.

The VOICE of Zola, from behind, startles them.

                    ZOLA (OC)

        Soup? Who has soup? They are going to
        give you soup?

Henrik and Antolina turn to see another woman, ZOLA — matronly, harsh - and her daughter, ANNA — eight,

street urchin looks, in the doorway. They are dressed
the same - ragged, wrinkled clothes.

                    ZOLA

        Why do you get soup while Anna and I
        starve?

                    Antolina

        We get nothing, widow Zola. Mind your
        own business.

                    ZOLA

        Do not take that tone with me, child.

                    HENRIK

        Both of you stop. The soldiers said they
        will feed us some of their magic soup,
        and they ask nothing from us.

                    ZOLA

        Then why are you taking your hidden
        water to them?

                    HENRIK

        Hidden water? What hidden water? Who
        ever heard of 'hidden' water?

Zola looks past Henrik to Antolina, who was putting
a jug back under a floor board, then up to Rifka on a
chair. She takes a CORK out of the nostril of a mounted
elk's HEAD on the wall and water runs out into a
tankard Rifka holds.

Henrik looks down at his basin in shame, then back up.

                    HENRIK

        Umm, we... we...

                    ZOLA

        You told us last week you had no water,
        Antolina.

                    Antolina

        We didn't, Zola. We... father?

There is a tense beat between them. Then

                    HENRIK

        We found it.

Henrik hurries out of the room, sloshing water.

EXT. COOKING POT — DAY

Mikah's pot is filled with water now.

                         MIKAH

          Oh, yes. That topped it off nicely,
          Henrik, thank you very much.

                         HENRIK

          It is nothing compared to your soup, my
          friend. By the way, uh...

                         MIKAH

          Yes?

                         HENRIK

          When will, um, it be...

                         TEODORO

          Finished?

                         PASHE

          Ready to eat?

                         HENRIK

          Yes.

                         MIKAH

          A little longer yet.

Mikah looks over Henrik's shoulder and sees some other
VILLAGERS approaching angrily.

Henrik follows his gaze and sees Zola heading up a
small group.

                         HENRIK

          Blast! Lousy gossip. A thousand curses
          on her.

Zola and her platoon stop as their SHADOWS cover Henrik
and Mikah.

                         ZOLA

          Why do you feed his family and not ours?

                         MIKAH

          Pardon me?

                         ZOLA

          You plan to feed only them. My family is
          hungry also. Why do you not feed us as
          well?

                         PASHE

          We extended the invitation to the entire
          village.

Zola peers into the pot.

                         ZOLA

          There is not enough there to even feed
          yourselves.

                         TEODORO

          It's magic.

                         ZOLA

          Magic. Hah! There is no way you can feed
          the village from that small pot.

                         MIKAH

          We can't?

                         ZOLA

          No.

Mikah looks to Henrik, then back to Zola.

                         MIKAH

          Are you sure?

                         ZOLA

          Are you deaf as well as stupid?

                         MIKAH

          What do we do?

EXT. ZOLA'S COTTAGE - DAY

Zola drects as LOTHAR — 40s - 50s, a stoic mountain -
drags a heavy iron CAULDRON out of the house and sets
it on a cart.

The cart is pulled away by an old gray DONKEY.

EXT. COOKING POT — DAY

The donkey cart pulls up to Mikah. Zola gestures
proudly.

                    ZOLA

You see? Put your magic soup in there,
then it will feed enough.

                    MIKAH

How do you know?

                    ZOLA

Because I am a cook. Ask my brother.
Right Lothar?

                    LOTHAR

She cooks.

                    ZOLA

In good years I fed the whole village
from that.

                    PASHE

You are a cook? What do you cook?

                    ZOLA

I was a cook. But I could cook anything!
Ask Lothar. Lothar?

                    LOTHAR

Anything.

                    ZOLA

I could cook anything.

                    MIKAH

Ah, then you must have made stone soup
before.

Some of the other skeptical villagers stare at Zola,
she fidgets nervously. She sweats it.

                    ZOLA

    Only once...

"Ahhhs" go up from the crowd.

                    MIKAH

    Great, then perhaps you would like to
    help, eh?

Zola fidgets and looks at the faces of her neighbors,
silently challenging her.

> ZOLA

It is your soup; good cooks never
interfere with

> TEODORO

We don't mind.

> MIKAH

A good cook welcomes knowledgeable help.
But if you don't want to.

> ZOLA

I really can't, because I... Lothar?

> LOTHAR

Help.

> ZOLA

Shut up Lothar.

Lothar shrugs and sits on the edge of the donkey cart.
Mikah stands.

> MIKAH

Terrific. Pashe, Teodoro, help me get
this cauldron set up over our fire.

A man moves forward.

> MAN

That small fire will never heat that pot.
You need a bigger one.

> MIKAH

Oh, I don't think so; we have plenty of
wood, see?

He motions to the small pile of STICKS they have set by
the fire. Most of it looks wet.

> MAN

Hah! You couldn't burn your thumb with
that pile of twigs.

Teodoro fiddles with the fire, then abruptly pulls his
singed THUMB away and sticks it in his mouth.

> MAN

I will get you some better wood.

                         PASHE

     Please, we don't want to take anything
     from you kind people. The pot is one
     thing, but...

                         MAN

     If you do it your way, none of us will
     ever eat.

He turns and leaves among NODS and WHISPERS from the
throng. Mikah, Pashe and Teodoro start the task of
unloading the cauldron.

EXT. COOK FIRE - DAY

The cauldron sits atop a huge fire and Mikah empties
his tiny pot into it, the stone falls with a deep,
resonating clang.

                         MIKAH

     Ahh! Smell that.

                         TEODOR

     Is there enough water, Mikah?

                         MIKAH

     Ssshh, Teodoro.

                         HENRIK

     What? Why do you whisper? Is there not
     enough, we have no more.

                         MIKAH

     We did not ask, Henrik. This... will
     have to do.

Some of the other villagers pay close attention.

                         MIKAH

     We will have to make this work. Do not
     worry, if it comes down to it, we,
     ourselves - and maybe just one or two
     more - will do without.

The villagers shuffle nervously. Treslyn furtively
raises her HAND.

                         TRESLYN

     Uh, there may be some water left at the
     bottom of the well.

Everyone looks toward the boarded up WELL.

                    PASHE

     It looks dry to me.

                    HENRIK

     After the last soldiers came through,
     they took all the water they could
     carry. Then they told us that the well
     was dry, and boarded it up.

                    MIKAH

     Terrible. To look down into your own
     well and see no water at the bottom.

The villagers stare at each other for a moment,
embarrassed at the obvious question.

                    HENRIK

     They... they told me it was... dry.

EXT. WELL - FOLLOWING

BOARDS BEND and BREAK as Teodoro pries them with his
bayoneted rifle as a lever. They all look into it.

                    WOMAN

     Water! There is water down there. They
     lied to us.

                    MAN

     We have been dying for months, Henrik
     and we had water all along.

                    ZOLA

     It has refilled for us. Little miracles
     happen all the time.

Henrik makes a face and silently mocks Zola. Lothar
catches Henrik's gaze. Lothar is not happy. Henrik
licks his lips and stops his mocking.

                    ZOLA

     Things may be starting to get better.

The crowd's tired faces smile a little and nod.

                    TEODORO

     Maybe they poisoned it.

Everyone stops dead for a few seconds and stares
daggers at Teodoro.

                        TEODORO

          I'm just saying, is all. They could have
          dropped a dead goat down there. Or a
          bale of Sickweed... or half a goat and
          three handfulls of sickweed, or...

Pashe WHAPS him upside his head.

                        PASHE

          Whose side are you on?

                        ZOLA

          Someone should test it.

They all stare at Teodoro, who smiles weakly, panics,
then points.

They follow his direction and look toward the old, gray
donkey, who flicks his ear at a fly and utters what would
pass for a "HUH?"

EXT. WELL - DAY

The villagers pour WATER from a bucket into a PAN,
sit it in front of the donkey and FORCE its head
down into it.

The donkey DRINKS greedily then comes up for air. The
villagers all pause breathlessly. The donkey starts to
make noises and staggers a little. The villagers wince.

                        DONKEY

          BBBBUUUUURP.

EXT. CAULDRON OVER THE FIRE - LATER

The cauldron now BRIMS with water, and steam rolls off
in voluminous wisps.

All the villagers gather around, smiling, watching the
soup boil.

Mikah, Teodoro and Pashe sit a little way off. Mikah
CARVES a small TOY out of wood. The toy looks a bit
like a Russian Matreshka doll.

Mikah rubs some charcoal across the doll's face, then
blows off the excess dust. The black highlights the
carved features. He hands it to Anna, and she joins her
friends in play.

Henrik wanders by, craning to look into the cauldron.

                              MIKAH
          How's it doing, Zola?

                              HENRIK
          Ha, Lothar's donkey knows more about
          cooking than her.

Mikah ignores the comment. Zola feints a blow with the
spoon, Henrik backs off. Zola stirs the soup.

                              ZOLA
          It is doing, um, fine. It looks rather
          plain... and thin, still.

                              MIKAH
          Perfect.

                              ZOLA
          Don't you have anything else to liven it
          up just a bit?

                              PASHE
          Nope. Doesn't need it.

                              ZOLA
          Potatoes, beets... anything?

                              TEODORO
          Nope. Doesn't need it.

                              HENRIK
          Lentils? You have lentils?

                         MIKAH/PASHE/TEODORO
          Doesn't need it.

The three start to wander away from the fire. The folks
around the pot look at each other and at the thin soup.

                              ZOLA
          I don't care what he says. It looks
          plain. We should check their packs. They
          hold out on us I bet.

Treslyn stands near the cauldron, watching.

                              TRESLYN
          No. We shouldn't repay their generosity
          with ...

                         ZOLA

     YOU eat hot water, I am getting some of
     their food.

Zola looks to Mikah and the other two as they PLAY with
the KIDS and talk to each other; then she sneaks over
to their BED ROLLS.

She pokes around for a few moments, then finds Mikah's
bulging PACK. Just as she reaches inside, Mikah is over
her, and he snatches up the pack in one hand.

                         MIKAH

     Okay, okay. I will add more. But I warn
     you, it may ruin the whole thing.

                         ZOLA

     Aha! I told you so.

She gestures toward the others around the cauldron,
they lower their gazes as Mikah steps over to the pot.
He reaches into his pack, making faces as he fishes
around.

                         MIKAH

     I hope you are all satisfied. This may
     very well destroy the soup for everyone.

He sighs heavily and closes his eyes. Quickly, he pulls
out another STONE and plops it into the cauldron.

                         MIKAH

     There. Fancy enough for you now?

He angrily tosses his pack on the ground and stalks
away. The rest of the villagers scowl at Zola.

An older man, JON, timidly motions with his hand.

                         JON

     I... I think I may have a potato or two
     at my house.

                         ZOLA

     Jon? You have potatoes, Jon? You said
     you had no potatoes, Jon.

                         JON

     Actually, my son found them in our old
     garden from last season.

                    MIKAH

          Absolutely not. We want nothing...

                    ZOLA

          Quiet, thin-soup maker.

She moves closer to Jon as she eyes Mikah.

                    ZOLA

          I guess your potatoes would liven it up
          a bit, Jon.

                    TEODORO

          Ahh, you are an unselfish saint, my
          friend. An extra big portion for you.

                    JON

          No, I will take what everyone else has.
          I only have one or two potatoes.

EXT. COOKING FIRE - LATER

Jon puts down a huge SACK of potatoes by the cauldron.
Zola looks at the sack, then up at Jon.

                    ZOLA

          Just a few, eh?

                    JON

          I... I have no knife to cut them with,
          though.

                    MIKAH

          Use mine.

He sticks his bayonet into the sack.

                    MIKAH

          I would do it, but they are your
          potatoes, and I strongly protest the use
          of any of your food in this soup.

He walks away and the others whisper behind his back.

                    ZOLA

          "I strongly protest the use of any of
          our food..." Who does he think he is?

                    Antolina

          Come, we will help you, Jon, we are not
          lazy like he is.

EXT. COOKING SITE — DAY

On a make-shift table, villagers help get the potatoes out and clean them.

Jon cuts them up with the bayonet, then the kids help pour them into the cauldron.

EXT. VILLAGE SQUARE — DAY

Pashe, Teodoro and Henrik sit on logs near each other. There is awkward silence as Henrik tries to concentrate on the cauldron.

Pashe clears his throat.

> PASHE
>
> So, who were these soldiers that stole
> all your food?

Henrik only barely takes his eyes off the cauldron and speaks quickly.

> HENRIK
>
> Just soldiers, they are all alike.

Pashe and Teodoro look down at their uniforms and back up. Henrik catches this, smiles weakly, and tears his eyes off the soup, paying more attention to his comrades.

> HENRIK
>
> Some months ago, toward the end of the
> war, a group of deserters came through.
> They took what they wanted, burned the
> rest of it.

He motions toward a field covered by dark, scraggly grass.

> HENRIK
>
> Then they left. We had a bad year with
> the crops, so there was not a lot to
> begin with.

> TEODORO
>
> Didn't you get help from surrounding
> villages?

> HENRIK
>
> No, we do not truck with others.

>   TEODORO
>
> Why?

>   MAN
>
> Why should we believe others have it any
> different?

>   PASHE
>
> Are there other villages still nearby?

>   WOMAN
>
> Just a few. But they have their own
> problems. Children from those villages
> come here to beg for food.

>   PASHE
>
> It is very kind of you to feed the
> neighboring children.

Henrik looks away, he half-mumbles.

>   HENRIK
>
> I did not say we fed them.

Pashe and Teodoro look at each other, Pashe shakes his
head slowly.

>   TEODORO
>
>   Well, at least you don't chase them off
>   with rocks and switches.

Henrik glances at Teodoro guiltily and hangs his head,
staring at the ground.

EXT. — VILLAGE SQUARE - DAY

Mikah plays with the kids. Each of the children has
some kind of wooden toy.

>   Rifka
>
> Thank you so much for the gift.

>   MIKAH
>
> You are very welcome, Rifka. It isn't
> much.

>   Rifka
>
> It is more than I had before you came.

                         MIKAH

     It was here before, you just didn't see
     it. Look there is another, and another.

He points at other pieces of wood lying about.

                         MIKAH

     See?

                         Rifka

     That one looks like a pig.

                         MIKAH

     Then we'll make it a pig.

He picks up the piece of wood and takes out his knife
and starts to carve as the other kids gather around.

A sharp CRY of pain is heard from Jon.

                         JON

     Angel of Mercy, I have cut off my hand!

Mikah, Teodoro and Pashe hurry over to Jon and the
others. Jon is bleeding, but his fingers are all there.

                         Antolina

     Oh, it's just a little cut, Jon, stop
     carrying on so.

                         JON

     On the last potato, too. Ooh, it hurts.

                         MIKAH

     Here, brother, take a bandage.

He pulls a rolled BANDAGE from his pocket and offers it
to Jon.

                         JON

     No! It was your cursed blade that cut
     me.

                         MIKAH

     I know, so it should be my bandage that
     mends you. Take it. Please.

Jon takes the bandage and Anna and Zola help wrap his
finger. Another villager looks at the blood and makes
a face.

                         VILLAGER

     He got blood on the potatoes. I will not
     eat them.

Mikah sees a few others make a face at the potatoes.

                          MIKAH

     Every day my friends, every day we all
     eat our own blood. And sweat, and tears.
     If you eat something that is completely
     clean, it will not fill your stomach.

The people ruminate on that for a minute. Teodoro
starts to say something, Pashe stops him with a curt
gesture.

Jon looks up at Pashe.

                           JON

     What did he mean?

Pashe shrugs "don't look at me." Jon scrunches up his
face in thought.

                           JON

     Now my head hurts, too.

                         TEODORO

     The pain goes away eventually.

Mikah wipes his hands on his pants as he looks into the
pot and frowns.

                          MIKAH

     Really should not have added all
     those potatoes without some carrots or
     something to break up the color, give it
     some texture.

                        Antolina

What color? What's wrong?

                          MIKAH

     Well, I haven't seen it too often. But
     sometimes when there are too many
     potatoes in this soup it can... Ah, my
     survival instinct runs away with me.

The villagers stare at him like he just said they were
all going to die.

                        MAN

       We have beets!

                       WOMAN

         Will celery help? I have celery.

People begin to rush off in different directions. Mikah
speaks barely loud enough to be heard.

                       MIKAH

         Nonsense. I forbid you. Stop.

Treslyn eyes Mikah through the group of rushing
villagers. Their eyes meet. Mikah smiles at her. She
watches the villagers scurry about.

INT. COTTAGE — DAY

A woman scoops up a small pile of beets from under a
mattress and rushes out of the room.

INT. ANOTHER HOUSE — DAY

A man KNOCKS on a spot on the wall twice and a SACK
with greens hanging out FALLS from the ceiling.

INT. YET ANOTHER HOUSE — DAY

A woman pulls out VEGETABLES that looked like they were
part of a PAINTING hanging on the wall.

EXT. RIFKA'S HOUSE — DAY

Henrik pulls a SACK from his doorway and throws it on a
WHEELBARROW.

EXT. RIFKA'S NEIGHBOR'S HOUSE — DAY

The neighbor lifts a larger BUNDLE onto his wheelbarrow
and shoots Henrik a look.

THE TWO SCENES ARE INTER-CUT

Henrik reaches under his porch and pulls out three
EGGPLANTS and puts them on his barrow and smiles wryly
at his neighbor.

The neighbor yanks a flower out of a POT on his porch,
then pulls a good size PUMPKIN out from underneath. He
sneers over at Henrik and gestures "what else you got?"

Henrik thinks a moment, then reaches down the front of
his baggy TROUSERS and pulls out a large ZUCCHINI.

He makes a cocky head-nod and tosses the zucchini onto
his barrow and looks over to his neighbor.

The neighbor STARES at Henrik with a raised eyebrow and disturbed look, then pushes his wheelbarrow away.

Henrik looks down at the zucchini, sneaks embarrassed glances around, then smiles meekly and wheels his food away as well.

EXT. VILLAGE SQUARE — DAY

A large TABLE has been set up near the fire, and people work at preparing the vegetables and dumping them into the pot.

Mikah, Teodoro and Pashe breathe in the aroma and smile.

> TEODORO
>
> This will be a great soup.

> PASHE
>
> The best.

> HENRIK
>
> I can not wait. I want to test it, it smells so good.

> TEODORO
>
> Yeah! Let's just get a little...

Teodoro grabs a LADLE as Henrik approaches with a SPOON to taste it. Pashe slaps the ladle out of Teodoro's hand, and stops Henrik by standing in his path.

> PASHE
>
> No.

> HENRIK
>
> What will it hurt, I just want a taste.

> TEODORO
>
> Yeah, what can it hurt...?

Pashe makes a face at Teodoro as he speaks, trying to give him the high sign.

> PASHE
>
> One of the conditions with stone soup:
> you cannot eat it until it's finished.

> MAN
>
> Bah, what rubbish. Let us taste it.

Villagers all push forward, nodding.

                    ALL

          Yes! Let us taste. What will it hurt?

Mikah looks at the villagers faces as they converge on
the cooking pot. He tenses up as they approach.

                  TEODORO

          I'm sorry. What do we do? We can't stop
          them all.

                   MIKAH

          Alright. Then we won't.

                  HENRIK

          Ha! I knew it. They are going to take it
          all for... what did you say?

Mikah resumes a relaxed demeanor and turns to his
friends, his back to the cauldron and villagers.

                   MIKAH

          Pashe, Teodoro, let them taste. I will
          work on the markers. Now, how many will
          we need.

He turns and starts to COUNT heads as the villagers
push toward the soup. They STOP when they see what
Mikah is doing.

                  HENRIK

          Markers? For what, markers?

                   MIKAH

          So your children and grandchildren will
          know which grave to visit each week,
          of course. Now I've lost count. Okay,
          One... two... three...

                  WOMAN

          Graves? The soup is poisoned?

                  TEODORO

          No. Just... uh, not ready.

                   PASHE

          You should have seen what happened last
          time, eh, Teodoro!

He pats Mikah on the back and starts to help him count.

                    WOMAN

    What happened?

                    MAN

    Yes, what?

                    MIKAH

    Oh, it was a long time ago. Go ahead and
    eat.

                    HENRIK

    No, don't force us to do things we don't
    want to do. Tell us the story.

                    PASHE

    I think you should tell them.

                    TEODORO

    Yeah, tell us; I mean them.

                    MIKAH

    As you wish. Many years ago, when I was
    given this stone, the old man who gave
    it to me also gave me this warning.

Steam from the cauldron obscures Mikah somewhat from
the rest of the group.

EXT. SMALL VILLAGE — NIGHT

A young MAN makes a soup over a fire in a very run-down
village. Many people gather about him as he works.

                    MIKAH (VO)

    When the old man was a young man and was
    making this soup for the first time, the
    people he made it for could not wait to
    taste it.

Some villagers pick up broken bowls and cups and move
toward the pot. The man pleads emphatically with them
to stop.

                    MIKAH (VO)

    He tried to get them to hold off just
    a little longer, but they would not
    listen. Finally, a few of the people
    took a sip.

A woman sips from a cracked bowl and smiles. A man sloppily drinks from a tankard.

                    MIKAH (VO)

        They smiled at first, they went "oooh"
        and "mmm" and "my, this is rather
        tasty."

Many smiling people drink from bowls and rub their stomachs in appreciation.

                    MIKAH (VO)

        Soon their smiles broadened and their
        toes left the earth as they floated on
        the wisps of steam that carried the
        scent of the magical soup. They could
        not stop smiling and licking their lips,
        they were in rapture.

People drift about the campsite with exaggerated smiles on their faces, they dance with bowls and mugs. A man snuggles his wooden spoon.

EXT. MIKAH'S COOKING SITE — DAY

The villagers don't move a muscle, many are poised to take a dip of the soup.

                    MIKAH

        Their mouths watered for more, watered
        so much for just one more taste of the
        divine broth, that they drowned; the lot
        of them. Drowned in their own saliva.

Teodoro gawks, completely lost in the story. Pashe watches the crowd.

                    MIKAH

        You see, this magical soup is at its
        most potent from the start, and the
        flavor spreads as it cooks.

WISPS of steam that look like beets and potatoes and celery appear faintly, then curl back and vanish into the cauldron.

                    MIKAH

        So that by the time it is finished,
        everybody gets exactly what they need.

The townspeople stare at Mikah, fixed on his every word.

When he is done, they sigh and pull back, then sit and stare forlornly at the cauldron again.

Teodoro fidgets, then leans in and whispers to Mikah.

> TEODORO
>
> Did that really happen?

> MIKAH
>
> Do you believe it, Teodoro?

> TEODORO
>
> I have not heard that story before. It sounded good.

> MIKAH
>
> Then it was a good story.

EXT. COUNTRY ROAD — DAY

Gurkin crouches on the road, studying tracks. He looks off in a few directions, then stands.

A horse trots up to him with Drakko astride.

> DRAKKO
>
> Which way, Gurkin?

> GURKIN
>
> Hard to say my Lord...

> DRAKKO
>
> It will be even more harder to say when I remove your sound-maker from atop your shoulders, Gurkin.

> GURKIN
>
> He seems to have headed due west, oh Mighty Body-Part Remover. But his tracks have been muddled by some other group on foot.

> DRAKKO
>
> Soldiers?

> GURKIN
>
> Could be, not many, though. Maybe three. Drakko surveys the countryside.

> DRAKKO
>
> How long?

                    GURKIN

     Most of the feet are average. There's
     this one print, looks like a size 12, if
     I'm not mistaken...

Drakko closes his eyes and sighs.

                    DRAKKO

     How long - ago?

                    GURKIN

     Oh. Less than a day, Snarling Ruler
     Over-All.

Drakko grunts and trots his horse away. Gurkin wipes
his brow and follows.

EXT. EDGE OF TOWN — DAY

A RAGGEDY MAN shuffles furtively toward the village. He
frequently looks behind him, but sees no one following.

He lifts his nose into the air, sniffing intently, then
shoots glances around as he shimmies along the edge of
a building.

A DOOR opens, and a WOMAN exits the building carrying a
BASKET with BREAD loaves in it. She does not notice the
raggedy man.

The man licks his lips and follows at safe distance.

EXT. VILLAGE SQUARE — DAY

Teodoro stands in a small circle of children showing
them the patches and insignias on his uniform. Pashe
stands nearby chuckling. He is fiddling with a handful
of spongy moss.

                    TEODORO

     And this one here, the one with the
     Badger on it... I'm not quite sure what
     that one is for either. I think it's for
     digging holes and snarling at people.

The children laugh and touch the hash marks on
Teodoro's sleeve.

                    TEODORO

     Those are called hash marks. You get one
     every time you eat breakfast.

>   PASHE
>
>   Teodor, please, where do you come up
>   with this stuff?

Pashe looks away and sees Treslyn watching them, smiling.

Their gazes meet, then she shies away.

Pashe half-smiles and waves too late.

EXT. VILLAGE SQUARE - DAY

Mikah sits with Rifka on stumps a short distance from Teodoro. Mikah sharpens his knife as Rifka watches.

>   MIKAH
>
>   Do you like the knife?
>
>   Rifka
>
>   Yes, it is very nice. Where did you
>   get it?
>
>   MIKAH
>
>   I got it in the war.
>
>   Rifka
>
>   Did you take it from a dead soldier?
>
>   MIKAH
>
>   No. He gave it to me before he died.
>
>   Rifka
>
>   Was he your friend?
>
>   MIKAH
>
>   He could have been. At the time, he was
>   my enemy.

Mikah adjusts on his stump and shows the knife to Rifka.

>   MIKAH
>
>   He attacked me one night with this. I
>   took it from him and cut him first. With
>   his dying breath he asked me to keep it.
>
>   Rifka
>
>   Why?

                    MIKAH

     I'm not really sure. I think he wanted
     to remind me that... We do things some-
     times without thinking, because we're
     told to.

Mikah looks at the shiny blade of the knife and sees
his reflection. Behind him, the IMAGE of another MAN in
uniform appears in the reflection.

                    MIKAH

     Without thinking, yet always remember-
     ing. He wanted to forget, I think. He
     let me take his weapon too easily.

The man's reflection FADES, and only Mikah's is left.

                    Rifka

     Did you kill anyone else with it?

Mikah comes out of his reverie and continues to sharpen
the blade.

                    MIKAH

     I have not killed anyone else since
     that day.

Mikah displays the knife.

                    MIKAH

     It is a tool. You can destroy with it,
     or you can create with it. Your heart
     will tell you when each has its time,
     eh?

                    Rifka

     I guess.

Rifka holds up a doll Mikah had carved.

                    Rifka

     Thank you for the doll for my sister.

                    MIKAH

     She may not want it.

                    Rifka

     I think she will want it some day. She
     doesn't trust strangers since...

> MIKAH

I understand.

> Rifka

Thank you.

Rifka skips away with the doll.

Antolina approaches Mikah.

> Antolina

You tell a lot of stories. How is it a soldier learns to tell stories?

> MIKAH

I have learned many things in the last seven years, sister.

Antolina softens a bit and smiles.

> Antolina

Antolina. You may call me Antolina.

> MIKAH

Antolina. One of the biggest things I learned is that sometimes a good story is all you need.

> Antolina

A story can not feed your family.

> MIKAH

You may be right.

Antolina looks at him for a moment, then turns her gaze toward the villagers, all talking and laughing together.

> Antolina

I haven't seen these people together for a long time. I've forgotten most of their names already.

> MIKAH

Then go and get to know them again. I'm sure you all have stories to share now.

Antolina sees Zola and Anna walk past. She hesitates, then gets up and heads toward them.

Antolina

Widow Zola, Anna... wait a moment.

EXT. VILLAGE SQUARE - DAY

Treslyn walks over to Pasha and Teodoro, who are
talking by the cauldron. Pashe has fashioned a garland
from the moss clumps. She stares for a minute or so
until Pashe and Teodoro look at her.

PASHE

May we help you?

TRESLYN

I was wondering... could you help me at
the Inn?

TEODORO

Pashe and I are a team, we will help you
together. What do you need?

INT. DINING HALL - DAY

Treslyn opens two large double doors from the outside.
Pashe, Teodoro and she enter the large, dusty HALL full
of tables and chairs covered with sheets and webs.

TRESLYN

In better times we used this hall for
special gatherings and events.

PASHE

It looks like you haven't used it in a
while.

TRESLYN

We've had nothing to celebrate.

TEODORO

You're alive. That's a celebration.

TRESLYN

We are not alive.

TEODORO

What?

TRESLYN

We've learned to hate and fear. Learned
to hide. We've gotten very good at it

> after all these years. We don't take to
> strangers at all. We even hide from our-
> selves, hate and fear each other.

PASHE

The war is over.

TRESLYN

Damage is done.

PASHE

Why did you ask us here?

TRESLYN

I don't know. Maybe, do you think we
could clean this up?

Teodoro makes a face and shakes his head.

TEODORO

You tell us that story, then you expect
us to do your cleaning for you?

Treslyn and Pashe stare at each other, oblivious of
everything but themselves while Teodoro rants.

TEODORO

Well I don't think so. I used to clean
the bathrooms in an Inn, and if you
don't think that people leave a mess
when they leave a rented room, let me
tell you something. This one guy left a
bag of boiled nuts. The room was filled
with bugs. And don't even get me started on the linens... oh my gosh, they're
stained with...

Pashe comes out of his trance, waves him silent.

PASHE

Teodor. I think she means to start
cleaning the wounds.

She nods and half smiles.

TEODOR

And now we're doctors? Who do you think
we are? Of course I did have to help de-
liver a baby during the war. Yes, it was

                         a baby cow, and it did bite me, but when
                         you look at it...

                              PASHE

                    Teodoro. Shut up and help.

They begin to take chairs off of tables. Teodoro is
handed a broom.

EXT. DINING HALL - DAY

Mikah watches Treslyn, Pashe and Teodoro through a
window at the side of the building. Pashe and Treslyn
seem to be hitting it off well.

EXT. VILLAGE STREET - DAY

The raggedy man slinks along an alley, staying as close
to the wall as possible.

He stops and rolls up one sleeve enough to show a rusty
MANACLE with two links of chain still attached. He rubs
his wrist and TUGS in vain at the iron RING.

He draws a KNIFE from his belt, starts to position it
to cut his manacled hand off. He sees a piece of PURPLE
CLOTH stuck on the blade. He pulls the cloth off and
puts the knife away.

He starts to slump, but then his nose goes up to the
air again and he inhales deeply.

He starts down the alley again with renewed vigor.

EXT. - VILLAGE SQUARE — DAY

Henrik, Lothar and some other men sit around, watching
the goings-on and not really relating to each other.

                              HENRIK

                    I hate this waiting. All I can think of
                    is the food.

                               MAN

                    Take your mind off it, Henrik. Your
                    Antolina and Zola seem to have.

He motions toward where Antolina and Zola talk at a
table, they laugh and talk quickly.

Henrik screws up his face and turns towards Lothar.

                              HENRIK

                    Do they just not understand that we

> can't change the way things are? Why do
> they insist?

Lothar juts out his lower lip and shrugs.

Henrik appeals to the other men sitting nearby,

                    HENRIK

> We have survived the way things are,
> have we not?

Some of the men nod kind of noncommittally and murmur
vague answers.

                    HENRIK

> It is bad that we try to change the way
> things are, nothing good will come from
> it. We can not expect things to get
> better, and we can not change.

The men stare blankly at Henrik. Lothar glances around
at the circle.

                    LOTHAR

> Soldiers.

                    MAN

> What?

                    LOTHAR

> Soldiers.

                    HENRIK

> What are you going on about, Lothar? You
> and your convoluted notions.

                    MAN

> I think...

                    HENRIK

> Oh, so you're taking his side now? Why
> would you listen to him and not me?

                    MAN

> Henrik, I think all Lothar means is
> that, well, the soldiers changed the way
> things were. Didn't they?

The other men all nod affirmatively.

                    MAN

     And if they could change things, then
     why can't we?

                    LOTHAR

     Change.

Henrik scowls at the man, as the rest of the men nod
more enthusiastically.

                    MAN 2

     That would take a lot, but... We would
     not need to hide in our houses anymore,
     we could get out and...

Henrik cuts him off sharply.

                    HENRIK

     You keep throwing that word in my face
     night and day. There is no such thing
     as faith. What are we supposed to have
     faith in, I ask you? That we can change
     the path of our future? That we can put
     aside our petty differences and help one
     another - rebuild and endure? Don't try
     to speak to me of faith... any of you.

There is a brief silence. One man shakes his head as if
to clear it.

                    MAN

     No one has mentioned that word, Henrik.
     Except you.

                    LOTHAR

     You.

Henrik boils, he spits his words at Lothar.

                    HENRIK

     You and your big mouth.

Henrik gets up and storms away. The other men all start
to talk excitedly.

INT. DINING HALL - DAY

Treslyn and Pashe set a table with goblets, cloth
napkins and utensils.

Teodoro struggles with a centerpiece, a huge vase of
flowers with carved birds on sticks.

> TEODOR
>
> No no no, the birdie needs to stay on
> the log. Put the flowers on the other
> side, move the moss.

The children all giggle as they make a mess of things.
One little child SMILES up at Teodor, who grimaces and
gives up.

> TEODOR
>
> Perfect.

> TRESLYN
>
> Your friend is good with children.

> PASHE
>
> That's because he is one himself.

> TRESLYN
>
> He fought in the war?

Pashe stares at Teodoro.

> PASHE
>
> He's no soldier. He was in prison for
> refusing to fight. When they stormed the
> city, the prison was destroyed. We found
> him wandering, dazed.

> TRESLYN
>
> Why wouldn't he fight?

> PASHE
>
> His family was on the other side.

Treslyn blinks, she looks over at Teodoro, then back
at Pashe.

> TRESLYN
>
> He... he doesn't look...

> PASHE
>
> Up close, they almost never do.

Treslyn looks away and busies herself with folding
napkins.

> TRESLYN
>
> And what of your family.

                    PASHE

     My village was completely wiped out
     at the beginning of the war. My wife...
     I don't even know where I am going
     home to.

                   TRESLYN

     You will find a home.

                    PASHE

     I had hoped, once. No more.

Treslyn glances at him quickly.

                   TRESLYN

     There is always hope, Pashe. Always. I
     believe that. Your other friend knows
     that.

                    PASHE

     Yes, he has great hopes, great beliefs.
     I wish I were more like him.

                   TRESLYN

     There is nothing wrong with you as
     you are.

Pashe smiles nervously, Treslyn blushes slightly. A
howl breaks up the awkward silence.

Pashe and Treslyn look up at Teodoro, who has gotten
his HAND jammed between two tables that the children
are pushing together.

                   TEODOR

     Back, pull it back!

The children quickly pull the table back and Teodoro
FALLS backward, his backside meeting quickly with A
handful of FORKS, tines out, that another child brings
to set on the table.

Teodoro wails and dances about madly, holding his butt.

                   TEODORO

     That was me. My fault entirely.

Teodoro pulls a huge serving fork out from behind him
and hands it to another child.

TEODORO

You may want to re-wash that one.

EXT. - VILLAGE SQUARE - DAY

There is a festival-like atmosphere. People laugh and
help each other with simple chores — stacking wood,
cleaning plates, repairing chairs, etc.

Rifka and her friends play nearby. Mikah and some other
people are in a circle watching another villager juggle
flaming sticks.

MIKAH

You are truly gifted, my friend. It must
be very rewarding to hear people laugh
and cheer your skills.

JUGGLER

Ah, it has been quite some time since
I have heard laughter in this town, or
seen smiles on their faces. I thank you.

MIKAH

Me? I've done nothing.

JUGGLER

I manipulate burning wood and sand-filled
bags. You pull the shroud of death and
gloom from an entire village.

The juggler finishes the routine to the applause of all
watching, and takes a bow. He winks at Mikah, who takes
a tiny bow at the waist.

A villager, NARGEZ, addresses the juggler

NARGEZ

I had no idea you could do such tricks,
where have you been all these years?

JUGGLER

I live two houses down from you, Nargez.

NARGEZ

You do?

Nargez' daughter tugs at his sleeve

                    DAUGHTER

     He's the shiftless buffoon you told me to
     stay away from, daddy.

Nargez blushes all the way to his soul.

                    NARGEZ

     I... I... was talking about that other
     man who lives the other way, honey.

The juggler chuckles.

                    JUGGLER

     No harm, friend.

A woman throws a good-natured scowl at Nargez.

                    WOMAN

     Do you mean my husband, Nargez? What
     is wrong with him? Are you too good to
     mingle with a carpenter?

                    JON

     Garret is a carpenter? Since when?

                    WOMAN

     Who do you think made the tables at the
     Inn?

                    NARGEZ

     I... I...

                    MAN

     How about me, Nargez, I'm a tailor.

                    JON

     You're a tailor? Why do we not have
     decent clothes then?

                    MAN

     Nobody asks. Nobody has any material.

                    WOMAN

     I have material. Can you make shoes?

                    WOMAN

     I can make shoes.

                    MAN 2

     You can make shoes?

                              MAN 3

          I can make buckles.

                            WOMAN 3

          I fix farm tools.

                              MAN 4

          My wife and I prepare crops for storage.

                            WOMAN 4

          I can cut hair, and cure coughs, as
          well.

The villagers all start to talk noisily about what they
can do. Mikah turns to the juggler.

                            MIKAH

          Another nice trick my friend. It seems
          there was a village here after all.

EXT. VILLAGE SQUARE - DAY

Mikah carves a doll while sitting on a stump near the
cauldron.

Some adult villagers sit and watch. Children play with
other dolls nearby.

In the far background, the Raggedy Man can be seen
wandering about.

                            WOMAN

          Why do you carve so many dolls?

                            MIKAH

          Because there are so many children.

                            WOMAN

          Why do you make that kind of doll?

Mikah looks up from his work and cocks his head at
the woman.

                            MIKAH

          Do you really want to know? The story is
          a bit difficult to understand.

The woman nods. The other adults follow suit slowly.

                            MIKAH

          Well then. This is a story I heard from
          a man during the war. There once were a

people, called the Rolly-Polly, who were
held in siege by a fierce tribe a long,
long time ago.

Rifka and some children come and sit closer to Mikah.

                    Rifka

What did the Rolly-Polly people do?

As Mikah begins to talk, the WISPS of steam from the
cauldron TWIST and bend and take the shape of WARRIORS
on horseback, and foot soldiers with axes and spears.

                    MIKAH

        The People never gave up, never sur-
        rendered. Every time the great Warlord
        attacked and beat back the Rolly-Polly's
        forces...

The wisps of steam blend into a REAL SCENE of

EXT. BATTLEFIELD - DAY

A battle rages between large, fierce warriors in animal
skins, and plain-looking people in leather armor.

The hoard of warriors attacks viciously, driving the
plain people back.

                    MIKAH (VO)

        ... the People bounced back, fought
        hard, and held their ground.

The People PUSH BACK from against the wall of mountains
behind them.

                    MAN

        So what happened?

                    MIKAH

        The Warlord managed to trap the
        leader of the Rolly-Polly. The Warlord
        gave this leader one chance to save his
        people.

INT. WARLORD'S TENT - DAY

The Leader, tied with ropes, is brought before the
Warlord, who sits on a wooden throne. The Leader is
pushed to the floor at the throne's feet.

The Warlord growls and shakes his fist at the Rolly
Polly, who only listens with a calm face.

                    MIKAH (VO)

     The Warlord told him that if he could
     bring great treasure, then his people
     would be put to death quickly. If not,
     then they would be tortured slowly.

EXT. VILLAGE SQUARE - DAY

                     ZOLA

     That is not much of a choice.

                    MIKAH

     Sometimes you have very little choice
     in life. What matters is how you deal
     with it.

                     ANNA

     What did the Rolly-Polly Leader do?

Henrik waves at Anna quickly.

                    HENRIK

     Hush, girl. Do not try to understand —
     this is adult conversation.

Henrik turns back to Mikah, very attentive.

                    HENRIK

     What did the Rolly-Polly Leader do?

                    MIKAH

     The next day, the Rolly Polly leader
     brought the warrior a small, plain box
     containing one of these dolls.

INT. WARLORD'S TENT - DAY

The Rolly-Polly Leader opens the box and takes out a
doll that looks much like the one Mikah is carving,
only more ornate.

                    MIKAH (VO)

     The Warlord sneered and threw it to the
     floor and laughed at the Leader. "Is this
     the best you can do?" the warlord shout-
     ed through peels of laughter.

The Warlord throws the doll to the floor and shouts at
the Rolly Polly leader.

                    MIKAH (VO)

     But the Leader smiled as the doll rolled
     a short distance and righted itself.

The Warlord grabs the doll, tosses it down again and
laughs. The doll wobbles and comes back up. The Warlord
is vexed.

                    MIKAH (VO)

          The warrior grew angry and kicked the
          doll, pushed it down. Always it wobbled
          and stood upright. The Rolly-Polly Lead-
          er told the Warlord that this was the
          greatest treasure his people had, and no
          army could ever take it away.

The Warlord struggles to keep the doll down, but it
pops back up each time. Finally the doll gets away from
the Warlord's hands, rolls out the door and is lost
down the hill that the tent is perched on.

The Warlord is furious.

He wheels on the Rolly-Polly leader a STRIKES him down
to the floor. The Rolly-Polly leader slowly gets up, and
smiles.

                    MIKAH (VO)

          Eventually, the great Warlord tired.
          He could not break the spirit of these
          people who would not stay down when trod
          upon. His troops grew weary, his sup-
          plies dwindled.

EXT. RAINY BATTLEFIELD — NIGHT

The warlord SLUMPS in his saddle as he leads his small,
ragged army away in the rain. A wagon drives over the
Rolly-Polly doll and pushes it into the mud.

The doll sits a bit, then rights itself.

EXT. VILLAGE SQUARE - DAY

Mikah glances around at the adults. Some have quizzical
looks on their faces. They each look at the others not
wanting to register confusion or lack of understanding.

                    MIKAH

     The Warlord was never heard from again.

                    Antolina

      How did these people do it? Soldiers are
      strong, they have many weapons.

                    MIKAH

      Where there is a common goal among a
      people, faith and inner strength, any-
      thing is possible.

He puts down the doll he was carving and pushes it
over. It falls to the ground, then bounces back up. The
children start to knock their dolls down as well. The
adults sit and watch.

                    MIKAH

      Understand?

They all nod very unconvincingly.

                    HENRIK

      Oh yes, I see. Very good story.

Henrik tries to lean inconspicuously toward Anna and
whispers.

                    HENRIK

      What does "dwindled" mean?

EXT. VILLAGE SQUARE - DAY

The Raggedy man snoops around the cauldron, sniffing
deeply at the wafting steam. Henrik, who is tending the
pot, eyes the man suspiciously.

                    HENRIK

      I do not know you, friend. Are you from
      here?

The man almost jumps at Henrik's voice. He stares at
the pot and licks his lips.

                    HENRIK

      Are... are you hungry? Do you want to
      eat?

Henrik motions at the pot. The man seems to understand.
He nods slowly.

Another villager approaches and looks at the man.

                    VILLAGER

      Hey, hey you.

He approaches the raggedy man and touches his sleeve.

> VILLAGER
>
> What are you doing here? That soup isn't
> ready yet, are you trying to kill us
> all?

The strange man shrinks away from the hand and draws a knife from his cloak, he brandishes it at Henrik and the other villager.

The raggedy man shouts in another language. Henrik gasps and stares.

> HENRIK
>
> Taburki. He's from Taburk.

> VILLAGER
>
> Lousy thieves. Hey, over here, Taburki!

The villager shouts to some nearby people and waves them over.

> VILLAGER
>
> We have a thief among us, over here.

A small crowd gathers around the strange man, who gets very agitated and nervous.

> HENRIK
>
> Easy there, Taburki. Don't make us go
> Rolly-Polly on you.

The Taburki shouts again in his language.

INT. DINING HALL - DAY

Teodoro, a number of fingers bandaged now, holds a small child up to put a candle in a chandelier. A loud din is heard outside. He puts the child down.

Teodor, Pashe and Treslyn turn toward the door.

> PASHE
>
> What is that?

> TRESLYN
>
> I heard the name Taburk.

> TEODOR
>
> What's a Taburk?

                              TRESLYN

          Trouble. Maybe.

She runs toward the door, Pashe follows, motioning to
Teodoro.

                               PASHE

          Watch the children, Teodor.

Teodoro pulls the other children toward him.

                               TEODOR

          Come here, let's play a game... that
          doesn't involve squishing, poking,
          crushing or burning any part of Uncle
          Teodoro.

EXT. COUNTRY ROAD - DAY

Drakko and his band travel at a slow pace. Gurkin and
Drakko squint at the road as they ride.

                               DRAKKO

          What say you, Gurkin?

                               GURKIN

          We will catch up quickly, most Angry
          Destroyer of Property. They seem to head
          for that small village we occupied a few
          months ago.

                               DRAKKO

          Which one? The one we pillaged, burned
          and spat on?

                               GURKIN

          No, Drakko. That was back east. This is
          the one we sacked, bullied and demoral-
          ized.

                               DRAKKO

          We didn't spit on it?

                               GURKIN

          We might have, we get pretty sloppy
          when we're bullying. Yes, we more than
          probably spitted on them. With a great
          quantity of moisture.

Drakko smiles broadly, rubs his chin and stares ahead, down the road.

                    DRAKKO

          This will be funner the second time
          around.

Gurkin stops and looks to the ground.

                    GURKIN

          Those other tracks again, Drakko. The
          large fast-moving group. Very fresh,
          probably nearby. Do you wish to pursue?

Drakko thinks a moment, scratches his face stubble.

                    DRAKKO

          You say there are more than us?

                    GURKIN

          Yes, more than double our size, but
          lightly equipped. If we surprise them,
          we might win. If not, they will sing of
          our crushing defeat for years to come.
          We will die in a glorious battle. Our
          entrails strewn from tree to boulder to
          furry creature. Our heads mounted on...

                    DRAKKO

          We continue to the village as planned.
          There will be no resistance at all.

Drakko laughs maniacally, Gurkin joins in, relieved.

                    GURKIN

          Yes, Big Bulging Scurrilous Leader, no
          resistance at all.

EXT. - VILLAGE SQUARE - DAY

A CROWD has gathered around the Taburki. Someone makes
a grab for the man, but is stopped by the SLASH of the
knife.

A huge HAND grabs the Taburki's knife hand firmly. It is
Lothar, from behind the assailant.

Mikah appears next to Lothar. He spies the manacle on
the Taburki's wrist.

                    MIKAH

          What's the problem?

LOTHAR

Taburki.

Mikah looks to Rifka for answers.

Rifka

Taburk is a village a few days away from
here.

Antolina

They are not like us.

MIKAH

How?

HENRIK

They are different.

MIKAH

How?

ZOLA

They're bad.

MIKAH

How?

ZOLA

Look, he has been a prisoner.

She gestures at the manacle.

MIKAH

For what reason?

ZOLA

What does it matter? We have heard
stories, and now this criminal appears
and proves it.

WOMAN

They always have been trouble. We have
always been warned about them, since we
were children.

MIKAH

They steal from you? They hurt you? They
part their hair differently?

                    Rifka

          There are a lot of stories about the
          dangers of the Taburki.

                    WOMAN

          He has a knife!

Mikah nonchalantly pulls out his own and waves it.

                    MIKAH

          Me too.

The Taburki stares at Mikah and his knife, he shifts
toward Mikah.

Mikah scrutinizes the other knife.

                    MIKAH

          His is not a good knife. It must be hard
          to work with. Would you like mine?

Mikah holds his knife out, handle first. The Taburki
glares uncertainly. The villagers stare.

Mikah walks closer.

                    MIKAH

          Take it. It's a good knife.

Mikah approaches with the knife on his open palm. The
Taburki fidgets.

Rifka and her sister watch frightened.

Amid gasps, the Taburki lunges forward and grabs the
knife from Mikah's hand, and brandishes both.

Lothar makes a move, Mikah waves him back.

The Taburki weighs the two knives in his hands and
makes a face. Then he nods a "not bad" face. He looks
Mikah's knife up and down, then holds out his own knife
to Mikah.

The Taburki then takes out a small medallion he wears,
and offers it as well.

                    MIKAH

          You know good workmanship. An excellent
          trade.

Mikah takes both the offerings and nods.

The Taburki sheathes Mikah's knife and eyes Mikah
warily.

Mikah sheaths the Taburk's knife, and hangs the medallion and chain around his own neck.

> MIKAH
>
> Thank you.

He looks at Henrik.

> MIKAH
>
> He's a thief?

Henrik mutters.

> HENRIK
>
> I didn't make up the stories.

> MIKAH
>
> There is a name for stories like those.

> HENRIK
>
> What is it?

> MIKAH
>
> I forget.

Mikah motions for the Taburki to sit, which he does.

EXT. COOKING AREA — DAY

Zola bites her lip as she looks into the swirling soup.

> Antolina
>
> What is wrong, Zola?

> ZOLA
>
> Nothing really. Just thought how well some meat would go in this stew.

> Antolina
>
> I was thinking the same thing. Do you have any?

> ZOLA
>
> No, I would bring it if I did, but we had the last of a rabbit months ago.

Jon approaches with Lothar.

> JON
>
> We have Rabbit?

                    Antolina
      No, we were just thinking about meat.
                     LOTHAR

      Venison.

                      ZOLA

      How I wish I had some venison; what I
      could do with that.

                     HENRIK

      I remember your venison, Zola, from
      a festival years ago. You worked
      magic with that stag, so tender and
      juicy and...

Henrik's mind wanders, Zola looks at him and blushes.

                      ZOLA

      Why Henrik, you've never mentioned that
      to me before. Thank you.

Now it is Henrik's turn to blush. He shuffles his feet
and mutters.

                      JON

      How did we get that stag?

They stare at each other unable to answer.

                     HENRIK

      Come with me.

EXT. STREET AT EDGE OF TOWN - DAY

Pashe, the Taburki, and Henrik walk to a workshop. The
workshop is boarded up, but a door has been removed.
Many tools and weapons lean in piles on the walls.

                     HENRIK

      All our weapons and tools were
      destroyed. No one knows how to fix
      bows, or

The Taburki looks a bow up and down. He nods and says
something in his language and motions toward the bow.

                     PASHE

      It looks like someone does now.

                         HENRIK

          This bow was designed by our village
          ages ago. Its secret died with the
          craftsman who made it. I doubt anyone
          can fix it, let alone hunt with it again.

INT. WORKSHOP - DAY

Henrik and the Taburki stand by the workbench near the
open doors. Mikah, Zola, Pashe and Jon stand outside
watching in.

The Taburki holds up the bow and gives it a few test
twangs.

                         HENRIK

          Amazing.

The Taburki walks outside with the bow, admiring it and
the arrows in a quiver at his side.

He looks up suddenly toward Mikah. Quickly and nimbly,
he grabs up an arrow, nocks it and aims.

                         PASHE

          Look out!

                         HENRIK

          I knew it, he deceived us.

                         MIKAH

          Nobody move.

A tense moment passes, gazes move about the small
gathering from face to face, but mostly between Mikah
and the Taburki.

Finally Zola, who is closest, makes a move toward the
Taburki.

                         ZOLA

          Run!

                         HENRIK

          Zola, no!

Before she reaches him, the Taburki lets the arrow fly.
It sails past Mikah, missing him easily.

Zola can not stop her assault in time, her fist connects
with the Taburki's face and he goes down hard.

Mikah looks at the Taburki on the ground with Zola
crouching above.

                          MIKAH

         Impressive.

                          HENRIK

         Yeah. G... good shot.

He stares at Zola, then smiles proudly around the
gathering and gestures toward her.

                          HENRIK

         She's my neighbor.

The Tabuki looks past Mikah. Mikah follows the line of
site and stares.

                          MIKAH

         Nice shot. That should be enough to feed
         the whole village.

The Taburki nods, says something in his language.

EXT. VILLAGE SQUARE — DAY

A group of people, lead by Zola, prepares MEAT for
dinner. A large section of an animal is roasting over
another fire on a SPIT, slowly turned by Lothar.

Antolina offers a CUP of water to the Taburki, who is
having his manacle removed by a villager.

Teodoro, Pashe, Treslyn stand by the cauldron, sniffing.

                          PASHE

         Ahh, I think it is ready. Smell that.

They all take huge lungfulls of the steam through their
noses.

                          TRESLYN

         Your magic stone is wonderful. What a
         delicious aroma.

The Taburki's attention is pulled away abruptly. He
SNIFFS the air away from the pot. A look of concern
crosses his face.

Teodoro catches this look.

                          TEODORO

         What is it my friend?

The Taburki is agitated, he speaks quickly in his own
tongue and frantically starts to scan the edges of the
village.

                         PASHE

          He's worried, but about what?

Teodoro makes a GESTURE toward the Taburki, but is
STOPPED by a quick halting motion by the Taburki.
The Taburki sniffs again and his face changes, he smiles
and nods.

The Taburki says something curtly, points away from the
square and hurries out, disappearing around a corner.

Henrik passes with a platter of meat to drop in the
soup pot and looks toward the Taburki.

                         HENRIK

          Hmmph. Taburki, go figure.

INT. DINING HALL — DAY

Pashe, Teodoro and Mikah stand in the doorway admiring
the work done. The hall is beautifully decorated, and
well lit by sconces and candles.

Garlands of the moss adorn the beams, window and door
frames. The moss seams to sparkle in the candle light.

                         MIKAH

          My friends, I think we are almost ready.

                         TEODORO

          Almost? We've food enough for three
          villages outside. These people are
          talking to each other, working together.

                         PASHE

          I hate to agree with Teodoro. Things
          look good. Their troubles are past.

Mikah looks outside up to the sky. The SOUNDS of the
Village Square can be heard.

                         MIKAH

          The past is a good teacher. I have
          learned much, and my lessons have taught
          me that there is a much greater trial to
          come before we can move on.

190

                    TEODORO

     Why do you ruin everything by making us
     think all the time?

                    MIKAH

     The pain will leave soon Teodor, and the
     muscle it leaves will be stronger.

Mikah massages Teodoro on the head and walks out. Pashe
laughs at Teodoro and slaps his back.

                    TEODORO

        Is he ever wrong?

                    PASHE

        Yes, many times.

                    TEODORO

        Is he wrong now?

                    PASHE

        No.

                    TEODORO

        Can we go home?

                    PASHE

        When it is time.

Pashe follows Mikah outside.

                    TEODORO

        Can't we ever just eat and leave?

He slumps and follows his friends out.

EXT. COUNTRY ROAD — DAY

Drakko and his band of thugs charge up to the top
of a hill where Gurkin crouches, motioning them
down as well.

Drakko dismounts, crouches and approaches Gurkin.

                    DRAKKO

        What is this, Gurkin?

Gurkin pats the ground with his open hand.

                    GURKIN

        It is a hill, a rather nice one too, I

> might add, as far as hills go. See this
> soft moss here...

Drakko closes his eyes and grinds his teeth. Gurkin
catches himself.

>   GURKIN
>
> They are down there, my lord. I saw a
> handful or so just outside that village
> at the base of that next hill. See?

Drakko squints into the distance to where Gurkin
points.

>   DRAKKO
>
> Where are they now?

>   GURKIN
>
> I don't know, But they have not left the
> village.

>   DRAKKO
>
> They have nothing?

>   GURKIN
>
> No, my Impossibly Massive General.

>   DRAKKO
>
> Then why are they still here?

Drakko watches a bit longer, then stands and walks back
to his horse.

>   DRAKKO
>
> Let's rest a bit, then take them at
> dusk.

A henchman gets on all fours at Drakko's feet. Drakko
steps on his back, pushing his face into the dirt, and
lifts himself up onto his horse and turns to ride away.

>   DRAKKO
>
> This time we don't even leave the grass.

Gurkin pulls his face from the ground, spits clods out.

>   GURKIN
>
> Thank you, Quite Disgustingly Evil One.
> You are too good to us.

INT. DINING HALL — DAY

Pashe and Treslyn fill cups with water out of a large pitcher.

Teodoro and some children put bread on the tables at the other end of the hall.

> TRESLYN

I can't believe we are about to dine together again after so long. And the food — it is almost like a dream.

> PASHE

The food is good, and the company is even better.

Treslyn smiles shyly and continues her work.

> TRESLYN

Have you been together long?

> PASHE

The three of us?

Treslyn nods affirmatively.

> PASHE

It seems we have always been together. You know about Teodor.

Pashe stares into space and muses a bit.

> PASHE

The "Magic Man" and I met just before the war, in the great city north of the Tyrus sea. On a trip to a fishing village.

> TRESLYN

You were a fisherman?

> PASHE

No. I was a merchant. I bought and sold things. I feel I was rather good.

> TRESLYN

And he?

> PASHE

I don't know, it never came up. We met, got along — it seemed there was nothing he couldn't do.

They watch Teodoro and the children for awhile, laughing and playing at their job.

                    PASHE

        When the war was over, I had nowhere to go, so I traveled with him. I have no idea what I'm going to do.

                    TRESLYN

        We have many skilled people in this village, we used to have many things to trade. It looks as though we may still.

                    PASHE

        Yes, it does.

                    TRESLYN

        Would you... would you stay and

                    PASHE

        Stay and what?

Treslyn searches for words, she can not look Pashe in the face.

                    TRESLYN

        Help us rebuild? Teach us to trade?

Pashe looks away and makes a face. Treslyn does the same, looking as though she regrets the words.

                    PASHE

        Selling trinkets does not hold the importance with me it once did.

                    TRESLYN

        What would it take to keep you here?

They look at one another and slowly begin to smile.

EXT. VILLAGE SQUARE — DAY

Mikah addresses the people from near the cooking area.

                    MIKAH

        Good news everyone, it's time to eat.

Loud CHEERS and applause go up from everyone. Mikah glances toward Zola and Lothar at the stag spit.

Zola makes a "perfecto" sign and nudges Lothar, who nods his head in agreement.

                         MIKAH

        The dining hall is ready, so my friends
        and I will...

Before he can finish, villagers start to move about,
gathering items. Henrik directs the action.

                        HENRIK

        Rubia, round up the children. Jon, get
        the serving utensils. Zola, we will need
        a huge platter for the meat.

They start to move like a well-oiled machine, oblivious
to Mikah.

                         MIKAH

        ... just stand here and watch you.

                          JON

        Henrik, Zola, where are the large bowls
        for the soup?

                        HENRIK

        Zola and I will get them. Do you mind,
        Zola?

Zola smiles as she looks at Henrik, his hand
outstretched to her. Their eyes lock and you can almost
hear violin music playing.

                         ZOLA

        Not at all. This way, Henrik.

They start to walk away together. Rifka is at
Mikah's side.

                         Rifka

        Thank you for all you have done.

                         MIKAH

        I can truly say I have done very little,
        Rifka. May I ask one last thing of you,
        though?

                         Rifka

        Of us? What?

                         MIKAH

        Would you mind if my friends and I
        stayed to eat with you?

                    Rifka

          Of course, you may all stay, even your
          new friends.

                    MIKAH

          Our what? Who...

Rifka points, Mikah glances around the outskirts of the
square.

Drakko's men are standing at each of the different
entrances to the square.

                    MIKAH

          Go to your father, Rifka, be brave, no
          matter what. Go, now.

Rifka glances at the men in furs and then hurries away.
Gradually the villagers start to notice the men too,
and they all grow quiet until an uneasy silence engulfs
the plaza.

                    TEODORO

          Right again.

                    MIKAH

          It's not something I'm happy about,

                    Teodoro.

          At one entrance, the small group of
          raiders PARTS and the huge black horse
          bearing Drakko trots slowly through,
          followed by toady Gurkin and a larger
          group of raiders.

Drakko surveys the area, SNIFFING at the air. He rides
toward the center of the square.

The soldiers FILE in casually but confidently.

Villagers back away toward the cooking area trying to
HIDE the cauldron as the raiders strut around.

The intruders finally settle near the well.

                    DRAKKO

          Who opened the well?

No one answers. Drakko grows impatient

                         DRAKKO

         Who opened up the well? I told you it
         was dry.

Again, no answer. Drakko grabs a MAN who is close by
and pulls him in closer.

                         DRAKKO

         You?

                          MAN

         N... no.

                         DRAKKO

         Somebody did. It might as well be you. I
         told you what would happen.

Drakko un-slings his club with one brawny arm and holds
it high, ready to strike.

He stops, his nose lifts to the wind and he sniffs.

                         DRAKKO

         What is that?

The villagers all shuffle nervously.

Drakko throws the man aside and glares at the
villagers.

                         DRAKKO

         What is that smell?

                         WOMAN

         What smell?

                          MAN

         Oh, that is the uh, garbage dump, east
         of town.

                         DRAKKO

         Garbage? Gurkin, that smell like
         garbage?

Gurkin shakes his head and sniffs. All the soldiers
sniff.

                         GURKIN

         No, my Profoundly Enlarged Tyrant.
         Smells like chicken. Dead chicken.
         Roasted with vegetables to provide fiber.

                    ZOLA

        Chicken, hah. That's venison.

She catches herself too late, covering her mouth with
both hands. All eyes are on her. Drakko dismounts.

                    DRAKKO

        You feast while we have been on the road
        for weeks and weeks starving away to
        skin and bones?

He motions toward Gurkin, who stands holding his pants
up, scratching his huge gut and sucking his teeth.

                    DRAKKO

        Gurkin, find it.

Gurkin grabs a few more men and begins to go through
the food stuffs on the tables, picking things up and
sniffing them.

                    DRAKKO

        Where did this food pile come from? You
        held back on us? You lied to Drakko?
        You.

He POINTS at Henrik deliberately. Henrik swallows hard
and stares back.

                    HENRIK

        Me?

                    DRAKKO

        You look like the leader of these
        pathetic people. Where is that smell
        coming from?

Henrik is frozen, he stares at Drakko and barely
whispers.

                    HENRIK

        I look like a leader?

Zola is by his side and takes his arm.

                    ZOLA

        It comes from the next village over.

The villagers all clump together blocking the cauldron,
eyes wide and scared.

                         GURKIN

          Hmmm... could it be? Yes. I think I
          found it, Drakko.

EXT. VILLAGE SQUARE - DAY

The soldiers gather around the simmering cauldron
smelling deeply. Drakko takes a huge wooden ladle from
a table and dips up a steaming spoonful.

He snaps his fingers and a couple of lackeys blow on the
hot soup for him. Then he downs the entire portion and
chews like a pig.

                         DRAKKO

            Mmmmmm. Mmmmm. Good. Who made this?

The villagers stand and stare at the soldiers in
silence. Then Mikah's voice booms over everyone.

                         MIKAH

           I did.

Everyone turns to see Mikah, Pashe and Teodoro standing
apart from the other villagers.

Gurkin draws his notched cutlass, but Drakko holds his
arm down.

                         DRAKKO

           You? You are not from here. Who are you?

Mikah looks Drakko and the raiders up and down.

                         MIKAH

           I am the soup maker. This is Pashe and
           Teodoro. We made the soup.

Zola fidgets and SHAKES her head angrily.

                         DRAKKO

           Good soup, my friend. Mind if we eat?

                         TEODORO

           You have not helped make it, and you
           don't look like you've missed too many
           meals.

Mikah shhhs him.

                        MIKAH

        He said he was hungry, he may eat. There
        is plenty. If the rest of you don't
        mind.

Mikah looks to the villagers, who stand frightened and
unmoving. Some shake their heads.

Mikah sighs and makes a gesture of "help yourself" to
the raiders.

                        DRAKKO

        Thanks, friend.

The soldiers grab up bowls and mugs and start to take
out huge dripping scoops of the soup. They grab up
handfuls of fresh bread and eat sloppily and noisily.

Mikah looks at Zola and Henrik, who say nothing. Zola
drops her gaze to the ground and turns away.

Gurkin farts and grins as he tosses a half-eaten chunk
of bread toward the fire.

                        GURKIN

        Good food. Take all the bread and
        utensils, men. And grab that carcass.

He points with a food-covered hand toward what's left
of the stag on the spit.

                        DRAKKO

        Thank you for sharing, my good people. I
        hope you don't mind if we take a little
        water and a few other things with us.

                        GURKIN

        We only get into town once in a while,
        so we need to stock up.

                        JON

        As long as there is some soup left.

                        DRAKKO

        Huh? There's some left?

He looks into the cauldron, which is not even a quarter
empty.

DRAKKO

> Hmmm, sure is. Gurkin, make sure you
> share this with the rest of these
> people.

Gurkin and two other raiders chuckle, then LEAN into the cauldron with their shoulders, giving a mighty HEAVE and push it over.

The contents SPILL out onto the ground, spreading to the villagers, who look on in shock.

The stones come out last. Drakko picks one up.

DRAKKO

> What's this? You try to poison us? Who
> put this in there?

Mikah holds up a finger.

MIKAH

> I did.

Gurkin grabs Mikah and drags him over to Drakko.

GURKIN

> Are you trying to poison our Lumbering,
> Odorous Leader Drakko? Even though you
> can't, 'cause he's too powerful?

MIKAH

> No, it was part of the soup.

DRAKKO

> Rock soup? Who makes soup from Rocks?

Mikah starts to speak, but Henrik cuts him off.

HENRIK

> It's a stone.

Drakko reels on Henrik.

DRAKKO

> What?

HENRIK

> Nothing.

GURKIN

> Did you call Drakko a liar? Inferring
> that he lies? Even though if he did,

>   they'd be some of the best lies you ever
>   heard...

                    HENRIK

>   I... I just said it's a stone.

Mikah looks up at Henrik, and a soft smile creeps across his face.

                    MIKAH

>   We make stone soup. My friends, Pashe,
>   Teodor and I.

                    JON

>   Those... those were my potatoes.

                    WOMAN

>   And my beets.

                    MAN

>   We gave the water, quit taking all the
>   credit.

                    WOMAN 2

>   I made biscuits.

Many villagers find their voice and start to talk all at once.

Drakko whips the club off his back and sounds a loud, ringing GONG on the cauldron.

                    DRAKKO

>   Shut up. Everybody.

Drakko pulls Mikah closer and breathes in his face.

                    DRAKKO

>   Nobody makes soup from rocks. What is
>   this here for?

                    MIKAH

>   Its magic.

Drakko looks at the stone in his hand. A laughing FACE appears in the STEAM drifting from the stone, then dissipates.

                    DRAKKO

>   Bah!

He abruptly WHACKS one of his FLUNKIES in the forehead
with the stone. The flunky goes cross-eyed and falls
backward to the ground.

The rest of the raiders laugh and point.

                    DRAKKO

          What do you think, Gurkin?

                    GURKIN

          Wondrous in it's powers, oh Gigantic
          Seething Wizard.

                    DRAKKO

          Great, I keep it then.

                    MIKAH

          I wish you wouldn't.

                    DRAKKO

          What did you say?

                    MIKAH

          I said I wish you wouldn't. I need to
          keep that for...

Drakko picks up Mikah with one arm and throws him
against a tree. Mikah falls to the ground with a groan.

                    DRAKKO

          Nobody tells Drakko what to do.

The villagers gasp. Pashe and Teodoro rush to
Mikah's side.

                    PASHE

          Are you alright? Talk to me.

                    TEODORO

          He's dead. I know it, he's dead.

Mikah shakes his head to clear it.

                    MIKAH

          Thank you for the encouraging words,
          Teodoro.

                    PASHE

          What now?

Mikah eyes the villagers and the soldiers, glaring at
each other.

                    MIKAH

    Now we see what empty stomachs and full
    heads and hearts can do.

                    DRAKKO

    Leave my sight. All of you. Gurkin,
    prepare for pillaging.

Drakko and his men start to gather up their things, and
pack away stuff from the village.

                    GURKIN

    You heard Drakko, nothing else to see
    here. Cowering should be done in your
    houses. Please prepare your dwellings
    for incineration. Try to pile combus-
    tible items in the center of your main
    room. If you have lamp oil, please soak
    your walls and floors, this will help
    save time and expedite...

Gurkin finds a rolly-polly doll on a table and tosses it
aside. It rights itself.

                    GURKIN

    Ooh, that's interesting.

Gurkin does a double take. He pushes it down and it
pops back up. He motions toward Drakko.

                    GURKIN

    Putrid Muscular One, look at this.

Drakko turns from his task of glaring at people toward
Gurkin. He sees the doll, Gurkin pushes it.

                    DRAKKO

    Huh? Let me see that.

Drakko strides to the doll and stomps it down. It stays
momentarily, then pops up.

                    DRAKKO

    Rrrrrrgh.

He stomps it again and again. He looks up and does a
double-take.

The villagers have amassed around the band of raiders.
They do not look scared, they do not look like they are
leaving.

                              Rifka

        Stop it, that is for my sister.

Drakko turns slowly toward Rifka, his eyes filled with
anger.

                              DRAKKO

        Who dares tell me to stop?

Rifka fidgets. She looks to the doll, over to Mikah and
back. She opens her mouth to speak but is cut off by
Treslyn.

                              TRESLYN

        I did.

Pashe's eyes widen he tries to wave to Treslyn to stop.

Drakko glares at Rifka, then over to Treslyn.

                              DRAKKO

          I'll eat your head while you watch, you
          insolent

                              TRESLYN

          You have taken what you want, please
          leave that alone.

Gurkin is beside himself, sputtering and gesturing and
waiting for Drakko to say something warlord-like.

Drakko picks up the doll and heaves it at a nearby
stone wall. The doll splinters.

Drakko takes a few huge strides toward Treslyn,
but just before he is in her face, Pashe steps between
the two.

Treslyn whispers to Pashe.

                              TRESLYN

          I am not afraid of him, Pashe.

                              PASHE

          That's okay, I'm afraid enough for both
          of us.

Drakko reels back a fist to strike at Pashe.

An object THUNKS off of Drakko's head and lands on the
grass nearby. It is another doll.

Everyone looks in the direction the doll came from.

Henrik stands alone, lowering his hand slowly. He shrugs and smiles sheepishly.

                    HENRIK

        It slipped. It's slippery. I was trying
        to...

                    Antolina

        He was trying to hit your huge fat
        bottom.

                    HENRIK

        Yes, I was trying to hit your... oh no
        no no wait.

Henrik thinks a moment, looking at the faces of his neighbors.

His gaze rests on Zola's face. She smiles proudly. Henrik turns back to Drakko unafraid.

                    HENRIK

        You have plundered our village for the
        last time. You will leave - now.

There is a short silence as Drakko and Henrik glare at each other.

Another doll hits Drakko, then another.

Soon dolls are flying everywhere. The soldiers draw weapons and form a prickly huddle near Drakko, who brandishes his battle club.

                    DRAKKO

        You will pay for that. Kill them all!
        Drakko raises his club above his head
        to strike.

Suddenly, an ARROW pierces Drakko's hand, pinning it to his weapon.

                    DRAKKO

        Aaaargh!

Mikah and Teodoro look in the direction the arrow came from. At the head of large CONTINGENT stands the Taburki with a bow. Many other strong men stand behind him with weapons at the ready.

Drakko's group is greatly outnumbered.

                    GURKIN

          Taburki, a lot of them this time. You
          know what to do men.

Gurkin points his CUTLASS in the Taburki's general
direction, his pants fall.

The soldiers look to the Taburkis for a tense beat.

Mechanically, as one, they DROP their weapons and take
off at a manic TEAR out the other side of the square,
with Taburkis and villagers in hot pursuit.

Gurkin takes a few steps and falls flat on his face,
ankles tangled in trousers.

Drakko nurses his gun hand and backs up as other
villagers close in on him.

                    DRAKKO

          I will make you a deal. I will let you
          keep half of all I have if you help me
          fight the Taburki dogs. I'll give you...

                    ZOLA

          It is not yours to give.

The Taburki sees Mikah and goes to his side. He pulls
out a bandage for the cut on Mikah's head.

                    MIKAH

          Thank you, my friend. It is very good to
          see you again.

                    TABURKI

          Good friend.

                    PASHE

          Yes. Good friend.

Antolina looks at the food on the ground as her father
hugs her.

                    Antolina

          Father, the food is all gone.

                    HENRIK

          No, Antolina, it is still here.
          We just need to clean up and start over.
          Eh, Zola?

Zola takes his hand and pulls her daughter close to her.

                         ZOLA

     Anna and I would be proud to help. How
     do we begin?

Henrik looks over at Mikah and his friends.

                         HENRIK

     We have what we know now, that is where
     we start.

They all begin to pick up loaves and plates, and other things strewn by the raiders.

EXT. VILLAGE SQUARE — DAY

Mikah, Pashe and Teodoro are bent over their knapsacks packing their belongings.

Treslyn helps Pashe pack his, she eyes him a little nervously. Pashe calmly nods to her as if to say "it's okay."

Henrik KNEELS at the side of the grave of Elana, he is speaking softly, no one can hear.

Villagers stop and shake hands or offer hugs and farewells. Some children fetch items for the trio.

A little girl brings a doll for Teodoro.

                         TEODORO

     For me? Thank you very much, what is her
     name?

                         GIRL

     I named her Tanya, after me, so you will
     always remember us.

Teodoro stops his packing and gives the girl a huge hug.

                         TEODORO

     How could I do anything but remember
     you?

Teodoro packs the doll in his knapsack.

Lothar and Zola approach Mikah. Zola holds a small bundle.

ZOLA

You are leaving? For sure?

MIKAH

I have taken advantage of you kind
people for more than is fair.

ZOLA

Bah, there is plenty. Here, I have some
fresh bread to take with you.

LOTHAR

Fresh.

MIKAH

Thank you Lothar, Zola. You are the
finest cook I have ever met.

ZOLA

My kitchen has never seen such a wonder-
ful meal as you made yesterday. I will
never forget you.

LOTHAR

Never.

Zola hugs Mikah, Lothar gives him a powerful handshake,
and they wander off.

TEODORO

We may never make it out of town. Pashe,
pack faster, it will be dark before...

Mikah and Teodoro watch as Pashe packs slower and
slower.

MIKAH

This is another day of new beginnings,
eh, old friend?

Pashe smiles meekly.

TEODORO

What?

MIKAH

I think Pashe has found his village,
Teodor.

> TEODORO

What?

Pashe stands upright and he and Treslyn glance at each other.

> PASHE

I am sorry, but we... we.

> TEODORO

What?

> MIKAH

No need for apologies or explanations. It is time you started anew. I wish you both the best life has to offer. I will not forget all you have done for me, Pashe.

> PASHE

Me... done for you? In six years all I have done is

> MIKAH

You have been my friend, and you have always been there for me. That has made my life bearable.

> TEODORO

What? Is he dying? Why am I always the last to know? It was the Sickweed wasn't it? We slept on Sickweed.

> PASHE

Teodor, my friend, I am staying here with Treslyn. We want to be part of each other's lives.

> TEODORO

Staying? Was it something I said?

Teodoro is near tears, he pouts and sticks out his lower lip. Treslyn hugs him.

> TRESLYN

You are one of the kindest, happiest men I know, sweet Teodoro. Don't be sad.

                    MIKAH

     It isn't so bad, we can visit.

                    PASHE

     Ahh, you are always like a child my
     friend.

                   TEODORO

     A child? Am not. You're the child, you
     big...

A little boy runs past and taps Teodoro on the arm

                     BOY

     You're it, Uncle Teodoro.

The child runs off, Teodoro immediately chases after
the boy.

Pashe, Treslyn and Mikah laugh.

Henrik walks up beside Zola. He wears an ornate vest
emblazoned with the symbol from Elana's grave marker.

                    MIKAH

     Henrik, you've been keeping this
     village's faith after all.

                   HENRIK

     I have let them down. I buried myself
     the day my wife died...

Zola takes his hand gently.

                    ZOLA

     And I will dig you out, Henrik. We will
     rebuild. Faith Keepers work in pairs.

Henrik smiles, he and Zola stare deeply into each
other's eyes. Smiles all around.

EXT. EDGE OF TOWN — DAY

Mikah and Teodoro have their gear on and are ready to
leave.

Pashe and Treslyn and the villagers form a half circle
around them.

Antolina, Henrik, Zola and Rifka are at the front of
the congregation.

>   Antolina
>   Bless you. Thank you again.

>   MIKAH

>   You are too kind, and I am undeserving
>   of your thanks.

>   HENRIK

>   I am ashamed of my behavior toward you,
>   my friends, please forgive me. You are
>   welcome here anytime. Any time at all.

>   TEODORO

>   We will be back, I promise.

Teodoro shakes hands with Pashe, then hugs him
emotionally. Rifka looks up at Mikah sadly.

>   MIKAH

>   Rifka, I have almost forgotten. I have
>   something to give you, it is not much,
>   but I want you to have it.

Rifka perks up a bit.

>   Rifka

>   What is it?

Mikah produces his magic stone from his pocket.

>   MIKAH

>   You know its power, use it wisely and it
>   will do you a world of good.

Rifka takes the stone and smiles. Mikah pats her head
and stands up again and waves.

>   MIKAH

>   Good bye, my friends, may you all live
>   and love for many years.

Mikah and Teodoro walk off down the dirt road away from
the village. The villagers wave and shout as they go.

Slowly, the villagers turn from the road and start back
to their homes. Pashe and Treslyn are the last
to leave.

EXT. COUNTRY ROAD - DAY

Mikah and Teodoro walk at a leisurely pace, chatting
quietly.

Mikah's attention is taken by a rustling in the bushes. He motions for Teodoro to stop.

                         MIKAH

         Who's there?

Silence. Mikah and Teodoro scan the bushes for a second.

Mikah shrugs, and they continue walking.

An arrow whizzes by and perches in a tree just in front of Mikah and Teodoro. They stop.

                         TEODORO

         The marauders!

He dives for cover behind a fallen tree. A commotion and CAT's WAIL shoot forth, Teodoro yelps. An animal zips away into the woods.

                         TEODORO

         Wildcat. My fault entirely.

The Taburki steps out into the path, bow in hand, a pack and bedroll in his other hand.

Mikah and the Taburki look at each other for a moment. Mikah smiles and motions for the Taburki to join him.

                         MIKAH

         I would consider it an honor, my friend.

The Taburki motions to where Teodoro is and asks a question in his language.

                         MIKAH

         He's alright. He missed the Rashweed
         bush.

Mikah and the Taburki start to walk again. Teodoro gets up, dusts himself off and hurries after them, catching up quickly.

                         TEODORO

         But... but wait...

Teodoro glances back and forth at Mikah and the Taburki a few times. Mikah smiles.

                         MIKAH

         Yes, Teodoro?

                         TEODORO

          You gave away the magic stone.

                         MIKAH

          Yes, I did.

                         TEODORO

          But they don't need it anymore.

                         MIKAH

          Maybe.

                         TEODORO

          What are we going to do now, we still
          have many miles to go, through some
          pretty inhospitable country.

                         MIKAH

          So?

Teodoro makes a lot of GESTURES as he tries to put the
words together. The Taburki tries to avoid the rabid
movements.

                         TEODORO

          We have no magic stone now.

Mikah chuckles and shakes his head.

                         MIKAH

          Teodoro, you make my soul laugh.

Teodoro walks on, complaining and whining, trying to
make the Taburki understand their plight.

                         TEODORO

          What will happen next time we need to
          eat, or the time after that? Maybe we
          will not be so lucky, or we'll be at a
          cannibal village.

Teodoro's face registers new concern and his hands flail
about, panicky.

                         TEODORO

          Oh, that would be great, "oh wait, I
          think I have an arm here somewhere," and
          you, just handing our magic away like it
          was some common bauble or something.

Mikah stops and nonchalantly looks down at the ground.

He bends over and picks up an odd shaped STONE, turning it over in his hands and brushing it off.

A WISP of dust flies off the stone, and a FACE appears ever so briefly and WINKS before the dust FADES into the air.

Mikah nods in approval and tucks it into a POCKET at the side of his pack.

                    MIKAH

        Don't worry; I have another, you know.

                    TEODORO

        What?

Teodoro scrambles up to Mikah's side, his eyes widening.

                    TEODORO

        How many magic stones did that old man
        give you? Where did he get so many magic
        stones?

Mikah laughs, still shaking his head as they walk on. Teodoro nudges the Taburki, who smiles.

                    TEODORO

        How come I never got a magic stone?
        I got a doll. You get magic stones,
        Pashe gets a partner and a village.
        I got a doll at the last two villages,
        and a key-ring at the village before
        that. I'll probably get an ashtray at
        the next one...

Teodoro grumbles under his breath, and Mikah and the Taburki laugh louder as they start down a hill and out of view.

FADE OUT

THE END

APOCALYPSE... WHEN?

Three Screenplays

Sometimes I have dark dreams. Not nightmares, per se, just kinda dark. And sometimes I remember them long enough after I wake up to write them down. APOCALYPSE... WHEN? is an example of that.

As part of my obnoxiously poor sleep regimen, I often have times where I wake up in the dead of night with an incredibly heavy, dark, feeling of dread, or maybe foreboding. It could be foreboding-adjacent. Whatever the case, I wake up, and everything feels hyper-still and quiet; my eyes pop open, and I know they are wider than they need to be.

I can't quite put my finger on it, but something feels off. Something feels like The End is near, and I sit there and wait for It but It (so far) never comes. And after I lay there staring into the abyss that I just know is waiting to jump out at me for what seems like eons, the feeling goes away, and I settle into the comfortable insomniatic rut that feels like a warm sweater.

It wasn't difficult to parlay that into the story you are about to read next. Because if I felt that way - waiting and waiting for The End to happen - then chances were likely that someone else did as well. And then I got to feeling sorry for the poor guys whose

One Job it is to kick The End into gear, The Four Horsemen of the Apocalypse. Sitting around on the Other Side, waiting... waiting... for eons; maybe playing solitaire, maybe turning an ear in the direction of a sound... was that The Call...? Is it time NOW? Do we ride at Dusk? Does the Ace go at the top of the stack next to the King, or does it go down next to the Two?

Then, as feels natural, I just added that ol' dark humor to the whole thing, amped up the sibling bullshit commensurate with the intolerably boring wait - and then slapped a "Dad always liked you best" on top.

What I ended up with was this ridiculous story of knowing what your purpose is, but not being able to actually do it, sprinkled with some little bits of sarcastic societal commentary that still make me laugh when I read it today.

Saddle up, The End is nigh.

FADE IN

EXT. BUSY CITY STREET - DAY

A city BUS pulls away from the sidewalk as a woman and
her daughter run up and bang on the door.

SUSAN, 30's, dressed just this side of professional,
ROBIN, 10, has a smart, mischievous face.

                         SUSAN
          No, no, wait. I'm sorry, please wait.

The bus stops, the door opens and the two start to get
on. The girl stops on the first step and watches

As Susan rushes over to a homeless MAN who sits on the
sidewalk. She fishes some CHANGE out of her purse, hands
it to the man and hurries back onto the bus.

The bus pulls away and heads down the busy street.

INT. CITY BUS — FOLLOWING

The bus is half full of tired riders. SUSAN shakes her
head as she and ROBIN sit toward the front of the bus.

Susan puts her bags under the seat and looks out at a
CRAZY street PREACHER ranting and waving a sign on the
sidewalk.

Robin's backpack is on her lap; she has a book-shaped
TROPHY in her hands.

                    SUSAN

          This is ridiculous; we almost miss this
          bus every day.

                    ROBIN

          Sorry, mom.

                    SUSAN

          Just try to get out on time please.

Robin makes the trophy a little more conspicuous.

                    SUSAN

          How was school today, sweetie?

                    ROBIN

          Boring.

                    SUSAN

          Why was it boring?

                    ROBIN

          We were supposed to discuss half-life
          and carbon dating, and all we did was
          play with popcorn kernels in a shoe box.

                    SUSAN

          It's fifth grade, honey, what do you
          expect?

                    ROBIN

          I want to go to Farmington Academy.

                    SUSAN

          We've discussed that. The bus trip alone
          would add over an hour.

Robin sulks, shifts the trophy again. Susan perks up,
changes the subject.

                    SUSAN

          Anything fun happen today? Anything you
          particularly liked?

                    ROBIN

          Well, yeah, actually there was.

                    SUSAN

Ooh, what?

                    ROBIN

Sean Kensington brought his father in
today for career day.

                    SUSAN

Really? Your little friend from Spanish
Club? What does his father do?

                    ROBIN

He sends people to Hell.

A woman in the seat next to them gasps and stares.

                    SUSAN

Well, that's a pretty neat

(beat)

Pardon me?

                    ROBIN

He's a preacher, and he said we're all
going to burn in Hell when the End of
the World comes.

                    SUSAN

I'm sure he didn't say...

                    ROBIN

Yeah, he did. If we don't listen to
him, that's where we're going.

                    SUSAN

And where was the teacher while he was
saying all this?

                    ROBIN

She had to go grade tests, and when she
came back, most of the kids were crying.
It was great.

                    SUSAN

Well, I think I'm going to have to have
a talk with your teacher, I find that
highly irresponsible.

Susan shakes her head and stares out the window at the gathering clouds. Robin puts the trophy back in her pack.

The woman in the next seat stares at Robin with a dour face. Robin leans toward the woman.

> ROBIN
>
> The Four Horsemen of the Apocalypse will wipe out every living creature. Everybody.

The woman harrumphs, and directs her attention elsewhere.

> SUSAN
>
> That's enough, Robin. First of all, those type of "preachers" only talk that way to scare other people into attending their church so that they can make more money from donations. And second of all, there's no such thing as horsemen who come to destroy the earth.

> ROBIN
>
> I don't know, he sounded very sure of himself.

> SUSAN
>
> And how do I sound?

They look at each other a beat, then turn away.

> ROBIN
>
> I wonder how someone gets the job of Pestilence, or Famine or...

> SUSAN
>
> Stop it. They're figurative beings created so people would have something to focus on.

Susan waves her hands around, attracting attention from other riders and the driver.

> SUSAN
>
> Because when you label the intangible, or make it into something familiar, like a person who does this or that, it's not so scary anymore.

Robin looks at her mother with an eyebrow raised.

                    SUSAN

          That "Armageddon" isn't going to happen,
          and those horsemen just plain don't
          exist. Okay?

She stares sternly at Robin, who stares back.

                    SUSAN

          Okay?

                    ROBIN

          Okay. They don't exist.

EXT. OTHERWORLDLY PLAINS - NIGHT

Three huge, black, red-eyed WAR HORSES ride across the
dusty, rocky plain. The sky is an odd purple/green
color, clouds roiling madly. Lightning flashes, shapes
of riders can be seen on the horses' backs.

They get closer. One of the figures, FAMINE, is portly
with a round, unshaven face. He wears raiment trimmed
out with bones. His helmet is fashioned like some sort
of skull.

Figure two, PESTILENCE, is tall and gaunt and has a
sickly pallor. Clasps and buckles in the shape of
insects highlight his long flowing robes.

The third rider, WAR, is of a mighty build with a
strong, bearded face and dark eyes. His braids fall
over tarnished armor and leather straps. The haft of a
great axe shows over his shoulder.

                    WAR

          There!

He points toward a looming, shadowy STRONGHOLD up ahead
in the dusky night. One window spills eerie light out
into the dark.

                    WAR

          Hah!

The horses gallop faster and charge toward the
stronghold.

EXT. BUILDING — FOLLOWING

The horses stop ABRUPTLY at a hitching post. Famine
FLIES out of his saddle, over his horse's head and

crashes into the building through a closed WINDOW.

War and Pestilence look to each other and shake their heads. They dismount and enter the building.

INT. GREAT ROOM — FOLLOWING

Wall SCONCES burst alight with flames as War and Pestilence enter the cavernous, rustically appointed room. It is decorated in early Gothic, heavy timbers, stone, iron, etc. A sweeping stairway leads upstairs.

A huge stone fireplace dominates the room, and a long, heavy wooden TABLE with chairs sits before it.

Famine is face down on the floor near the window.

> WAR
>
> Brother, where are you? Where is he, Pestilence?

> PESTILENCE
>
> He's obviously gone again, War.

> FAMINE
>
> I'm okay guys, thanks.

Famine dusts himself off and gets awkwardly to his feet. He nonchalantly yanks away a jagged piece of wooden WINDOW FRAME that protrudes from his chest.

> WAR
>
> His room.

> FAMINE
>
> Your concern is warming, brothers.

> PESTILENCE
>
> Learn how to ride, Famine, or skip along behind us.

> FAMINE
>
> I'll skip your jaundiced head on the lake.

> WAR
>
> Enough. Let's find him.

> PESTILENCE
>
> I tell you he's not here.

War snarls and storms up the stairs. Pestilence and Famine stare at each other a beat.

                    FAMINE

          How would you know anything?

                    PESTILENCE

          Because at family gatherings, while you
          and War are eating and fighting and try-
          ing to decide which hole in your bodies
          the best noise comes out of,

Famine makes a face as he scratches absentmindedly at his butt.

                    PESTILENCE

          I actually talk with - and listen to -
          our elusive brother. And treat him
          decently. And... spy on him in his room.

                    FAMINE

          Brown nose.

                    PESTILENCE

          Envious boor.

                    FAMINE

          Over-educated fairy.

                    PESTILENCE

          Jackass.

                    FAMINE

          I know you are, but what am I?

Pestilence rolls his eyes and turns away.

                    FAMINE

          Ha, I win.

Pestilence gestures back toward Famine, who is immediately attacked by a swarm of hideous biting locusts. He flails his arms about.

                    FAMINE

          Ow! Ow! No fair.

Int. Hallway — same

At the top of the stairs, War stops at a wooden door. He pounds his fist on it.

                    WAR

     Brother! Open up. Is it time for the
     smashy thing?

No answer.

                    WAR

     Brother? Do we ride tonight? Answer me.

War starts kicking and pulling crazily at the door. His
brothers come up behind him.

                  FAMINE

     He's probably sharpening his sickle.

                PESTILENCE

     Takes one to know one, lonely boy.

                    WAR

     Death!

Putting his shoulder to the door he gives a great
shove. He waves his brothers over. Famine eagerly
joins him.

Pestilence just stares.

                PESTILENCE

     Surely you can't be serious. I don't do
     physical...

War grabs Pestilence by the shoulder and he and Famine
shove Pestilence hard against the door numerous times.
The door suddenly gives inward.

                  FAMINE

     Whoa.

They fall forward into a room cluttered with
bookshelves lined with huge, old tomes and rolled-up
scrolls. Charts cover the walls. Oddities adorn the
desk and tables.

The brothers look up from the floor. An immense,
muscular WOLF, chained to the wall just a few feet
away, drools down at them.

                    WAR

     Ha. The chompy, bitey thing is all
     chained up. Ain't you, Fenrir, you
     flee-encrusted drool-rag?

The three start to chuckle nervously, then with more confidence.

The wolf gives a slight TUG of its head and the heavy chain SNAPS in three places. He crouches slightly, showing many big teeth.

                              WAR

          Steaming poo.

The wolf LUNGES forward as the brothers scramble to their feet.

                            FAMINE

          Mommy.

INT. GREAT ROOM - NIGHT

The brothers, disheveled and bruised, sit around the large, rough-hewn wooden table. The TICKING of an old CLOCK is the only action going on here.

Pestilence has a grooming KIT in front of him. He dabs at a cut on his arm.

Famine slouches, his head propped up on one hand. In front of him on the table is an APPLE, which he wilts and rejuvenates again and again with a finger motion. The motion and noise it creates is monotonous.

War stares at Pestilence, gets bored. Then he stares at Famine and his apple. Up, down. Up, down. Up, down. He finally jumps up and throws his chair across the room.

                              WAR

          Arrrgh! He leaves us again!

Pestilence doesn't even look up.

                          PESTILENCE

          Ooh, can't put anything over on you.
          Big, empty house; he's gone a hundred
          times a week; and we told you three
          times.

Pestilence examines his fingernails and tsk-tsks.

                          PESTILENCE

          Only took you thirty minutes to piece it
          together.

> FAMINE

Took him forty just last week, he's getting better.

> PESTILENCE

And only one vein throbbing on his forehead.

> FAMINE

A crown says his butt is all twitchy and
spasmodic.

Famine laughs like a fool. Pestilence, holding a
mirror, dabs at a scratch on his face and grins
slightly. War is seething.

> WAR

Rrrraagh!

He whips the AXE off his back, grabs Famine by the
throat, lifts him off his chair and shoves the head of
the axe up under Famine's chin.

> WAR

Take it back.

> FAMINE

What?

> WAR

Take it back or I'll rip you from head
to toe and feed you to the wolf.

> FAMINE

Crying out loud War, we're just playing.
Right Pestilence?

He turns pleadingly to Pestilence, who just looks at
himself in the mirror trying to ignore them. Finally he
slumps and turns his head toward them.

> WAR

Well?

Pestilence SIGHS heavily and delivers deadpan.

> PESTILENCE

We were only playing. You are so very
smart. The nerve of us. And I mean
really.

War glares a moment, then drops Famine to the floor. War spins and SPLITS the table in two with one mighty arc of his axe.

                    PESTILENCE

        Well, that's the last time THAT table
        pisses anyone off.

                    WAR

        Who does he think he is? Running off
        every time he fancies, while we sit in
        this stink hole.

War starts to WHACK at other pieces of furniture and décor in the room.

                    PESTILENCE

        Ooh, much better. That really pulls the
        whole room together.

                    FAMINE

        He's right you know.

                    PESTILENCE

        Pardon me?

                    FAMINE

        He's right. All we ever get to do is
        practice, while Death gets to go out
        into the real world. We've been here
        forever.

Pestilence watches as War chews on the back of a fur-upholstered chair, spits out some hairs and throws the seat against a wall.

                    PESTILENCE

        As much as I hate to admit it, I do
        believe something stinks here. And it
        isn't just Nutjob over there.

War grabs a candelabra from the mantle and BITES a thick CANDLE in half. He makes a surprised face, nods, and starts to eat the remaining piece.

                    FAMINE

        Let's make him take us.

War offers a candle piece to Pestilence.

                    PESTILENCE

          Thank you, no; I walk upright.

          (to Famine)

          What was that, Brother?

                    FAMINE

          Next time he goes, we go.

War GROWLS angrily through a mouthful of tallow.

                    WAR

          We're missing all the excitement.

INT. COMFORTABLE, CRAMPED APARTMENT - NIGHT

A small FISH NET sloshes around in a fish bowl, trying
to snare a floating ex-GOLDFISH.

Susan, the scooper, finally snags the dead fish and plops
it into a baggie.

Robin stands next to her, a pout creeping into her
face.

                    SUSAN

          I'm sorry he's dead, Honey. These things
          happen sometimes.

                    ROBIN

          I guess so.

She is near tears. Susan tries to re-direct her
attention.

                    SUSAN

          We can have a funeral for him, a nice
          service before we... er... flush

                    ROBIN

          NO! Not that.

Susan winces, then pats Robin on the shoulder.

                    SUSAN

          Let's go have a service for poor Mr...
          what was his name?

                    ROBIN

          His name was Stanley. It isn't fair; He
          was my best friend and now he's going to
          hell.

Robin cries and runs away. Susan stands holding the dripping baggie and net. She stares at the little lifeless body.

INT. SUSAN'S APARTMENT - NIGHT

Susan and Robin eat dinner at the small table in the "dining nook" of the kitchen.

Robin picks at her plate with a fork.

> SUSAN
>
> Robin, please eat your dinner, it's going to get cold.

> ROBIN
>
> I'm not hungry.

Susan watches her daughter for a few seconds, then puts her fork down.

> SUSAN
>
> Honey, Mr... Stanley is not going to Hell. There is no Hell for Goldfish. I mean, what could a goldfish possibly do to deserve Hell?

Robin ignores the remark and continues picking.

> SUSAN
>
> Hog the pellets? Start a fight with the Tetras?

Robin continues to ignore her mother.

Susan giggles nervously. Robin snaps at her.

> ROBIN
>
> What do you know anyway? You didn't even know his name, you didn't notice that I won a trophy for the reading marathon - there isn't a single book in that school that I don't know about - you pick me up late every day and you know nothing about anything.

She storms away from the table and a few seconds later a door is slammed shut in another area of the apartment.

Susan sits at the table looking completely dejected. Now it is her turn to pick at her food with a fork.

A door is heard opening, a few seconds later Robin
returns to the nook. She stands frowning in front of
Susan.

> ROBIN
>
> Did you at least remember the costume
> that I need for the school play
> tomorrow?

Susan looks at Robin, trying her hardest to not let her
"No; what costume?" face show.

> SUSAN
>
> Of course I did. I just need to iron it.
> It'll be waiting for you in the morning.

The two stare each other down for a few seconds.
Robin's furrowed brow softens a bit.

> ROBIN
>
> You sure?

> SUSAN
>
> Sure.

> ROBIN
>
> Positive?

> SUSAN
>
> Positive.

Robin's eyes narrow to slits.

> ROBIN
>
> Thank you for the turtle costume.

> SUSAN
>
> You're welcome for the turtle costume.

Robin knits up her eyebrows again and frowns mightily,
then stomps off to her room.

> ROBIN
>
> It wasn't a turtle costume; it was
> a seven-banded armadillo. Nice try,
> though. Good night.

Susan smacks her forehead, then throws her elbows on
the table and cradles her head I her hands. One of her
elbows messily squishes her food.

Susan closes her eyes.

INT. GREAT ROOM - NIGHT

War, Pestilence and Famine SLEEP in chairs about the room. Three empty candlesticks and tallow pieces litter the small end-table in front of War, who SNORES like a monsoon, crumbs dotting his beard.

Pestilence FIDGETS in his sleep, his hand jerking now and again.

Famine COOS like a baby.

The main door to the room CREAKS open slightly and a shadowy FIGURE appears in the doorway.

The figure is tall, robed and dark. It seems to look at the three sleeping brothers for a moment, then comes in, closing the door.

The figure's hands pull the hood down from the head, and a man's face is seen. This is DEATH, very handsome, neatly trimmed beard, long thick hair - dark, penetrating eyes.

Death crosses the room and looks down at Famine, then at Pestilence. When he turns again

War stands directly in front of Death, wide awake - and angry.

                         WAR

          Long night, brother?

INT. GREATROOM - NIGHT

Death sits in a chair at the split table, War paces in front of him, Famine stands behind and Pestilence sits next to him.

                         WAR

          That is still not good enough, brother.
          You cheat us.

                         DEATH

          Pestilence, please, talk some sense
          into...

                         WAR

          No! You not talk sense, I want fair
          for me.

> PESTILENCE
>
> Oh, excellent talking words, War. You
> speak so goodly.

> WAR
>
> Flattery won't change my mind. We want
> to go out into the other worlds, Death.

> DEATH
>
> We? All of you actually agreed on some-
> thing? Famine?

He glances back at Famine, who smiles sheepishly and
shrugs, sweating bullets as he looks to War.

War is incredulous, he glares at Famine.

Death looks at Pestilence.

> DEATH
>
> You?

Pestilence looks to War and then to the cringing
Famine, then to War again, before looking to Death.

> PESTILENCE
>
> Personally, I can wait till The Call;
> but War seems to think...

War explodes in rage, he lunges at Pestilence.

> WAR
>
> You filthy... I'll squish you into paste.

> PESTILENCE
>
> Oh, get over yourself.

As War GRABS at Pestilence, Pestilence turns into a
SWARM of FLIES and disperses, leaving War grasping
crazily at flitting bugs.

War, fist raised to strike, turns at Famine, who nearly
inhales all the air out of the room.

> FAMINE
>
> Not in the face.

> DEATH
>
> Leave him alone, War.

> WAR
>
> Shut up.

                    DEATH

        Don't hit him.

War pulls two nasty-looking heavy blades out of his
robes and brandishes them.

                    WAR

        You're gonna pay, fat boy - we agreed.

                    FAMINE

        But... but... I'm a chicken. You know
        that.

                    WAR

        Then I'm gonna carve you up with the
        slicey thing.

                    DEATH

        Back off, War.

War lunges at Famine and is within fillet reach when
Death reaches up and lightly TOUCHES War's chest.

War drops to the floor like a sack of lead weights.

Pestilence REFORMS and stands at Famine's side.

                    PESTILENCE

        I can't believe you lost your spine like
        that.

                    FAMINE

        At least I was honest, you cringing
        little weasel.

                    DEATH

        Both of you stop it. Pick him up and
        get him to his room, he's going to be
        a little angry when he gets up.

                    FAMINE

        That'll be something new.

                    PESTILENCE

        You might well have said, "He's going to
        be a little angry when he's walking. Or
        sitting. Or being."

INT. DEATH'S ROOM - NIGHT

Death sits at his desk. Fenrir lies by his side,

snoring. The mesmerizing TIC-TOC of an old clock keeps them company.

Death pores over a large, dusty TOME with exotic binding on his desk, reading intently.

He makes a face, grabs another book and flips open to a page with CHARTS and scans quickly using a finger.

> DEATH
>
> I thought so.

He sighs and shuts the chart book and tosses it on his cluttered desk. He lowers a hand to Fenrir and SCRITCHES the wolf's ears.

> DEATH
>
> Keep an eye on things, okay?

Fenrir growls softly.

EXT. HALLWAY OUTSIDE DEATH'S ROOM - SAME TIME

Pestilence PEEKS through the KEYHOLE, watching Death at the desk.

EXT. ALLEY WITH TRASH BINS - NIGHT

Susan looks at the dead goldfish in the baggie in her hand.

> SUSAN
>
> Poor little guy.

She opens the trash bin and tosses the baggie in.

A voice startles her.

> VOICE (TOM)
>
> You're pretty brave, There are germs all over that dumpster.

Susan turns to see TOM - 30's, handsome, guy next door - at the mouth of the alley.

> SUSAN
>
> Hi Tom. Stanley died.

> TOM
>
> Robin's goldfish? I'm sorry.

They walk into the building together.

INT. BUILDING STAIRWELL - FOLLOWING

Tom and Susan climb the stairs.

                    SUSAN

     I don't know why things like this affect
     her so easily. It's just a fish.

                    TOM

     Some people just feel things deeper; she
     empathizes with others, that's all. It's
     a good trait.

                    SUSAN

     How do you handle all those people at
     the hospital that you know won't make
     it.

                    TOM

     I was blessed with not being a big
     feeler. I wouldn't be any good as a
     doctor if every single case hit me
     deeply. But somebody has to care.

They get to the top of the stairs. Tom goes to the
LEFT, Susan turns RIGHT.

                    TOM

     If there weren't people like Robin that
     can feel for others - and with whom
     others can connect - the world would be
     in pretty bad shape.

                    SUSAN

     I guess so. Thanks, Tom.

                    TOM

     Knowing when to step in and when to let
     it go, though - that's a tough nut to
     crack.

INT. FAMINE'S ROOM - NIGHT

Famine sits on his bed reading a book and cracking nuts
with his TEETH. Nutshells litter the bed and floor.

There is a KNOCK at the door.

                    FAMINE

     Mmmm?

Knocking again.

                        FAMINE

          Mmmmaaahh?

The door opens and Pestilence enters, glancing behind
him.

                      PESTILENCE

          Brother, he leaves again.

                        FAMINE

          So?

                      PESTILENCE

          What do you mean, "so?" Don't you want
          to see where he goes?

Famine shrugs, mumbles through a cracking nut.

                        FAMINE

          Mmmm-mm.

                      PESTILENCE

          What is with you? This was your idea.

                        FAMINE

          The more I thought about it, the less I
          cared. Nuts?

He offers the bag to Pestilence, who slaps it away.

                      PESTILENCE

          You're scared.

                        FAMINE

          Am not.

                      PESTILENCE

          Are too. You're getting cold feet.

                        FAMINE

          Nu-uhn. You're just mad cause I won't go
          along with your dumb plan.

                      PESTILENCE

          You're dumb.

                        FAMINE

          You are.

> PESTILENCE

You are... aaarg. Now you've got me
doing it. Stop being a baby and come
with me to tell War. We have to act
soon.

> FAMINE

No, I'm not riding that stupid...

> PESTILENCE

Ah-HA!

Famine shakes his head and gets really into his nut
cracking.

> PESTILENCE

You're afraid of the horse.

Famine doesn't answer: his face shows the truth. He
pouts, nutshells sticking to his quivering lower lip.

> PESTILENCE

Tell me, what good is an Apocalypse
rider without his horse?

> FAMINE

It's not my fault, I got the mean one,
I swear it. He, he does things to tease
me, and he bit me last night. He has the
Crazy Eye.

He grabs Famine by the sleeve, spilling nuts all over
the bed, and hauls him up.

EXT. WAR'S ROOM - NIGHT

Famine and Pestilence are at the door, they knock
hesitantly.

> PESTILENCE

War? You awake?

No answer. Knocking.

> PESTILENCE

War, we need to talk to you.

> FAMINE

He's still dead, we'd better go.

Famine turns to leave, Pestilence pulls him back.

                         PESTILENCE

          Go on in.

                          FAMINE

          You go in, he cut off my arms last time.

                         PESTILENCE

          Go see if he's up, or I'll give you
          diarrhea again.

Famine winces, holds up a balled FIST.

                          FAMINE

          Axes-Spiders-Apples?

                         PESTILENCE

          Okay.

They do a modified "rock-paper-scissors" with Famine
coming up the loser.

                         PESTILENCE

          Hah, apples smash spiders. Go.

Famine grumbles and slowly opens the door and enters.

INT. WAR'S ROOM - SAME TIME

Famine enters the room, there is very little light from
a candle in one corner. The room is a disaster area;
everything is broken, ripped, crushed or bent.

A large WEAPONS rack lines one wall, covered with many
gruesome-looking killing utensils.

A huge SHAPE lies on the bed.

                          FAMINE

          Brother? Is that you? Are you...

War jumps from behind the door and grabs Famine, head-
butting him hard.

                           WAR

          Rrraaah!

War swings Famine around like a rag doll before Jamming
him into the doorway.

War holds Famine steady and starts slamming the door on
his head repeatedly. Famine whimpers and flails about
helplessly.

INT. HALLWAY OUTSIDE WAR'S ROOM - SAME TIME

Pestilence grabs the doorway with both hands and tries to push War back into room with his FOOT.

Famine grabs at Pestilence spastically, pulling his brother's PANTS down a little at a time while trying to pull himself out of the room.

War BITES at Pestilence's FOOT every time it comes close, tearing off bits of leather each time.

Unseen, Death stands watching the show, shaking his head.

                         DEATH

          You three can't even be in the same room
          two minutes without trying to stave each
          other's brains in. And I say "trying,"
          because between the three of you, you
          have not one full brain. You will
          always stay here because you simply
          aren't disciplined enough to go off into
          other worlds. You are children. Ugly,
          stupid, quarreling children.

The three brothers stop their fighting and stare up at Death.

War has his FINGERS dug into Famine's NOSTRILS and is trying to pull them off.

Famine has Pestilence's UNDERSHORTS stretched way out in his FIST.

Pestilence smiles weakly and covers his CROTCH with his hand.

Death walks away.

Pestilence frowns.

                      PESTILENCE

          Thanks guys. Way to go. I can always
          count on you two to screw things up.

War snarls and WHACKS Famine on the head.

Famine yelps and LETS GO of the underpants - which SNAP pestilence in the CROTCH with a loud THWACK.

Pestilence falls to the floor in the FETAL position, War and Famine laugh stupidly.

INT. SUSAN'S APARTMENT - DAY

Susan is asleep on the table, draped over a fuzzy armadillo COSTUME. The table is littered with crafty materials. Robin walks in, already dressed for school, carrying her backpack.

                         ROBIN

          Mom.

Susan doesn't stir, but she sleepily replies, barely moving her lips.

                         SUSAN

               I'll have that report on your desk in
               five minutes, Mr. Phalan.

Robin looks at the costume and her sleeping mother. She tries to see more of the costume under Susan's head and arms. She looks at her mother again, and gently TOUCHES her mother's hair.

                         ROBIN

               Thanks Mommy.

Susan jerk's bolt upright in her chair, wild eyed and incoherent.

                         SUSAN

          What time is it?

                         ROBIN

          Seven thirty.

Susan stares about the room, resting her focus on Robin.

                         SUSAN

          Oh no.

INT. BUILDING STAIRWELL - DAY

Susan and Robin fly down the stairs, at the same time Tom, in a scrubs top, is coming in the door.

                         TOM

               Morning ladies how...

                         SUSAN

               Great. That's nice. Late.

Tom watches them stumble down the last few stairs before racing for the door.

                    TOM

          Careful, you're gonna kill yourself one
          of these days.

                    ROBIN

          Bye Mr. Harrington.

Tom smiles and watches them go. Then he gets a look of
concern, shakes his head, and goes up the stairs.

EXT. CITY STREET - DAY

Susan and Robin sprint down the street toward the bus
stop. Susan's skirt and blouse really don't match, she
has two different shoes on her feet and their matching
pair in her hands.

Robin has one arm through a sleeve of her jacket and
the rest of the jacket, along with the armadillo
costume, is trailing along behind her.

                    ROBIN

          Um... I also need two boxes of cookies.

Susan glares down at Robin, her anger softened by love.

                    SUSAN

          Right.

She screeches to a complete halt at a sidewalk FRUIT
STAND, taking three seconds to grab a bag of mixed
fruit, throw money at the vendor, and grab her change.
Then they are off again at a tear.

                    ROBIN

          Nutritionally speaking, that's probably
          better for them anyway.

EXT. BUS STOP - DAY

The bus is just starting to close its doors, Susan jams
her LEG into the back doors and yanks Robin inside.

A homeless WOMAN and her DAUGHTER stand nearby, Susan
makes eye contact and hands over the change from the
vendor, smiling quickly but genuinely. Then she hops on
the bus.

INT. BUSY OFFICE - DAY

Susan rushes into a cubicle and throws her bag and her
shoes onto the desk, glances at a picture of her and
Robin that is pinned to the wall, and begins to change
her shoes.

DOMINIQUE, 30's, loud dresser and outgoing, approaches
with a stack of files.

                         DOMINIQUE

         You're way late, Sue. Phalan wants to
         see you. He isn't happy.

                         SUSAN

         He's never happy.

Susan struggles with her shoes as she looks up at
Dominique. Dominique sees the concern and desperation
in Susan's smile, and notices that she is merely
changing one mismatched pair of shoes for the other
mismatched pair.

Dominique takes two matching shoes away from Susan and
pats her shoulder, looks her in the eye.

                         DOMINIQUE

          He's really not happy this time.

EXT. SCHOOL PLAYGROUND - DAY

Susan stands next to a gate in the fence surrounding
the school. A bell rings and within seconds SCHOOLKIDS
stream from the building.

Susan spots Robin and waves.

                         SUSAN

         Over here sweetie.

Robin looks up and smiles, then frowns slightly.

                         ROBIN

         How come you're so early?

                         SUSAN

         I got all my work done so quick, Mr.
         Phalan let me go.

She puts her arm around Robin and they start to walk
down the sidewalk. Robin looks up at her mom.

                         ROBIN

         I'm sorry mom, that was my fault.

                         SUSAN

         Nonsense, sweetie, some people just
         don't work together well. Want to get an
         ice cream?

Robin looks down at the ground as she walks, pouting.

                         ROBIN

          No thanks, save your money; the wolf is
          coming to the door.

INT. GREAT ROOM - NIGHT

Death opens the door, peers in, then enters and ducks
quickly.

Nothing happens.

He looks around the room, in the same state of
disrepair, then cocks his head.

                         DEATH

          Brothers?

No response.

Death walks deeper into the room, hands on his hips,
looking around.

                         DEATH

          Pestilence? Hello. Famine?

          (pause)

          Big dumb angry guy?

Death chuckles to himself. Nothing.

Death heads for the stairs.

INT. HALLWAY OUTSIDE WAR'S ROOM - FOLLOWING

Death opens the door slowly and looks in. The room is
still a mess. Death notices war's weapon rack - weapons
are MISSING.

                         DEATH

          Hmm, there's no practice today.

He goes down the hall to the next door and starts to
knock when something catches his attention further down
the hall. He turns to look and sees

SPLINTERS of wood at the turn in the hall. He cocks his
head and muses, then a thought grabs his mind.

He throws open the door to Famine's room. The room is
neat, the bed made, flower arrangement, a huge mint on
the pillow.

Death rushes down the hall and turns the corner to his room. The floor is littered with huge chunks of door and twisted hinges.

                         DEATH

        Brothers, what are you... ?

He rushes into his room - it is in SHAMBLES. Papers and books are thrown everywhere. He looks to his bookshelf; there is a noticeable GAP where a huge tome is missing.

                         DEATH

        Earth. What have they done? Fenrir?

A WHIMPER wafts up from behind Death's bed. Death jumps on the bed and looks behind it.

Fenrir lies on the floor, all skin and BONES, GNATS swarming around his ears, BRUISED and swollen in places.

                         DEATH

        Oh dear - they've learned to work
        together. This is not good.

Death whirls around the desk like a dervish, tosses papers, knocks things over; Searches frantically.

He finally picks up an ornate wooden BOX, open and empty.

                         DEATH

        They have the key. And The Book. That
        means...

EXT. OTHERWORLDY PLAINS - NIGHT

The sky roils with weird colors and clouds. The brothers sit atop their horses, giddy. They dance from side to side, play with their armor straps, chanting in an off-key sing-song

                        BROTHERS

        We're going to ride to the Apocalypse.
        We're going to ride to the Apocalypse.
        Lala la lala la, lala la lala la!

In the air in front of them, a dark swirling mass appears; lightening crackles at its center; wind picks up, blowing dust and leaves.

                    PESTILENCE

          It's working.

The horses start to rear up, stamping at the earth,
sending sparks flying from their hooves. Famine is
having a difficult time controlling his horse.

                      FAMINE

          Guys... I can't... hey guys...

                       WAR

          Get ready... ready... more ready...

The swirling mass opens wider, big enough now to allow
many riders through.

                    PESTILENCE

     NOW!

                       WAR

     Now what?

                    PESTILENCE

          What do you think? NOW!

Pestilence charges his horse through, War follows.

Famine's horse bucks and kicks. Famine is thrown from
the saddle, his foot caught in the stirrup, he is
dragged through screaming.

EXT. STREET - DAY

Insert - hand written sign: THE END IS NEAR

Crazy Street Preacher trudges down the sidewalk
carrying his sign, people largely ignore him as he
goes by.

                     PREACHER

          Repent! The hour of your reckoning is at
          hand. Armageddon is upon us.

A young upwardly bound PROFESSIONAL passes, snooty.

                      YUPPIE

          Not today, pops, I got a huge meeting.

                     PREACHER

          The end of the world waits for no man.

A WOMAN pushes past him

                            WOMAN

          I guess I'm safe then, huh sweetie?

Preacher gets jostled, pushed and bumped until he is
shoved into a side alley. He trudges into the alley,
dragging his sign behind him.

                          PREACHER

          Screw this, I need a cappuccino.

EXT. DESERT BATTLEFIELD - DAY

A raging TANK and small arms BATTLE carries on in the
desert valley. War stands high above on a sandy hill,
The Book from Death's room open in his hands.

He shakes his head in confusion, then turns toward
Pestilence and Famine, who sit on their horses behind
him.

He points down the hill at the battle.

                            WAR

          That wasn't me.

                        PESTILENCE

          Are you sure?

                            WAR

          I got here and they were like that.
          They're shooting each other and killing
          each other and I have no idea why.

                          FAMINE

          How long have you been here?

                            WAR

          Five minutes. The Book says this is
          where the Battle is supposed to start,
          and it's already going. Lousy liar book
          - smash it!

War tries to rip The Book into pieces, but cannot.

A loud shell BURST hits nearby. Everyone except War
FLINCHES and ducks the flying debris.

                            WAR

          I want one of those big explody things,
          though.

                    PESTILENCE

      Wow. They must have been going at it for
      a while.

                     FAMINE

      Bummer. Looks like they don't need your
      help. Long trip fer nuttin'.

Famine cracks a pecan with his teeth, then starts to
pick nut fragments out with his fingers. Pestilence and
War GLARE at Famine. Famine feels their gazes and looks
up from his task.

                     FAMINE

      I'm just saying.

War growls and mounts his horse, gallops off.

                    PESTILENCE

      Way to make him feel better.

                     FAMINE

      I'm just saying, is all. They're
      doing fine on their own. Whoa! Look at
      that one.

Pestilence rides after War. Famine tries to get his
mount to follow, but it SNAPS back at him, snorts,
rears up and runs away.

                     FAMINE

      Oh, not you too.

EXT. A WIDE RIVER IN THIRD WORLD COUNTRY - DAY

Pestilence stands at the bank of a FILTHY RIVER, War
and Famine stand next to him. BUGS fly about in noisy
swarms. RATS patrol the bank and forage. TRASH litters
the riverside, heaps of steaming junk.

People in tattered clothing bathe knee-deep in the
murky water.

                    PESTILENCE

      Oh that's just unsanitary. It's so
      beautiful.

                      WAR

      Good job, brother. I especially like the
      steaming donkey carcass there.

                    FAMINE

          (pointing)
     That one?

                     WAR

          (points elsewhere)
     No, that one over there, the one with
     the maggots and Ravens.

                    FAMINE

     That's not a raven that's a crow.

                     WAR

     Pretty damn big for a crow; that's a
     raven.

                    FAMINE

     You wouldn't know a raven if it pecked
     at your eyes and carried a little sign
     that said "I am a raven."

                     WAR

     Joke's on you. I can't even read.

                  PESTILENCE

     It wasn't me, you baboons.

Pestilence turns from the scene and stomps back to his
horse. War and Famine continue their babble as they
follow.

                  FAMINE/WAR

     Baboons!

                     WAR

     That would be cool; baboons eating a
     steaming donkey carcass.

                    FAMINE

     He has such good ideas.

INT. FAST FOOD RESTAURANT - DAY

War, Famine and Pestilence stand at the counter looking
down at the FOOD on people's TRAYS as they turn find a
seat.

They all look confused. Famine has his face all screwed
up, he sticks a FINGER into a burger on a KID'S tray

with a squish. The kid looks up at the three then
hurries away.

                         KID

     Mommy, that guy took my burger.

The burger stays stuck to Famine's finger like a
dripping, meaty donut ring.

                       FAMINE

     What the?

He pulls the burger off, and LICKS his gooey finger.

                       FAMINE

     This isn't even food. What is this
     "burger"? Taste this.

Famine offers his finger to War. War goes to take a LICK;
Pestilence puts up his hands and turns away

                     PESTILENCE

     Oh eew eew eeeeew.

War stops, thinks, then sniffs the finger instead.

                        WAR

     Hmm. Let me see that.

War takes the burger, bites it, SLOSHES the food around
in his mouth like a wine taster, then SPITS it away
onto Pestilences' back. Pestilence goes rigid.

                     PESTILENCE

     Oh no you didn't

He turns slowly as

War mashes his fist down on the burger, it squirts out
in Pestilences' face.

                     PESTILENCE

     Thank you, the suspense was killing me.

Famine starts to grab food off peoples' trays; takes
bites and spits. The people get angry and offended. A
large, husky, GUY with "manager" on his nametag comes
from behind the counter.

                       MANAGER

     What seems to be the problem here?

The three brothers, each with messy food on their faces and clothes stare back at the manager.

                          PESTILENCE

        Umm... do you have a bathroom?

EXT. CITY STREET - DAY

Famine runs from the restaurant with his arms covering his head. Pestilence backs out, hold his hands up to ward off an attack.

War, his arm TWISTED behind his back by the Manager, is unceremoniously escorted to the street, and tossed face down on the pavement.

                          MANAGER

        You try to come in here again, and I'm
        calling the cops.

The Manager goes back into the building. Pestilence and Famine stare around them at the city.

A city bus flies by them, bumping over War's body. They look down, then back up at each other. They start laughing.

EXT. CITY STREET - DAY

The brothers walk, dejectedly looking around them. War has faded tire marks on his face.

War sees PUNKS beating someone up in an alley. One looks over at him.

                          PUNK

        What are you looking at?

Pestilence sees a CAT chasing two RATS into a filthy gutter drain.

Famine sees a small BODEGA with streetside fruit trays almost empty; old-looking produce is all that's left.

                          WAR

        We're powerless here. Powerless.

                          FAMINE

        Did someone else beat us to it?
        Pestilence?

Pestilence stares at a trash heap teaming with flies.

                    PESTILENCE

          I'd have used bigger flies.

A gigantic ROACH slips from under the trash heap and
scurries into a crack in a building.

                    PESTILENCE

          Oh, rub it in my face why don't you?

EXT. SIDEWALK CAFE - DAY

Susan and Robin sit at a small table, empty ice cream
sundae cups in front of them. Susan wipes Robin's face
with a wet-nap.

                    SUSAN

          There you go sweetie, all gone.

Robin makes a face.

                    ROBIN

          I'm not a baby anymore, mom.

                    SUSAN

          I know, I'm sorry. You were just all
          sticky.

A waiter approaches the table, Susan motions to her.

                    SUSAN

          Just the check thanks.

The waiter NODS and goes into the cafe. Susan sees a
HELP WANTED sign in the window. Robin sees this.

                    ROBIN

          Tom is gonna be watching me for a few
          days, huh?

                    SUSAN

          Just until I find another job and get
          settled. You'll be in school most of the
          time anyway.

                    ROBIN

          I can get a job.

Susan smiles, and pats the hair down on Robin's head.

                    SUSAN

          You don't need to, honey. Everything's
          fine. Thank you, though. Couple days

>   until the weekend, I can find another one
>   easy; I've waited tables before.

Susan looks at her daughter, smiles faintly.

>   SUSAN
>   You just keep up with school. When
>   you're educated and you know what you're
>   doing, you'd have to be a complete
>   idiot not to be able to get a job in
>   your chosen field.

EXT. CITY STREET - DAY

War, Famine and Pestilence walk down the street. War
tries to copy the twisty arm move from the manager on
Famine, who is in pain.

Pestilence flips through the book shaking his head.

>   FAMINE
>   Ouch! What are you doing?

>   WAR
>   Hold still, I think I have it. He bent
>   it like this, right?

There is a sickening CRUNCH as War completely
dislocates Famine's shoulder.

Pestilence doesn't look up from the book.

>   PESTILENCE
>   Could you two please keep it down?

War plays with Famine's dangling limb like a cat plays
with a ball hanging on a piece of string.

>   WAR
>   Now that's cool.

>   FAMINE
>   Put it back... put it back.

>   WAR
>   "Put it back...?" I break, not unbreak.

War stops at a window in front of a video store. A
scene from DIE HARD plays on a screen. Bruce Willis
jams his arm against a wall to fix his shoulder.

War looks over at Famine. Grabs Famine by the scruff of
the neck - SLAMS him into a brick wall.

WAR

>   Feel better?

Famine slides slowly down the wall to the floor; he
whimpers pathetically as he goes down.

A guy with a baseball bat comes out of the store,
brandishing the bat, glaring at War. War snarls and
looks at the guy, then at his name tag:

insert: name tag "Jeff, Manager"

EXT. CITY STREET - DAY

The brothers sit on a bench. War has a swollen eye and
is playing with a new gap in his teeth with his tongue.
Pestilence studies The Book.

Famine stares at a hot dog CART with pretzels
displayed, shaking his head.

>   FAMINE

>   It's like this place is immune to us.

>   WAR

>   What says the Ready Thing?

>   PESTILENCE

>   I'm not sure. Maybe our powers only work
>   when we get The Call. We shouldn't even
>   be here, technically. According to this
>   we have another...

A WOMAN shoves past them, jostling Pestilence.

>   PESTILENCE

>   And these are some of the rudest people
>   I have ever met - and I've never even
>   met anyone before.

The Crazy Preacher passes, looks them over briefly.

>   PREACHER

>   Freaks.

>   PESTILENCE

>   Kiss my ass.

Other pedestrians pass by and give the brothers the
once-over.

>   MAN

>   Take a bath, dude.

War lifts his arm and SMELLS his underarm in loud, long
sniffs.

                          WOMAN
          That's attractive.

Famine finally gets up and lunges at the hot dog vendor,
grabs a handful of WIENERS from the hot water and
brandishes them in the vendor's face.

                          FAMINE
          Do you have ANY idea what is in these?
          Do you?

A MAN walks past Famine, leering at his garb. He
touches the STRAPS on Famine's armor, tugs a little as
he walks past.

                          MAN
          Give to me your leather... take from me
          my lace.

Famine gets distracted, smiles at the man.

                          FAMINE
          Thank you, I made this myself. The trim
          is actual fur from...

The hotdog vendor grabs Famine's nose with a pair of
hot TONGS from the grill, and TWISTS. The nose sizzles.

                          PESTILENCE
          Stop screwing around, Famine... there
          are more germs on that cart than even I
          can shake a stick at.

War lunges out into the street shaking his fists at the
sky...

                          WAR
          He is cheating us even here. Our brother
          keeps us from our glory.

...Just as a city BUS pulls up to the curb, Honks
loudly.

War snarls and whips out his axe, buries it in the
radiator of the bus, stopping the vehicle dead.

                          PESTILENCE
          Terrific; now we'll be at war with these
          great beasts.

The DRIVER exits the bus and surveys the damage.

                              DRIVER

          What the hell is your problem, man?

The driver tugs at War's axe, unable to remove it.

INT. CITY BUS - SAME TIME

Robin and Susan sit near the front, watching the scene
through the window..

                              ROBIN

              Mom look.

                              DRIVER

              I asked you a question, Grizzly Adams.

                              FAMINE

              We better get going.

                              DRIVER

              Bullshit, you guys are staying right
              here until the cops show up.

                              SUSAN

              They're not from around here.

                              ROBIN

              They look scared. Can we help them?

                              SUSAN

              I don't know honey, he did kinda break
              the bus.

EXT. CITY STREET - SAME TIME

                            PESTILENCE

              Excuse us sir, we're strangers here, and
              my brother didn't know...

                              DRIVER

              Are you kidding me? He didn't know he
              wasn't supposed to smash city property
              with an axe? You guys are damn sure gon-
              na get acquainted with our jail system.

Famine's lower lip starts to quiver, he looks near
tears. Pestilence rolls his eyes and sighs.

                              WAR

          You don't frighten us, mortal. Do you
          have any idea who we are? Do you? We're
          the Four Horsemen of the Apocalypse.

The driver looks them over. Famine has a handful of
dripping wieners, War has a mashed face with tire
tracks on it. Pestilence tries to smile friendly-like.

                            DRIVER

          Well it's obvious you ain't mathemati-
          cians, 'cause they's only three of you.

The driver spots a police CRUISER heading toward them
in the opposite lane. He waves his arms

                            DRIVER

          The Cops; Hey! Over here, police!

                            FAMINE

          What do we do now?

                              WAR

          This is my game. Follow my lead.

War starts toward the driver - TWO MORE squad cars
converge on the scene. War hesitates, then

YOINKS his axe from the bus and takes off at a sprint
past the driver. Pestilence and Famine stare after him.

                          PESTILENCE

          Discretion being the better part of
          valor this day.

                            FAMINE

          What?

                          PESTILENCE

          It means...

He TAKES OFF after War. Famine sees the police lights
flashing as the cruiser pulls in toward them, then he,
too takes off running.

INT. CITY BUS - SAME TIME

                            ROBIN

          Mom, did you hear him?

                    SUSAN

    Who?

                    ROBIN

    They're The Horsemen, three of them,
    anyway. They're here to send us to Hell.

                    SUSAN

    Oh Honey, they're strangers from another
    country...

                    ROBIN

    Cool!

Robin jumps out of her seat and EXITS the bus, Susan
chases her.

                    SUSAN

    Robin!

EXT. GRASSY, WOODED PARK - DAY

The three brothers stand panting, they look around the
empty park.

                    WAR

    Where are the horses?

                    PESTILENCE

    Famine was supposed to tie them up right
    over there. Famine?

Famine just stares blankly at the park. He grimaces.

                    WAR

    You did tie them up?

                    PESTILENCE

    You dropped the reins and ran, didn't
    you?

                    WAR

    Rrrargh!

                    FAMINE

    They barked at me; what was I supposed
    to do?

War jumps at Famine and gets him in a HEADLOCK. Famine
grabs at Pestilence as War pummels.

                         WAR

          You freakish little troll, I'll tear
          your ears off and eat them.

                      PESTILENCE

          While I don't share War's taste for
          delicacies, I would like to see you in
          pain. What are we supposed to do now?

Pestilence starts to slap Famine and kick his butt.

                        FAMINE

          They were gonna bite me! The big one has
          the Crazy Eye.

Famine starts to blubber loudly. Pestilence SWATS at
his head with a handkerchief. Famine tries to block the
assault.

Robin and Susan catch up with the brothers.

                        ROBIN

          Hey, are you guys for real?

The three brothers stop their frantic actions and stare
at Robin and Susan.

                      PESTILENCE

          Excuse me?

                        ROBIN

          Has it started already? Which one of you
          is Famine? Where are your steeds?

                        SUSAN

          Robin, stop it.

War grabs Famine by an EAR and drags him forward.

                         WAR

          Here he is. Why don't you ask him where
          the horses are?

                        SUSAN

          Are you gentlemen lost?

                      PESTILENCE

          We are new to this... place. Not really
          lost, per se; just kind of touring. We
          plan to come back some day and...

                    WAR

          Oh shut up, you ear-hurting windbag. We
          got bored waiting for The Book to call
          us, so we...

Pestilence's eyes get wide, he searches his ROBES and
the ground around them.

                  PESTILENCE

          The Book!

Recognition seeps into Famine and war's faces. They
look around the ground, pat themselves down.

                    WAR

          Bad thing.

                  FAMINE

          Nice move, Pestilence.

                  PESTILENCE

          Like you setting the horses free?

                  FAMINE

          I had three to watch; you had one little
          book.

                  PESTILENCE

          You have one little brain.

Pestilence SLAPS Famine.

                    WAR

          Don't hit him; YOU lost it.

War HITS Pestilence.

                  PESTILENCE

          I'll slap him if I want.

He slaps Famine TWICE. The second much harder and
louder than the first. Famine takes a swing at
Pestilence, who ducks, letting Famine crack War in
the jaw.

                  FAMINE

          Sorry... sorry

War slow burns, Famine cringes; Pestilence laughs.

                         PESTILENCE

          Sucks to be you, brother.

War lunges at the two, and the three brawl like rabid
monkeys. Susan and Robin look on helplessly.

From out of nowhere, the three horses charge past like
thunder. Famine's horse grabs him in it's teeth and
tosses him a few yards away.

The horses charge across the park and into the woods.
The brothers watch for a second, then take off running
after them.

                         PESTILENCE

          Thank you for your help.

                           ROBIN

          Wait - I have questions.

EXT. STREET - DAY

Susan and Robin walk along the sidewalk.

                           SUSAN

          They obviously need help, but you can't
          help people that don't allow it.

                           ROBIN

          We should find them.

                           SUSAN

          They're grown men, Honey; they can take
          care of themselves.

                           ROBIN

          Can we get something to eat?

                           SUSAN

          We just ate.

                           ROBIN

          Then why am I so hungry?

EXT. FOREST PARK - DAY

Famine shuffles around aimlessly, constantly turning
around to see what's behind him. He hears a noise and
spins again - nothing

                           FAMINE

          Here I am. All alone. Any big mean horse

> could easily get me here, alone like
> I am.

He walks toward a POND, across from which there is some kind of EVENT set up, white tents, and a stage.

                    FAMINE

> I wish I knew where my brothers were, so
> I didn't feel so alone and by myself.
> Ooh, a party.

Famine watches as WOMEN laugh and throw beach balls at each other by the tents. Flashes TWINKLE in the dimming light.

Famine stops, suddenly aware of the other heavy BREATHING besides his own. He turns to face

Crazy Eye. The horse pulls its lips back in a grotesque snarl.

                    FAMINE

> Nice Horsey.

The other two horses stand further behind Crazy Eye, pawing at the ground, snorting. Two FIGURES drop onto their backs from the trees - War and Pestilence.

                    WAR

> HAH!

Crazy Eye turns to see this, then back to Famine, he SQUINTS at the sweaty man.

                    FAMINE

> They... they made me do it.

Crazy Eye rears up, whinnying and snorting steam. He snaps at Famine.

                    FAMINE

> Not in the face!

EXT. PARK - DAY

Crazy Eye gallops across the pond, tossing Famine around like a dog with a chew toy in its mouth. Crazy Eye crashes through the tent at the far side and throws Famine aside, into a large wedding cake, then disappears into the woods.

A few seconds later War and Pestilence, on horseback, charge through the setup. Pestilence gets BUCKED from his horse, FLIES into a large cage holding dozens of white pigeons. The pigeons SCATTER.

War tries to control his steed, while laughing at the other two brothers, and when he looks forward again, it is just in time for a camera boom CRANE to peel him off the back of his horse with a loud CLANG.

The three brothers sit up and look around them, a dozen skinny MODELS in various revealing outfits watch in shock. Camera crew stares at the brothers.

                              FAMINE

          Look how emaciated they are. Did I do
          that? Are my powers back?

Pigeon droppings fall onto them in great number.

                            PESTILENCE

          That would be me, I guess.

                              WAR

          But no fighting. Where is the fighting

A burly DIRECTOR with an open shirt and beret walks up to War and BELTS him in the face.

                            DIRECTOR

          You focking ruined my shoot, osshole.

                         PESTILENCE/FAMINE

          There you go.

EXT. SCHOOL PARKING LOT - DAY

Susan messes with Robin's hair, then straitens her jacket.

                              SUSAN

          Have a great day, sweetie. See you
          later.

                              ROBIN

          Good luck with the interview, mom. I
          hope you get it.

                              SUSAN

          How hard can it be?

Robin turns to trot into the school, Susan turns and leaves.

A small group of KIDS moves in after Robin. One BOY has
the other kids looking over his shoulder. He holds THE
BOOK.

                         BOOK KID
          I found it at the bus stop, look at
          this, it has a map of the Earth...

EXT. SIDEWALK CAFE - DAY

Susan follows a tough-looking woman, MAUREEN, around as
she clears tables into a bussing cart.

                         MAUREEN
          Like I said, it's a lot of walking, you
          have a problem with that?

                         SUSAN
     No, no ma'am.

                         MAUREEN
     Good lord, call me Maureen.

In the back ground, the three Brothers, haggard and
covered with twigs, leaves, dirt and moldy cake wander
into the street.

They see Susan and cross the busy street in fits and
starts as cars honk and brake to avoid hitting them.

                         SUSAN
          Maureen. I can start whenever you need
          me to, and I can work any shift.

The brothers stop at the short fence surrounding the
cafe patio. They stare at Susan. Famine smiles and
waves.

Susan doesn't notice them.

                         MAUREEN
          Okay, look; I need someone like yester-
          day, so if you can start...

Maureen sees the three brothers, frowns; Susan's back
is to them.

                         MAUREEN
     No hand outs, bozos, take a hike.

                         PESTILENCE
     We just want to...

                    MAUREEN

     I said WALK. (to Susan) Anyway, if you
     can work a few hours tonight, you're
     hired.

War snarls and tries to walk forward, the FENCE stops
him. He SHAKES it, can't budge it. He tries to CHEW
on it.

Maureen pushes her cart aside and storms over. Susan
turns and sees them.

                    SUSAN

     You?!

                    PESTILENCE

     We saw you over there, and thought we
     might...

                    MAUREEN

     I told you bums to take a hike.

War stands and froths at the mouth in Maureen's face.

                    WAR

     I talk at her now, angry dish lady.

                    MAUREEN

     Have it your way, putz.

Maureen MACES War square in the eyes, he falls backward
grabbing at his face and swearing incoherently. He
falls into bushes and thrashes around some more.

                    MAUREEN

     You guys want some of this too?

                    PESTILENCE

     Thanks, no. But could you spray him
     again please?

                    SUSAN

     Maureen, wait, they aren't bums. They're
     lost.

                    MAUREEN

     These guys friends of yours?

Susan looks at Famine and Pestilence, who plead with
their eyes.

                    SUSAN

     Kind of.

                    MAUREEN

     You get them out of here, you still have
     a job. See you at five PM sharp.

Maureen grabs her bus cart and gets back to work.

EXT. FOUNTAIN PLAZA - DAY

Susan stands in front of the brothers, who sit on the
bench circling an ornate fountain. Pestilence has white
pigeons perched on him.

                    SUSAN

     You what?

                    PESTILENCE

     Apparently we will "never work in this
     Focking town again," according to Andre.

                    SUSAN

     Andre is...?

                    FAMINE

     The Director.

                    SUSAN

     And you got attacked by...

The three brothers look at each other, nod in agreement

                    PESTILENCE

     Horses.

                    WAR

     Pit bulls.

                    FAMINE

     Rugby players.

                    PESTILENCE

     You're the only person that has been
     nice to us. Will you help us?

Susan looks at the three dejected horsemen in front of
her. SQUIRRELS hop up on Pestilence's leg, FLIES circle
his head.

Famine's stomach GROWLS loudly.

A SQUIRREL hops onto War's leg. He grabs it and THROWS
it into a tree.

                         SUSAN

          Okay. But first, you've got to stop being
          so aggressive.

She points at War. He snarls.

                         SUSAN

          People don't like that. And what is the
          deal with you?

She looks at pigeon boy, who now has a large crow
perched on his head.

                       PESTILENCE

          Animals like me?

                          WAR

          See? THAT'S a raven.

                        FAMINE

          It's a crow.

She looks at Famine.

                         SUSAN

          You seem to be the only normal one.

Susan sighs and sits down next to Famine. Susan puffs.
She looks around the plaza.

                         SUSAN

          Well, we can't have you roaming the
          streets, that's for sure. You'll only
          get in to more trouble. You have money?

The three just look at her, blankly.

                         SUSAN

          Okay, no hotel. No friends in town?
          'Course not. How about the YMCA?

                       PESTILENCE

          That sounds like a nice place.

War and Famine turn and glare at him. Pestilence
shrugs; some pigeons leave.

                    ROBIN

          I guess there's only one place for you
          now.

INT. SUSAN'S APARTMENT - NIGHT

Susan enters and turns on the lights, Robin comes
in with Famine who looks around wide eyed. War and
Pestilence bring up the rear.

                    FAMINE

          Wow. Nice lair. Very cozy.

                    SUSAN

          It's not much, but there's room to sleep
          on the floor and the one couch.

                    WAR

          I call couch!

He shoves everyone aside a leaps on the couch,
whereupon the legs give way and the furniture crunches
to the floor.

                    FAMINE

          Sorry; he's a bit...

                    PESTILENCE

          ...loud and stupid.

                    ROBIN

          It's an old couch.

Famine rummages in the fridge.

                    FAMINE

          There's no food in here, either. And I
          just got here.

                    ROBIN

          We haven't gone shopping yet. Later we
          can go grab a burger.

                FAMINE/WAR/PESTILENCE

          No!

                    SUSAN

          Okay... maybe not a burger.

> PESTILENCE
>
> Do you have someplace I can freshen up a
> bit?

> WAR
>
> Yeah, and get a clean girdle for my
> sister as well.

> PESTILENCE
>
> Just because you wallow in your own
> stench, doesn't mean the rest of us
> have to.

War gets to his feet and strides toward Pestilence.

> WAR
>
> What did you just call me?

Pestilence looks confused. He gestures about.

> PESTILENCE
>
> A "wallow in your own stench?" What part
> of that sounded like a proper noun?

> ROBIN
>
> I know you guys must be tired and stuff.
> Uh, why don't you take turns in the
> bathroom, get cleaned up, and we'll go
> get something to eat. Okay?

War snarls at Pestilence, makes a grab for him.

Pestilence GESTURES. Nothing happens. He gestures
again.

Nothing.

War's hand grabs Pestilence's throat. War grins wide.
Pestilence gestures spasmodically.

> WAR
>
> What's the matter, Bugs? No swarm?

War pulls out a huge, ugly cutting implement and
brandishes it at Pestilence.

Famine covers his crotch and runs out of the room.

> FAMINE
>
> NO! Not the slicey thing!

                              SUSAN

          Whoa whoa whoa. Stop right there. I told
          you I can't have that in my house.

War turns his head to glare at Susan. Susan gulps. War
lets go of Pestilence and turns toward Susan.

                              WAR

          And what are you going to do about it?

Susan swallows hard. War moves his face closer and
snarls.

Susan MACES him square in the eyes.

War flails around and backs away clawing at his face.

                              WAR

          Ow ow, the burny hot! Burny hot!

He stops for a second, stares madly at Susan

                              WAR

          Where do you guys get that stuff?

Robin tugs at Pestilence's sleeve. He looks down at
her, she hands a large, heavy iron FRYING PAN to him.

Pestilence SLAMS the pan into War's FACE. The big angry
guy hits the floor.

Pestilence looks down at Robin.

                           PESTILENCE

          I like you.

INT. SUSAN'S APARTMENT - NIGHT

Robin sits at the table, the brothers stand, or sit on
the counter space around her.

                             ROBIN

          Okay, Mom is gonna be back with Tom real
          soon, so let's get your story strait.
          You are brothers with the Circus from...
          from...

She glances around the room, spots a magnet on the
fridge

Insert - magnet: Greetings from the Garden Sate!

                             ROBIN

          Jersey. You look like a Rafael...

She points at Pestilence; then at Famine.

>   ROBIN
>
> Your name is...

She sees as stack of bills on the table

>   ROBIN
>
> Bill. And you're Poindexter.

She points at War. He makes a face.

>   WAR
>
> Poindexter?

>   ROBIN
>
> It means, uh... mighty slayer of bears.

War nods, shakes out his shoulders.

>   WAR
>
> Poindexter. (tougher) POINDEXTER. Me
> good name.

>   ROBIN
>
> Can you guys remember that? It'll make
> things easier.

The brothers nod in agreement. The door opens and Susan
enters with Tom. Tom yawns, he's groggy.

>   SUSAN
>
> Okay, Tom can keep on eye on you before
> he leaves for work. I should be back by
> then and...

Susan looks at her watch.

>   SUSAN
>
> Oh no! I have to be at my new job in
> fifteen minutes.

She looks around the room at Robin and then at the
brothers. She looks at her watch.

>   SUSAN
>
> Robin...

>   ROBIN
>
> Pizza?

                    SUSAN

        Pizza. Do you mind? I didn't even ask,
        do you gentlemen like pizza?

The brothers look to Robin, she nods.

                  PESTILENCE

        We adore Pizza.

Susan runs to her room starts to pull clothes out of
the closet, she raises her VOICE so Robin can hear in
the other room.

                    SUSAN

        Tom, just order a few pizzas, Robin can
        write a check, I may be able to beat it
        to the bank on Friday.

Susan comes out of her room with a nicer blouse on. She
fixes her hair in a mirror.

                    SUSAN

        Will you be okay with... with... oh my
        gosh, I don't even know your names yet.

She turns ad looks at the brothers, who stare blankly
at her.

                    ROBIN

        Rafael, Bill and Poindexter.

She pints them out, they smile.

                   FAMINE

        We're with the circus.

                  PESTILENCE

        From Jersey.

                     WAR

        I sail with bears.

Susan's turn to stare blankly.

                    SUSAN

        I have to go. Lock the door. Tom, Thank
        you so much, sure you're okay?

                     TOM

        Sure, sure.

She gives Robin a kiss, grabs her purse and heads out the door. The brothers look to Robin. Robin looks to Tom.

                    ROBIN

     You're working nights again?

                    TOM

     Yeah. No big deal. You get a couple
     hours sleep and you can go all night.

INT. SUSAN'S BEDROOM - NIGHT

Tom snores loudly on the bed, face down. Robin and Famine peek in through the door before closing it.

                    FAMINE

     Now what?

Robin smiles.

INT. SUSAN'S APARTMENT - NIGHT

There are numerous pizza BOXES with varying amounts of pizza left in them littering the kitchen and living room. A dozen three-liter bottles of soda, all different flavors, scattered as well.

The radio plays loud pop music. Famine sits on the sofa using the remote to surf channels. He has two empty boxes next to him, and a big messy slice of loaded pizza in his hand.

                    FAMINE

     This stuff is incredible. It's got like
     everything in it. Calcium, vitamin C,
     dough.

Pestilence samples another slice of pizza from a box. He sees a ROACH on the wall. He smiles. TWO MORE scurry up to the first.

Robin sits by the open window, a basket of water BALLOONS by her on the table. She watches something below intently, then rockets a balloon out the window.

A CAT me-rows, hisses and noisily runs down the alley. Robin chuckles and throws another. It bangs on a trash can.

                    WAR

     Nice shot. Have you defeated the beasts
     yet?

                   ROBIN

     No. I've never even hit any.

War looks at the basket of balloons and frowns.

                    WAR

     These weapons are no good. I will fix
     them.

INT. SUSAN'S APARTMENT - NIGHT

Famine is intently watching Iron Chef on TV.

Pestilence plays with about a dozen roaches on the
table. They jump over a fork he holds out, build a
pyramid, dance for him.

War sets the basket full of balloons down next to Robin
with a thud.

                    WAR

     Try these.

                   ROBIN

     What did you do?

                    WAR

     Watch.

He takes one of the balloons in his hand raised over
his head, looks out the window.

He watches... watches... and throws.

From the street there is a loud crash and the sound of
a car skidding and braking.

                    WAR

     Much better. Famine come over hear and
     try this.

There is no response. Famine sits on the couch watching
TV - he is enthralled. A water balloon hits his head
with a satisfying BONK, then ricochets into a framed
picture on the wall, smashing it.

                   ROBIN

     They're frozen.

                              WAR

          What are you supposed to do, just fill
          them with water? "Oooh, watch out, I'm
          going to soak you."

A VOICE screams up from the street.

                            VOICE

          Hey. Hey, you!

War looks back down.

                              WAR

          Me?

                            VOICE

          Yeah. You the crazy bastard who threw
          that...

War whips out another balloon and rockets it out the
window. A loud THUNK cuts the man's tirade very short.

War laughs like a crazy man. Robin turns to Pestilence.

                            ROBIN

          Rafael, he can't do that, someone could
          get...

She sees the roaches performing all manner of tricks,
one dives off a three liter bottle into a cup of soda.

                            ROBIN

          Aaaah! Roaches!

She grabs a green can of spray from under the sink and
heads toward the table.

                            ROBIN

          I'll kill those suckers.

                          PESTILENCE

          No!

He GRABS her hand and they struggle. He tries to keep
her from spraying the roaches.

Famine gets up - a little woozy; he has a oozing WOUND
on his head.

                            FAMINE

          War, I'm telling, that hurt.

War shoots another frozen balloon out the window, and a painful shout is heard in retort.

                    WAR

          I'll give you something to cry about.

War grabs a large balloon and charges Famine, pinning him to the couch and starts WAILING on him.

Robin and Pestilence yank back and forth on the spray can, Robin gets it free and aims at the bugs, who cower against a pizza box.

Pestilence grabs the can away and sticks the business end in his mouth.

                  PESTILENCE

          Ha. Mmmph smee ooh goo it ow.

Robin grabs the can.

Famine whacks at War with a pizza box.

The bedroom door opens. Tom stands there with a raised eyebrow.

INT. SUSAN'S APARTMENT - NIGHT

Robin, Tom and the brothers sit in the living room. The room is straightened up, bags of trash by the door.

Not much talking, just kind of staring at each other. War glares menacingly at Tom the whole time. Tom is kind of uneasy, hard to keep his eyes open. Finally

                    TOM

          So, Robin says you guys are with the
          circus?

                  FAMINE

          Yes. From Jersey.

More silence.

                    TOM

          And what do you do with this circus?

                  FAMINE

          I am... food... doing.

                    TOM

          You're a cook? Like the circus chef?

Famine stares blankly, blinks.

> TOM
>
> You prepare the food for everyone, plan
> the meals, that kind of thing?

> FAMINE
>
> Right. That thing.

> TOM
>
> Rafael?

> PESTILENCE
>
> Me? I uh, I do the...

> ROBIN
>
> He takes care of the... pests, sanita-
> tion you get the idea.

> TOM
>
> Oh. Well, nothing wrong with that.
> Everybody has their place, right?

A SNARL starts to creep across War's lips. Tom glances
at Robin.

The door opens and Susan enters.

Tom gets up.

> SUSAN
>
> Hi Tom. Thank you so much for watching
> Robin while I was out. Everything okay?

War starts to show teeth.

> TOM
>
> Yeah, great. Well, I need to get going,
> Susan. I have to research this case...

> PESTILENCE
>
> I told you: monkey virus, meningitis,
> ringworm.

> TOM
>
> Right. I guess I'll see you around?

> SUSAN
>
> Sure, sorry, I'm not great company right
> now, I've got a lot going on.

                    TOM

     No big deal; we all do. Hope you guys
     get your luggage soon. See you later
     Robin.

He leaves. Susan smiles at Robin.

                   ROBIN

     How did it go?

                   SUSAN

     She wants to keep me on; and I may be
     able to get the early shift! Everything
     smells like roses.

INT. SUSAN'S APARTMENT - DAY

Famine waits at the bathroom door, Robin knocks at the
door.

                   ROBIN

     Pest... Rafael, you need to be courte-
     ous, there's only one bathroom and five
     of us here.

There is a moment of silence, then a flush; then the
door opens, Pestilence exits with a sheepish grin. A
second later Famine and Robin pinch their NOSES.

                 PESTILENCE

     Sorry - occupational hazard. Can't
     really do anything about it... I think
     it was the pizza. It's not that bad...
     is it?

War screams from the living room

                    WAR

     Aaah... burny!

                 PESTILENCE

     Oh, like yours doesn't stink?

Robin gets a can of spray from under the kitchen sink
and holds it out in front of her, spraying as she
enters the bathroom.

                   SUSAN

     Okay, look, if you guys are going to be
     here for awhile, we'll need to have some
     order to make things run smoothly.

She looks at the Brothers closely. Chews her lip.

                         SUSAN

        Honey, when does Goodwill open?

INT. GOODWILL STORE - DAY

Susan and the brothers enter the store - typical, lots
of clothes racks, a junk section at the back.

                         SUSAN

            Robin and I will help you pick out some
            clothes. Just take a look around, see
            what grabs you.

Series of shots:

A) changing room door opens, Famine exits wearing high
water cords and a button-down short sleeve shirt. Robin
shakes her head no.

B) Changing room door opens and Pestilence exits
wearing a powder blue tux. Susan stifles a laugh.
Pestilence looks around to see if anyone is looking.

C) Changing room door rattles, rattles harder; is
torn off its hinges. War exits wearing torn jeans, Doc
Martens and a Molly Hatchet T-shirt with a Frazetta
picture. Susan and Robin shrug a "sure - it works."

D) All three brothers exit at the same time. Famine
wears hippy duds from the sixties and a pair of rose
colored John Lennon glasses. Pestilence wears an ill-
fitting suit. War wears torn jeans and a Gwar T-shirt.
Susan and Robin just stare.

E) Famine wears Bermuda shorts, Hawaiian shirt and flip
flops, and playfully poses with a beach ball. He and
Robin laugh.

F) Pestilence sports a tweed suit with elbow patches;
looks as though he's ready for a day at the races in
England. Susan cocks her head and thinks.

G) War gets stuck in the doorframe and has to turn
sideways to exit. Torn jeans, George Michael T-shirt.
Robin starts to nod enthusiastically, Susan stops her.

EXT. SUSAN'S APARTMENT - DAY

Susan and Robin stand next to each other and look at
the brothers who are standing in the living room.

SUSAN

'Great - you'll blend in a bit more now.

They wear their Goodwill fashions. Famine has overalls and a white chef's shirt; Pestilence wears a cheap but nice suit and tie, and War has torn jeans and a Guns N Roses T-shirt with the word "Roses" crossed out in sharpie marker.

SUSAN

What do you think?

ROBIN

You guys look cool.

EXT. SUSAN'S APARTMENT BUILDING - DAY

The five stand on the sidewalk in front of the building. Susan hands Pestilence a key.

SUSAN

Here is the key, don't lose it.

WAR

Better not give it to him then

PESTILENCE

Don't start with me...

WAR

Key-Loser.

PESTILENCE

Dumb-Axe.

Robin shouts angrily, waves her hands.

ROBIN

Whatever - just don't lose it. That's our only spare. For crying out loud

They all look at her.

ROBIN

I'm sorry, I guess I'm just a little tired.

SUSAN

You guys can look around the city; here's some money for food and buses. We'll see you at four, okay?

                    PESTILENCE

     Thank you, Four. Right.

                      SUSAN

     If you get a chance, get some groceries
     for dinner tonight. I'll make it when I
     get home.

She hands the money to Famine, who smiles triumphantly
at War and Pestilence.

The smile is short lived, as War kicks him in the
shin hard, and Pestilence grabs the money when Famine
doubles over.

INT. GROCERY STORE - DAY

Famine walks the produce aisles, picking up items and
dropping them in a cart. He stops next to a produce
person stocking a bin.

                     FAMINE

     I've never seen so much food. And it's
     all edible?

                  PRODUCE PERSON

     Yep. Comes in fresh every day.

Famine mouths the words "fresh every day" in wide eyed
wonder.

                     FAMINE

     Your powers are strong. It would take me
     a week to rot all this.

                  PRODUCE PERSON

     You know how to cook, nothing goes to
     waste.

                     FAMINE

     Can you learn to cook here?

Produce person motions to the Cooking Station nearby.
The CHEF turns on her wireless mike.

                      CHEF

     Okay, we're going to show you how to
     cook with vegetables today. Anyone here
     know what Bok Choy is?

Famine lets out a gasp, he absentmindedly points at the
vegetables the producer person is putting out.

                         FAMINE

          Those are bad already.

The produce person looks at the produce in the bin,
smells them, makes a face and starts to remove them.

                    PRODUCE PERSON

          Huh. Thought these were fresh.

Famine grabs a large eggplant and walks over to the
cooking stage, holding the eggplant out to the chef.

                         CHEF

          Sorry sir, that's a Chinese eggplant.

INT. GROCERY STORE MEAT COUNTER - DAY

War and Pestilence look at all the meats under the
glass. War is bemused, and purses his lips.

                         WAR

          It all looks the same. Looks like dead
          enemies.

                      PESTILENCE

          Maybe we could ask for help.

A BUTCHER comes from out of the freezer - a side of
beef hangs from the ceiling in plain view.

                       BUTCHER

          Hey, what can I get for you guys?

                      PESTILENCE

          We need some... sirloin?

The butcher motions toward the beef hanging.

                       BUTCHER

          Oh, I'm just about to cut some new ones,
          can you come back in about an hour?

                         WAR

          Now. Meat now.

                       BUTCHER

          Sounds like you've already had too much

> red meat, buddy. Look I can't carve a
> whole side in two minutes, just give
> me...

War looks down at all the meat in the locker, then looks up at the hanging beef. He pulls out his two nasty blades and goes behind the counter, staring at the butcher.

                    WAR

> Waiting takes too long.

The butcher backs up. War strides into the meat locker and wails at the side of beef.

In short order, there are piles of expertly cut meats stacked on the counters.

War wipes his blades and puts them back.

                    BUTCHER

> Do you have a union card? Where'd you
> learn to do that?

EXT. SCHOOL PLAYGROUND - DAY

Robin eats her lunch at the end of a picnic table. At the table next to her three boys read The Book.

                    BOY 1

> What is that? Is that supposed to be a
> horse?

                    BOY 2

> What language is this in, I can't read
> any of this.

                    BOY 3

> It's in English, dumbass.

                    BOY 1

> This is the coolest book. I could read
> it all day.

A girl runs up to the boys, excited.

                    GIRL

> You guys see that dead bird Mike Connor
> found?

                    BOY 3

> Dead bird?

The three boys jump up and follow the girl away, leaving the book.

Robin eats, her eyes start to wander. She scans the playground to see if anyone is looking.

She gets up, sets her pack next to The Book, sits down.

INT. GROCERY STORE - DAY

Famine is handing items to the cooking stage chef like a child throwing sticks in a campfire.

                    FAMINE

          Cook these.

                    CHEF

          Shallots, these go great with poultry,
          wild game, and stew meats.

The chef slices up the shallots, and tosses them into a frying pan with hot oil. The pan SIZZLES and steam shoots up.

Famine hands the chef a pineapple.

                    CHEF

          If you hand me some mangoes and a
          papaya, I'll show you how to make a
          tropical chutney.

Famine squeals, claps his hands and goes to find the fruit.

War and Pestilence meander over to Famine. They have piles of meat wrapped in white paper.

                    FAMINE

          Whoa. We don't need all that, she just
          wanted one steak.

                    WAR

          Food for eating.

                    PESTILENCE

          Oh the nice gentleman said if we didn't
          report him, we could have all this for
          free.

Pestilence has locked his eyes on something at the end of the aisle. He walks sonambulently toward it.

                          WAR

          Brother? What is it?

Pestilence is staring in astonishment at a display for
Bug Killer. Large green cans of spray with pictures on
them of the spray wiping out big ugly bugs.

A woman steps up behind Pestilence, waits for him to
move.

                         WOMAN

          Oh this stuff is great. I killed two
          enormous roaches last week with this.
          BAM! Stopped in their tracks.

Pestilence tears up, puts a hand to his trembling mouth
and turns away from the display.

                       PESTILENCE

          Barbaric!

                         WOMAN

          No, it's very humane. They don't suffer,
          just one squirt and...

INT. SUSAN'S APARTMENT - DAY

Emeril Lagasse is on TV, doing his thing. Famine
watches from the kitchen as he works on dinner.

                        EMERIL

          BAM! We'll be back in just a moment, and
          we're gonna turn it up... another notch.

                        FAMINE

          No way he can make a sauce from that.
          He's like... the Anti-Me.

War and Pestilence walk in.

                       PESTILENCE

          Behemoth and I are going to go "look
          for The Book." Want to join us in our
          surely-doomed little venture?

                        FAMINE

          Can't - cooking.

                       PESTILENCE

          Thank heaven. Only one of you to
          baby-sit.

EXT. STREET IN BAD NEIGHBORHOOD - NIGHT

War and Pestilence peer down a dark alley, hesitant to go in.

                         WAR

          Are you sure you saw them run down this
          alley?

                         PESTILENCE

          Yes.

                         WAR

          Are you sure they were ours?

War just looks at his brother.

                         PESTILENCE

          Hmmm, let me see. Red eyes, steel
          hooves, breathing flames. Yeah.
          Pretty sure.

They start to inch into the alley.

EXT. FURTHER DOWN THE ALLEY - FOLLOWING

War and Pestilence stop at a loud noise.

                         WAR

          Hear that?

                         PESTILENCE

          Yes.

                         WAR

          Here's my plan.

                         PESTILENCE

          Oh no...

                         WAR

          Get them!

War charges down into the dark, Pestilence just stays
put.

A few seconds later War comes running back waving his
arms and screaming

                         WAR

          Plan change. Run away now.

The horses thunder behind War, they jump over he and Pestilence and charge out of the alley into the night. Immediately afterwards a roar is heard back down the alley, and a dozen motorcycles scream to a halt by the brothers.

The leader of the gang - CRUSHER, Big, bald, 40's - revs his engine and then all bikes shut down.

> CRUSHER
>
> You guys see a couple of bad-ass looking ponies come by here?

> PESTILENCE
>
> You mean our horses? Yes they...

> CRUSHER
>
> No, I mean our ponies, stick boy. They are outta this world, and I'm gonna get me one.

> PESTILENCE
>
> They're our horses.

Crusher gets off his bike, as do the rest of the gang. Some pull knives, some chains, and other fighting implements.

> LEADER
>
> I says they's mine. And we are going to take them.

Pestilence swaggers forward a step or two. Jerks a thumb toward War.

> PESTILENCE
>
> Over his dead body, you toothless hippo.

INT. SUSAN'S KITCHEN - NIGHT

Famine helps Susan gather food to take to the table. Robin and Pestilence set the table. War lays on the couch with an ice bag on his FACE, and two on his CROTCH.

Pestilence spots a big fat roach in the corner of the room, eyeing the table. He looks over at Susan, then back to the roach; shakes his head "no."

The roach eyes Susan, then back to Pestilence. Pestilence mouths the word "LATER," the roach nods, winks, and scurries away.

Susan and Famine enter the room with plates of food, setting them down on the table.

                         SUSAN

     Dinner is ready, hope you all like
     spaghetti.

                         FAMINE

     I caramelized the onions and peppers in
     a white wine sauce, and stirred in a
     browned garlic paste before adding the
     meat. It really brings out the earthy
     taste of the tomato sauce, which I made
     from scratch, by the way.

Everyone stares at Famine, he smiles.

War gets up, throws the ice bags down; grabs a handful of saucy spaghetti and raises it to his face. Robin coughs a little, hands him his fork. War drops the food and uses the fork.

                         FAMINE

     Let's eat before it goes bad.

                         ROBIN

     I'm so hungry, I could eat a horse.

                         PESTILENCE

     Just don't ask Poindexter to catch it
     for you.

                         WAR

     I know you are, but what am I?

                         PESTILENCE

     Very bad at witty retorts? Too large for
     most normal doorways? Dumber than a sack
     full of really, REALLY dumb things?

War doesn't look up, he just sends his right fist into Pestilence's face, knocking him across the room.

                         WAR

          I win.

Susan and Robin watch with a fork full of food halfway to their mouths.

EXT. BUS STOP - DAY

Susan looks down the street. The brothers stand behind them.

                              SUSAN

          There it is, Robin, let's go.

                              ROBIN

          Can't I hang out with them today, Mommy.

                              SUSAN

          No. Let's go... you guys have fun, see
          you tonight.

Robin hands a piece of paper to Pestilence, unseen by Susan. Pestilence winks at her.

                              ROBIN

          School it is, sorry guys.

                              WAR

          I never want to visit this placed called
          school.

                            PESTILENCE

          Oh I don't think you need to worry about
          that.

Susan and Robin just get on the bus, the doors close.

EXT. CITY STREET - DAY

City bus doors open, Robin gets out, War, Famine and Pestilence are waiting for her.

                              ROBIN

          You guys ready for some fun?

                             FAMINE

          Where are we going.

Robin turns around, points finger in the air.

                              ROBIN

            To the mall!

War is the only one who seems enthused.

                              WAR

          YES! We get to maul!

Robin coughs a bit, then walks down the street, they follow.

The bus drives away. Replacing it a few seconds later is a police squad car. It skids to a halt in front of a building, two COPS get out and rush to the entrance.

                    COP 1

          Cover me.

He rushes into the building. Cop 2 turns to look around the street. It is Death, no emotion, he turns and follows the other cop into the building.

                    DEATH

          I've got you, partner.

INT. VIDEO GAME ARCADE - DAY

On screen of Cop Shooting Crime Game. Nine Police and criminals run across the screen. A shot takes out a cop. Eight more quick shots drop the rest of the characters.

Game Over flashes on-screen.

A teenage boy stands next to Robin and War and watches, shakes his head.

                    TEEN

          Dude, that game totally pwn3d you.

War growls and slams his fist on the console, re-holsters the plastic gun.

                    WAR

          Games make head hurt.

                    ROBIN

          I keep telling you, you only shoot the
          bad guys.

                    WAR

          How can you tell the difference? They all
          have weapons.

                    TEEN

          Check this out, I'll show you how to
          beat this game.

The teen starts the game up, begins blasting away at the screen. War watches on with respect.

                         WAR

          You are a magnificent warrior.

                        TEEN

          Ain't no thang.

INT. MALL COOKING STORE DAY

Pestilence and Famine browse the gadgets.

                       FAMINE

          It's just like he described it on that
          show. Look!

He holds up an egg-separator.

                       FAMINE

          The yolk stays in the middle and the
          white flows out the edges. Genius.

                     PESTILENCE

          Wow, and look at the material it is made
          of. No germs can grow, it stays clean.

Three PUNKY BOYS and their GIRLFRIENDS wander by the
window and look in on them. They laugh and point.

                      PUNK 1

          Look at the fun boys picking out wedding
          presents.

                    GIRLFRIEND

          What is that, some kind of IUD?

                       FAMINE

          It's for our apartment. We're making
          quiche.

Pestilence looks at the skaters, looks at Famine.

                     PESTILENCE

          Oh.... no, I um... I don't know him.

Famine looks to Pestilence, confused.

                       FAMINE

          Wow. WOW.

The skaters slurp their slushies and walk away.

                      PUNK 2

          Losers.

                    FAMINE

          Ooh! A lemon zester!

INT. MALL MEN'S STORE - DAY

Pestilence browses through the suits on the rack. A
WOMAN in a sharp business suit comes up to him.

                    WOMAN

          May I help you find something, sir?

                    PESTILENCE

          Oh, no, I was just... looking.

                    WOMAN

          That is a great choice for you, it's
          Italian, vintage lines, hand made. What
          are you a 36 regular?

                    PESTILENCE

          I'm regular?

                    WOMAN

          Try it on.

                    PESTILENCE

          Oh no, I couldn't.. I... I...

She holds the sleeve out for him to feel.

                    WOMAN

          Feel that.

Pestilence does.

                    PESTILENCE

          ooooh... gimmee

INT. ARCADE - DAY

War has a CROWD of teenage boys around him, all
cheering him on as he plays a karate game. Robin is
there as well.

                    TEEN

          Dude, you are gonna beat this game too!
          You're awesome.

War works the joy stick and buttons, Robin gets very
animated, scary almost

                    ROBIN

          Kick his ass, kick his ASS!

The on-screen enemy goes down. The boys cheer. War
throws up his fists in triumph, the boys high five and
knock-knuckles.

Robin pumps her arm in victory.

                    ROBIN

          Yeah, baby.

                    TEEN

          You are so my hero, dog. I want to be
          like you when I grow up. Do you have a
          game system at home?

                    WAR

          You can do this in your lair?

INT. MALL - DAY

The brothers and Robin eat ice cream, giant cookies
and pretzels as walk past a JEWELRY STORE and sit on a
bench next to it.

                    FAMINE

          Oh, now I see why you eat this stuff.

                    WAR

          How do we get the things in Mall? Do we
          defeat the Leader of this Mall?

                    ROBIN

          No, that would get you thrown in jail.
          You have to pay for it with money.

                    WAR

          Where do we get money? Do we conquer the
          Lord of Money?

                    ROBIN

          You don't have to vanquish anyone, you
          need to get a job, like Mom has... or
          maybe sell something.

Pestilence watches people buying jewelry in the store.

He looks down at his jacket, and the big bug broach
pinned on it. He raises an eyebrow.

EXT. MALL PARKING LOT - DAY

Famine and Pestilence pile into a cab. War, loaded down with packages, stuffs the trunk full, then gets in the front seat.

The cab drives off.

EXT. SIDEWALK CAFE - DAY

Susan is on break, sits at a table staring off into space, she almost doesn't see

A MAN in a business suit briskly walks by, bumping her table; her purse drops and spills on the sidewalk.

The man who bumped her kneels to help her pick up her things. It is Death.

Susan doesn't look. She scoops almost everything into her bag and stands. Death stands, hands Susan her hairbrush.

                    DEATH
          I'm sorry, didn't see you there.

                    SUSAN
          That's okay, I wasn't paying attention.

                    DEATH
          Sure you're alright?

Susan nods, takes the brush, looks at Death.

                    SUSAN
          Do I know you? You look familiar. But I
          guess we'd remember meeting before, huh?

                    DEATH
          I know I would remember. Have a good
          day, sorry about that.

INT. SUSAN'S APARTMENT - NIGHT

War sits on the couch playing a Mortal Combat type of game on the TV on his new Video Game system - the mangled box lies nearby.

Famine sits at the table trying to figure out a pasta machine.

Pestilence, wearing a really nice suit, and Robin set up a large terrarium in the corner. Roaches, tarantulas and other bugs and lizards scurry around in it. Rubber chew toys lay on the table. Robin coughs as she eats a candy bar.

The door opens, Susan enters.

> SUSAN
>
> What is all this?

> FAMINE
>
> We went out to the big place with the stuff.

> SUSAN
>
> The mall?

She spots Robin helping Pestilence.

> SUSAN
>
> Robin, you skipped school and went to the mall?

No answer.

> SUSAN
>
> Get to your room right now young lady.

Robin coughs and shivers a bit.

> SUSAN
>
> We can not afford all this.

> PESTILENCE
>
> It's okay, we sold something.

Susan starts to get a little upset.

> ROBIN
>
> I just wanted to...

> SUSAN
>
> Go.

> ROBIN
>
> Can I get something to eat first?

> SUSAN
>
> NOW!

The brothers watch quietly, stopping whatever it is they are doing. Robin coughs, stops past Famine, grabbing a hunk of dough from his machine.

ROBIN

(back at Susan)

I hate you.

Silence.

PESTILENCE

Sorry, we just wanted to spend time with
her.

SUSAN

Yeah, well, there's plenty I want to do,
but I have to work for a living. I don't
have the luxury of playing with bugs.

War starts to get up and say something. Susan stops him
dead.

SUSAN

Not one word from you Poindexter. Just
shut it. Got me? And I do not like video
games in my house.

War sits back down pouting. Susan sighs and looks
around the room.

FAMINE

Dinner will be ready in...

SUSAN

I don't mean to be rude, but enough of
the fancy, unpronounceable medallions
of blah blah on toast points. Can't we
just have chicken or something? How long
are you guys going to be here? Don't you
have a circus to do?

Susan blows past the table on her way to her room.

INT. SUSAN'S APARTMENT - NIGHT

War sits and plays a video game. Famine reads from a
cookbook as he cuts pastry dough in the kitchen.

Pestilence walks in from the other room.

PESTILENCE

Brothers, we need to talk.

Nothing from the other two.

                         PESTILENCE

          Brothers? Hello?

                            WAR

          Can't talk. Destroying Temple of Ragnar.

                          FAMINE

          Malsouka. Baklava.

                         PESTILENCE

          What?

                          FAMINE

          Hello... phyllo pastry?

                         PESTILENCE

          She's sleeping... just had a bad day;
          but what she said is true.

                          FAMINE

          What?

                         PESTILENCE

          We have become complacent. Soft. We are
          forgetting our skills.

                          FAMINE

          Nonsense.

                            WAR

          Liar words.

Pestilence picks up a doily covered tray from next to
Famine - it has a nicely arranged assortment of petit
fours. Famine smiles sheepishly.

A techno voice comes from the TV

                        TECHNO VOICE

          You have found the Fluffy-Puff. You get
          three rainbows!

                         PESTILENCE

          We are forgetting why we are here.

                            WAR

          Dude, she said we could stay here. Duh.

Pestilence picks up a squeaky TOY from his terrarium
stand, squeaks it and waves it for War.

                    PESTILENCE

        Over here, boy... over here, pay atten-
        tion - focus that tiny little brain.

He drops the toy.

                    PESTILENCE

        I mean why we are HERE, in this realm.
        We need to get back to it, and we need
        to get back to where we belong.

                     FAMINE

        But there is so much more to do here.

                    PESTILENCE

        We're right back where we started.
        Worse.

Pestilence yanks the controller out of War's hands.

                      WAR

        Hey! I only need two more and I can
        unlock the heart of the Enchanted Pixie.

                    PESTILENCE

        You waste your talents, brothers, on
        things like pudding and...

                     FAMINE

        Pudding? That's creme brulee; and if you
        don't heat the sugar just right...

                    PESTILENCE

        You're not listening!

Pestilence waves his arms about. Behind him on the
table, the roach mimics him, waving it's legs about.
War and Famine see, but Pestilence does not.

                    PESTILENCE

        If we got The Call today, we wouldn't be
        able to do it.

                      WAR

        The Call has totally Pwn3d you, why
        don't you chill?

                     FAMINE

        Yeah, I mean, we don't even have the
        stupid book, remember?

> PESTILENCE

>> Then why aren't we looking for it?
>> (beat) Do you remember why we came here?
>> Doesn't it bother you that our brother
>> is still out doing what he does; while
>> we now do less with our skills than we
>> did before? He is winning again.

There is a heavy silence. A clock can be heard
ticking. Pestilence looks from War to Famine. Famine
puts down his wire whisk. War seethes.

> WAR

>> When I get my hands on the person that
>> took The Book, I'm gonna totally go
>> Apocalypse on their ass.

INT. APARTMENT HALLWAY - SAME TIME

Robin watches the brothers argue, one hand behind her
back clutches

The Book.

INT. ROBIN'S ROOM - DAY

Susan shakes Robin in bed, under the blankets

> SUSAN

>> Robin? Sweetie, you're going to be late
>> for school.

Robin doesn't move at first; then she moves her head a
little.

> ROBIN

>> (weakly)

>> I'm really tired mommy.

> SUSAN

>> Honey, I have to get to work. Are you
>> just faking so you can...?

She touches Robin's forehead, a look of concern crosses
Susan's face.

INT. KITCHEN - FOLLOWING

The brothers sit at the table eating breakfast. Susan
enters.

> SUSAN

>> Guys, we need to do something.

                    WAR

     I'm eating, does that count?

                    SUSAN

     Robin's sick, I have to stay home with
     her. But I can't afford to miss work.
     I'll get fired. If I get fired, we can't
     afford to live here, if we get evicted,
     you guys are evicted. If you guys are
     evicted...

Pestilence holds up a hand.

                 PESTILENCE

     We get the point. What can we do?

                    SUSAN

     I need to have my shift covered.

                    FAMINE

     So cover her shift; what do you need,
     some kind of tarp or blanket?

                    SUSAN

     No, not that kind of covering. Someone
     has to do my job.

War talks with his mouth full of food, spitting as he
speaks.

                    WAR

     Ha, what you want from us?

Susan stares at the three.

EXT. SIDEWALK CAFE - DAY

Pestilence takes an order from a COUPLE at a table.

                 PESTILENCE

     Sorry, could you repeat that again it
     makes no sense.

The man gets snippy.

                    MAN

     Are you deaf, or just stupid? I'm having
     the bagel and lox, large OJ no pulp; she
     will have the poached eggs with salsa,
     bran toast and a caramel machiado frappe
     with nutmeg shavings.

Pestilence just stares blankly.

War busses tables, noisily banging into people and tables as he goes.

                              WOMAN

          Watch it you clumsy oaf.

                              MAN

          What the hell, Dumbass? You spilled my
          chai.

War turns and snarls

                              WAR

          I'll cut off your head and suck your guts
          out through the hole where your head
          used to be.

                              MAN

          Wha... what did you say?

War gets a look from Pestilence across the room to take it easy.

                              WAR

          I said... pardon me; let me get you a
          fresh cup...

He turns away, pushing his cart.

                              WAR

          ... a fresh cup of stab you in the face,
          maggot butt.

INT. CAFE KITCHEN - DAY

Famine helps the kitchen staff prepare meals, he tastes some food from a tray that an assistant carries.

                              FAMINE

          What did you do with the sauce? It
          tastes bland. Take it back.

The assistant hurries away. Famine turns to the big stainless steal GRIDDLE where many orders are cooked at the same time: eggs next to ham next to hash browns next to steak next to pancakes.

                              FAMINE

          By all that is holy - NOOOOO!

Pestilence sticks an order on the order wheel, spins it back.

                    PESTILENCE

          Bunch of food that makes no sense, hold
          the appetite.

In the background, a patron holds up a fork to War as he walks past.

                    PATRON

          Could I get a clean fork please?

War head-butts him and keeps walking. The man SLUMPS into his plate.

                    WAR

          Fork you.

                    PESTILENCE

          This is going well, dontyouthink?

INT. HOSPITAL COMMISSARY - DAY

Tom sits at a table eating lunch and reading a paper. Another doctor comes up to him.

                    DOCTOR

          Hey Tom, you got a phone call at the
          desk.

                    TOM

          Who is it?

                    DOCTOR

          Said it's your neighbor.

Tom drops his paper and hurries out of the room.

EXT. CAFE - DAY

Pestilence is off to the side on the house phone. He tries to cover one ear so he can hear above the din.

                    PESTILENCE

          What? You are where? Hang on, Susan I
          can't hear. Hello; hello?

He tries to adjust, patrons wave at him.

                    MALE PATRON

          Hey buddy, where the hell are my eggs?

                    FEMALE PATRON

        Waiter, can I change my order?

Pestilence ignores them, War wanders near.

                         WAR

        Who talks at you?

                      PESTILENCE

        It's Susan, but I can't hear.

                    MALE PATRON 2

        Hey dipshit, can you clean this table so
        we can order already?

                   FEMALE PATRON 2

        When you two are done chatting to your
        "homies," can we get some service?

Pestilence hangs up, agitated.

                      PESTILENCE

        Go get Famine; something's wrong.

INT. HOSPITAL ROOM - NIGHT

Robin lays in bed, IV plugged into her arm. Susan sits
nearby in a chair flipping through a book "Riding to the
Apocalypse." Robin makes a sound, Susan looks up.

The door opens, Susan turns to see an ORDERLY enter.

                       ORDERLY

        Just here to check her vitals. Only take
        a minute.

When the orderly gets closer and reads the chart, it is
Death, dressed in scrubs.

                        DEATH

        Everything looks okay here. How are you
        doing?

                        SUSAN

        Okay.

Death looks at the book cover. He smiles.

                        DEATH

        Interesting book.

                         SUSAN

     This? Oh, it's actually hers.

                         DEATH

     Pretty heavy for such a little girl.

                         SUSAN

     I guess. She said it's full of trite
     postulation and zealous chatter about
     religious righteousness. They really
     aren't that way at all.

Death grins, looks Susan over.

                         DEATH

     Who isn't?

                         SUSAN

     The Four Horsemen. Well, three of them
     anyway. She's convinced they're living
     in our apartment. We haven't met Death,
     but his brothers think he's a pompous
     control freak with a need for constant
     attention.

                         DEATH

     You know them?

Death grabs Susan's arm.

                         DEATH

     Where are they? Tell me.

                         SUSAN

     Ouch, you're hurting my arm.

                         DEATH

     It won't kill you. Tell me where they
     are.

                         SUSAN

     What is your problem?

The door opens again and Tom enters; he sees the scene.

                         TOM

     What are you doing?

The orderly is now just some orderly, and he looks
confused. He tries to stammer an answer. Tom calls out
into the hall.

                         TOM

          Nurse! Get security up here right now.

EXT. CAFE - DAY

Famine has joined Pestilence and War by the phone.
Almost everyone is complaining at the tables. Maureen
walks up to them, shaking her head.

                       MAUREEN

          What the hell guys? There are tables
          that need taking care of, food is burn-
          ing on the grill, and you guys got your
          own little chat room going here?

                       FAMINE

          It's... it's...

                       MAUREEN

          It's time to get your sorry asses back
          to work, and I mean NOW.

                      PESTILENCE

          Maureen...

                       MAUREEN

          You can call me Boss.

                      PESTILENCE

          Boss, we need to go home real quick,
          there's something wrong there.

                       MAUREEN

          There's something worse going on here,
          you're fired.

                         WAR

          At least she didn't take our job away.
          Fire not so bad.

                       MAUREEN

          No, Dickbag, Me take job away. Me take
          all of your jobs away; including that
          sorry excuse for a waitress you call
          your friend. Now get out.

Maureen points out toward the street. Patrons complain
angrily as the three shuffle out of the patio and onto
the sidewalk.

                    MALE PATRON 2

        Hey, Mo, shake a leg, babe, I gotta get
        to work.

                    MALE PATRON 3

        Who the hell is in charge here? Can I
        get a freakin' chicken sandwich before
        the end of the world comes?

INT. ROBIN'S HOSPITAL ROOM - DAY

Robin sits in bed, propped up with pillows. Tom sits on
the edge of the bed, holding Robin's hand. Susan stands
nearby.

                    TOM

        Sorry, we've run every test we could
        here. We have no idea what it is. It
        seems like a flu bug, but it also acts
        like malnutrition. And then her blood
        pressure... it's elevated abnormally. It
        doesn't make any sense.

Susan and Robin eye each other. Tom sees this.

                    TOM

        Is there something you're not telling
        me?

Robin looks at Tom, she has guilt written all over her
face.

                    TOM

        It's okay, Robin; tell me.

INT. SUSAN'S APARTMENT - DAY

The three charge into the apartment, see no one is
there.

                    PESTILENCE

        Robin? Susan?

They check Susan's room, see the sheets messed up on
the bed. Famine goes to check Robins room.

                    FAMINE

        She's gone too.

                    WAR

        "Ooh, can't put anything over on you."
        Ha, how's that feel now? BURN!

                         PESTILENCE

          Not now, brother, something is wrong
          here, we need to...

He stops and his gaze is stuck on something on the floor
next to Susan's bed, he walks over and bends to pick it
up.

                            WAR

          Don't like my biting comeback, do you?
          Eat that you whack little dweeb.

Famine comes back in

                          FAMINE

          There's no note or anything. Where could
          they have gone?

Famine looks at Pestilence. War stops and looks at
Pestilence, he is holding The Book.

INT. ROBIN'S HOSPITAL ROOM - NIGHT

Tom crouches next to Robin, the machines nearby hum and
buzz intermittently.

                            TOM

          So you kept their book to keep them
          from leaving. It's just a book, they'll
          understand

                           ROBIN

          No, it isn't just a book, they're
          going to be very angry. They won't be
          my friends anymore.

                            TOM

          I'll talk to them for you, it'll be
          okay. Luckily, keeping someone's book
          from them doesn't exactly cause death.

Susan's eyes grow wide. She looks to her daughter's
chart hanging at the foot of the bed. The top sheet is
ripped right beneath where it says "Name: Spring, Robin
address:"

EXT. CITY STREET - NIGHT

War, Famine and Pestilence walk down the street. War
has the book in his hand, flailing it angrily about.

                    WAR

     She lies. Pagey thing not lost at all.
     Stuck with stupid things. Angry-making!

                 PESTILENCE

     Wow. Those were all real words, and yet
     he still doesn't make sense.

                  FAMINE

     There must be a good reason why she
     didn't tell us, War; maybe she didn't
     know what it was.

War motions toward Pestilence.

                    WAR

     Flappy mouth babbles about it every day.
     She meant to stop us. Destroy us.

                 PESTILENCE

     Right War; the little girl wanted to
     destroy three grown icons of total
     destruction. Get real.

                    WAR

     You real, I'm unreal.

                 PESTILENCE

     I won't even touch that one. Just give
     me The Book War.

                    WAR

     Take it from me, Bugs, just try...

Pestilence snatches it from War's hands with ease.

                 PESTILENCE

     Like taking candy from a big, loud guy
     with bad breath.

                    WAR

     Rrrrargh! Give it back, you lost it
     first.

                  FAMINE

     Actually, War, he's the one who stole it
     first, remember. You grabbed an almanac.

War snarls and grabs for his axe, but ends up only
pulling his T-shirt off.

                         PESTILENCE
          (deadpan)
          Look out Famine, he's got a cotton
          blend!

War jumps on Pestilence. Dark CLOUDS start to roil in
the sky.

                            WAR

          I want fair!

War pummels Pestilence mercilessly. Famine jumps on
War's back

                          FAMINE

          War, stop it, it isn't his fault.

War grabs Famine and throws him against a building,
smashing a huge HOLE in the wall. He turns back to
Pestilence, eyes red.

                            WAR

          You're the fly, and I am the... the...

Pestilence rolls his eyes

                         PESTILENCE

          Fly... swatter, maybe?

War leaps at him, but before he connects, Pestilence
dissipates into a cloud of gnats. War lands where
Pestilence was - right on top of The Book.

                            WAR

          Ha!

He starts to flip through the book.

Famine comes staggering out of the building, a two-by-
four protruding from his chest. He looks down, his body
becomes emaciated, the stud falls through his ribs and
drops to the ground. He resumes his normal shape again.

                          FAMINE

          Hey... guys...

INT. HOSPITAL LOBBY - DAY

Tom talks with a PATROLMAN by the front doors. Susan
stares out the window.

                    TOM

     I don't know, I've never seen this
     particular orderly before. Robin seems
     to think he knows the men staying with
     her mother.

                  OFFICER

     Do you think she could describe him for
     me?

                    TOM

     Sure, Susan?

They look to where Susan was standing - she's gone.

                    TOM

     Susan!

EXT. STREET - DAY

The sky is getting very DARK. LIGHTENING flashes in the
distance.

Pestilence reforms near Famine, they look at each
other.

                 PESTILENCE

     Did you see that? We're getting it back.
     War...

War looks up from the book, laughing, looking very evil
indeed.

                    WAR

     Ha ha ha - I know how to do it. I know
     how to summon the Steeds of the Apoc-
     alypse now. They wouldn't let us ride
     them until The Call -

                  FAMINE

     Don't do it War.

                 PESTILENCE

     Hopefully it will be a long, drawn-out
     ceremony, and we can keep him from...

War puts his FINGERS to his mouth and blows a long
sharp WHISTLE.

There is a thundering of hooves, and around the corner
the three steeds hurtle, manes flying.

PESTILENCE

That was kinda anti-climactic.

The horses stop next to War. A fourth horse storms up from the other direction and stops near as well.

WAR

Awesome, I get a Bonus Horse!

PESTILENCE

That's Death's, you synaptic midget.

People start to gather around the brothers, some are on their cell phones. People point and chatter.

PESTILENCE

War, we need to get off the street before
we attract attention.

WAR

I don't mind being attractive.

War starts to pull weapons off his steed, he throws on extra armor and robes from his saddle.

FAMINE

You know, if you'd trim your beard, you
have a real strong jawline...

A cab pulls up, Susan jumps out.

SUSAN

Okay, who are you guys... really.

FAMINE

Susan. Why did you keep The Book from
us?

SUSAN

Robin got it from a boy at school. She
didn't know... she told me what was in
it. Is it true?

FAMINE

Where is she?

SUSAN

She's very sick, she's in the hospital,
she getting worse by the hour.

PESTILENCE

What's the matter?

Susan hesitates. She looks to Famine

SUSAN

She has malnutrition...

She looks to Pestilence

SUSAN

...and some kind of bug they can't figure
out...

She looks to War

SUSAN

...and she was swearing like a sailor
and yelling at the doctors.

Pestilence looks down at the ground, Famine's jaw hangs
open. War smiles.

PESTILENCE

I'm sorry, you must think we're awful.

SUSAN

I know you're not like it says in there.
Those are just stories. I know you guys,
you're not bad.

Death steps out of the crowd.

DEATH

No, Susan, they aren't bad. But they are
what they are. Just as I am.

The three brothers look at Death. War runs over, whips
out a huge SWORD.

WAR

You lose this time, brother, I'm in
charge now. And now is The Time.

DEATH

No, brother, it is not. But when it is,
we will ride together.

A police cruiser pulls up, Tom jumps out and runs to
Susan.

                         TOM

          What's going on?

                        SUSAN

          It's all my fault. Robin's going to die.
          We're all going to die.

Tom pushes Susan toward the cruiser. The Patrolman
takes her to the safety of the car.

Tom charges over to War.

                         TOM

          What the hell are you doing, Poindexter
          You're scaring the only friend you have
          in this city.

War shoves Tom back toward the car with one hand. Tom
falls to the ground after hitting the hood of the car.

                         WAR

          I am War. W... W...

He can't spell it, why try

                         WAR

          I am War!

Patrolman pulls Tom into the car, then speeds off. Death
confronts War, Famine and Pestilence stand behind War.

                        DEATH

          What are you doing?

                         WAR

          Just getting fairness for me.

                        DEATH

          You have no idea what you are doing,
          War. There are protocols and processes
          that you must obey. You can't just
          decide to head out on your own. You
          could cause catastrophic events to ensue
          if you continue to...

From War's POV: Everything is muted, slow motion,
almost no sound. He sees Death, here's nonsensical
babbling. The crowd that is gathering sneers and points
at him.

He sees the punks from the mall, the Bikers from the

alley; patrons of the cafe. They all point and sneer, laugh, or yell at him.

He looks back at Death still babbling away. The scene takes on a pinkish hue.

Back to scene.

                    PUNK BOY

        Damn, he's bitch-slapping you.

                   GIRLFRIEND

        For a big guy, he sure is submissive.

People laugh and make faces. War grits his teeth. Pestilence sees the look on War's face.

                   PESTILENCE

        This is going to suck.

                    FAMINE

        At least they're not making fun of us.

A gang member gestures to Famine

                  GANG MEMBER

        Hey, lard-ass, why don't you change your
        baby's diaper; he looks like he went
        number 2.

POV from War: the scene is taking on a redder hue. Death is gesturing, the faces in the crowd become distorted and grotesque. The muted noise gets louder. He covers his ears.

Back to scene.

War grabs Death, lifts him high over his head and throws him into the side of a building.

The crowd stops dead.

                      WAR

        Rrrraaagh!

He swings the great sword, demolishes the closest vehicle to him - the crowd starts to disperse rapidly.

                   PESTILENCE

        Usually he uses the short form of
        "Rraagh," he must really be angry.

Crusher grabs a pipe from the ground and comes up behind War, he's poised to whack.

                        FAMINE

          I wouldn't do that.

Whack. The pipe crashes down on War's head, taking the
shape of the outline of his cranium.

War turns, grabs Crusher and tosses him through a
storefront window.

War stands facing Famine and Pestilence, his eyes red
with anger. He breathes like a racehorse after three
trips around the track.

                      PESTILENCE

          That's a new look for you, brother, why
          don't you...

GUNFIRE. Bullets rip into War and tear his armor.

Two police Cruisers are at the scene. The cops fire at
will.

                        FAMINE

          Hey - that's our brother.

Famine takes a step toward the cops, they fire at him,
he flails about trying to ward off the bullets.

Three more cruisers pull up to the scene, cops all over
the place, shot guns, small arms.

                      PESTILENCE

          All we need now is a big, senseless
          explosion.

War thrusts his sword into the pavement, a huge fissure
opens. There is a sound of ripping metal, and then
natural gas sprays out in a white fog.

War whips out a heavy blade from his belt, and strikes
the blade against the embedded sword.

Spark

BOOM.

                      PESTILENCE

          And there it is.

                        FAMINE

          How come he knows all the cool tricks?

War whirls on the cops, grabs an axe from his steed,
nasty looking heavy bladed knife in the other hand. He

trashes another car. His body is aflame, but he barely notices.

The cops unload on War, the shots jerk War around like a shooting gallery target.

PESTILENCE

That's quite enough of that.

He gestures toward the police, LOCUSTS stream from thin air and swarm around the cars.

An army of RATS and MICE exits a building and flows like a furry river, scattering cops and bystanders alike.

All manner of BUGS and nasty looking critters pour from beneath Pestilence's robes and scatter toward the city.

A tough COP makes his may toward Pestilence, aims his shotgun, but before he can pull the trigger, Famine waves at him and he withers to an emaciated form, too weak to hold the weapon - the gun drops.

War blows a whistle, the steeds charge to their sides, nostril flaring and snorting steam, eyes red and flickering, hooves cracking the pavement where they trample.

War swings into the saddle and brandishes his axe. He has smoke streaming from all over his body, his hair is aflame. His voice is deep, frightening.

WAR

Follow me, brothers.

He gallops off, sheering street lamps and signs, mowing down trees, trashing vehicles as he goes. Pandemonium wakes in his path.

Pestilence mounts his horse, he sees Famine's horse charge up to Famine, it's eyes a little weirder that other two, his nostrils blow smoke around in dizzying swirls.

PESTILENCE

He DOES have the Crazy Eye...

Famine mounts, he and Pestilence knock-knuckles, and charge after War.

FAMINE

I want flaming hair. How come he gets flaming hair?

INT. ROBIN'S HOSPITAL ROOM - NIGHT

Susan looks out the window and sees heavy smoke rising a few blocks away. Robin lies still in bed.

Tom enters from the hallway, he has a sense of urgency about him, yet tries to remain calm.

> TOM
>
> Susan, we're going to need to move your daughter, and you. There's a fire or something, nothing big, but it's moving toward us. I've got and ambulance downstairs.

> SUSAN
>
> It won't matter.

The lights in the room flicker and come back on. Smoke starts to waft past the window. Tom notices.

> TOM
>
> That's impossible, it can't be moving that fast...

Tom goes to the window and his eyes grow wide. Susan joins him.

In the street below, people on foot run hysterically away from the direction of the smoke. An army of cats, rats, raccoons, and other small animals flood toward them.

Swarms of biting and stinging insects whirl around the people. Some folks grow thin and weak and fall to the ground. Cars careen off other cars and buildings and crash.

Then they see

The Three Horsemen, charging full tilt behind everyone else. The horses seem to float on air, there eyes glowing, smoke streams from the figures, War's head crackles with flames, his axe cuts down everything in sight, signs, billboards, you name it.

> TOM
>
> What in God's name?

> SUSAN
>
> It's all my fault.

Tom goes to the bed, he starts to adjust the IV and other equipment for mobility.

                              TOM

          We need to get out of here now.

                              SUSAN

          She'll only get hurt if we go out there
          now. I need to talk to them.

                              TOM

          You will not talk to them, Susan, do
          you see what they are doing down there?
          Those are not your friends, they're,
          they're...

The sky starts to change colors - it takes on an eerie purple-greenish haze. Tiny FIREBALLS mixed with enormous HAILSTONES fall to Earth and explode on impact.

EXT. CITY STREETS - NIGHT

War spots the street gang on motorcycles, he bears down on them with gritted teeth.

                              CRUSHER

          Holy shit!

He rides away with his buddies; Pestilence throws a cloud of bugs at them. They are overwhelmed and fall, slapping and screaming, to the ground.

Famines rides past a crowd of pedestrians cowering behind an overturned truck, he wave his hand, the people start to wither, some hold their bellies. They stagger away.

War and his horse are airborne now, he ping-pongs between buildings, chopping huge chunks from everything.

The group of teenage boys from the arcade see him. They just stare horror-stricken.

                              TEEN

          Dude, what the hell? You're an asshole.

War heads for a WOMAN trying to push her baby CARRIAGE to safety, the teen darts toward her, just beating War.

Teen pushes the baby carriage and woman out of the way just as War reaches him. War snarls down at the prostrate boy.

> WAR
>
> Game Over.

INT. ROBIN'S HOSPITAL ROOM - NIGHT

Susan backs away from the window in shock. Tom takes her in his arms.

> TOM
>
> Now do you believe me? We need to get out of here. Susan... we need to move.

INT. STAIRWELL - NIGHT

Tom wheels Robin down the steps gingerly in a wheel chair. Susan carries a bag of supplies. The lights flicker, and dull thuds and noise can be heard through the walls

> ROBIN
>
> What's happening?

> TOM
>
> It's okay, there's a fire nearby, they are evacuating the building.

At a landing, a DOOR opens and an ORDERLY wearing SURGICAL GLOVES steps into the stairwell. It is Death, he takes the wheel chair handles.

> DEATH
>
> Let me help you with that doctor, you'll need to open the door at the bottom.

Death looks to Robin and says nothing, he shows no stress in his face.

> ROBIN
>
> I know you.

They make their way down the stairs.

EXT. STREETS - NIGHT

Complete pandemonium. Famine gestures at people who wither physically. Critters of all sorts, mostly rats, run in huge packs. Bugs swarm rotten food on sidewalk stands on store fronts.

But War is the worst. He hacks police and emergency vehicles into pieces. He tears up the road and buildings. He wades into crowds of fleeing people and throws them like frisbees.

Pestilence sees a WOMAN helping an old MAN to safety. He charges at them. The woman shields the old man with her body, and picks up piece of wood, brandishes it.

> WOMAN

Back off.

> PESTILENCE

Don't you know who we are?

> WOMAN

I don't care, I won't let you hurt this man.

Pestilence knits up his eyebrows and shakes his head. A WAVE of GIANT ROACHES heads for the woman and man. Pestilence jerks his head and the roaches head off in another direction.

He looks back at the woman's eyes, cocks his head, then charges off on his horse.

Famine rides up next to him.

> FAMINE

What are you doing brother? It is The Call; we have our orders.

> PESTILENCE

Something doesn't feel right. This isn't right.

> FAMINE

But War said...

> PESTILENCE

I've never known War to be right, brother, even when it came to highly personal things, such as "does he need to go to the bathroom," or "how many fingers am I holding up."

> FAMINE

But.... but if there was no Call, then...

                          PESTILENCE

          I'm afraid so.

Famine looks around at the destruction. Punks help
business people to safety, Homeless people gather
crying children into storefronts. People cringe in
alleys, staring about at the carnage, tears in their
eyes, hugging whomever is close.

Pestilence gestures about him, clouds of bugs
dissipate, rats stop in mid-charge, rear up and sniff
the air, then disappear into sewers and buildings.

Famine rears in his steed.

                           FAMINE

          Stop... No more.... No runny.

The steed ignores him, takes a snap at his hand on the
reins.

Famine snarls and yanks mightily on the reins, his
voice booms like a overloaded cannon.

                           FAMINE

          I said STOP, you shit-headed flea-bag.

The horse stops. It cringes as Famine dismounts. He
slaps it's head. Crazy Eye, snorts at him. Famine grabs
the harness and yanks.

                           FAMINE

          You want a matching one on the other
          side?

Crazy Eye lowers his head.

Famine walks past a fountain running red and muddy, the
water becomes clear and clean. People run to it and
drink and clean their faces.

EXT. STREET IN FRONT OF HOSPITAL - NIGHT

War is thrashing madly about. His axe has deep
scratches and notches in the blades. War's armor is
torn and covered in dirt and sweat - his is frightening
to see.

                            WAR

          That's what I'm talking about!!

Piles of cars and trucks encircle him, debris is strewn
all over the area, bodies litter the ground.

Pestilence and Famine ride to within a few yards of
him.

> PESTILENCE

Okay, get him to stop.

> FAMINE

Me? You get him to stop.

They pause a beat, then do the rock-paper-scissors
deal. Pestilence comes up short. He wanders closer to
War.

> PESTILENCE

Brother... have you got a minute?

War ignores him, he chops big pieces of stuff into
little pieces of stuff. Throws some at Pestilence.

> FAMINE

War, this isn't right.

> PESTILENCE

I don't know if we can stop him, and
even if we could, I wouldn't know how to
fix this.

War holds his arms out wide.

> WAR

This is what we've been missing. Feel
the power - nothing can stop us.

Around the corner an AMBULANCE careens at break neck
speed, it doesn't even slow down as it plows into War,
knocking him fifty feet into a wall.

The ambulance crashes into a pile of rubble. The
driver's door opens, Death steps out; Tom follows, as
does Susan.

> TOM

What are you doing. We need to get out
of here.

> DEATH

Enough.

War picks up and throws debris at the people running
around him. Throws at Death.

Death maneuvers around War walking slowly as he speaks.
He takes off one of his rubber gloves.

                    DEATH

        Look around you brother. Look what you
        have done

                    WAR

        What I was born to do. Like you,
        Brother.

                    DEATH

        Oh? Like me, born to kill?

                    WAR

        Yes.

                    DEATH

        But only I can kill. You destroy, you
        frighten, you make people fight.

                    WAR

        Then do your job - kill. We do ours.

Death steps over to a man lying on the ground under a
piece of a car. Death touches him with his ungloved
hand. The man drops dead.

                    DEATH

        Like this brother?

                    WAR

        Yes. That's the spirit.

Pestilence looks at War, then at Death, then at Tom and
Susan.

                    PESTILENCE

        Uh - oh.

                    FAMINE

        What?

                    PESTILENCE

        I think we messed up.

Death walks to another woman, puffing and leaning
against a building.

                          DEATH

          And this?

He touches her, she drops dead to the road.

                          SUSAN

          Stop it! Stop it! You're killing them.

                          DEATH

          No Susan, they are ready to die, it is
          The Call. I'm doing my job.

                          WAR

          Yes, we all are. You kill, I smash, he
          brings the bugs and he...

He motions to Pestilence and then to Famine.

                          WAR

          ...does stuff too.

War picks up a large piece of pipe from the ground, he
starts to smash things around him.

                          WAR

          Smashing, death, bugs... whatever he
          does...

Death touches another old man; who clutches at his
chest and then drops.

                          WAR

          Yes.

He smashes. Pestilence half-assedly sends a handful of
dragonflies from his hand.

Death touches another woman; a piano falls from above
and squashes her.

                          WAR

          Yes!

Death touches two people on the ground, a fissure opens
up and swallows them, flames shoot forth.

                          WAR

          YES!

Pestilence makes a face, he takes Famine under his arm.

PESTILENCE

You may not want to watch this.

Death smacks a bystander on the back; BABOONS leap from the rubble and drag the screaming man away.

Everyone looks at Death with "what the hell" faces.

PESTILENCE

You cheeky bastard... that was mine.

Death shrugs.

DEATH

The zoo got destroyed. Animals escaped.
I gotta use what there is.

He moves back toward the ambulance.

DEATH

Want me to keep going?

WAR

That's what we do, let's do it.

Death grabs Tom by the arm in his gloved hand.

SUSAN

No! Poindex... War, stop.

WAR

I don't care. Go go.

Death hesitates, he touches Tom's arm with his ungloved hand.

Tom drops to the ground.

SUSAN

Tom!

She runs to his side, shakes him.

SUSAN

Tom. Wake up. Don't die.

She starts to cry. Famine is already blubbering. Pestilence shakes his head.

PESTILENCE

War, stop. Enough already.

                    WAR

    Shut your funnel spider hole.

                 PESTILENCE

    War, I don't think you understand
    what...

                    WAR

    I don't need understanding, I need to
    smash.

                   DEATH

    And I need to kill.

Death grabs Susan by the arm with his gloved hand.

                   SUSAN

    No, no!(to Death) Why are you doing this
    to us?

Death looks at Susan with no emotion in his eyes, no
feeling.

                   DEATH

    I feel no anger toward you, and this is
    nothing personal, Susan.

The door to the ambulance opens slowly, Robin staggers
out, wearing her hospital gown. Groggy.

                   ROBIN

    Leave my mommy alone.

                   DEATH

    I can not. War won't let me.

Susan tries to wrestle free from Death's grasp.

                   ROBIN

    Mommy!

                 PESTILENCE

    War stop it now. Stop it! They've done
    nothing to us. She's our friend.

War stops smashing. He eyes Susan. Gnashes his teeth.
Starts to smash more, loses his drive.

                    WAR

    I don't care. I want fair for me.

Death shrugs. He reaches toward Susan with his ungloved hand.

Pestilence runs toward Death. Famine covers his face and turns away.

                    PESTILENCE

          No!

War just watches trying not care.

Robin rushes forward in a burst of strength.

Death's HAND is inches from Susan's shoulder.

Pestilence trips and falls, exploding into a cloud of bugs as he hits the ground.

Robin JAMS herself between Death and Susan. Death's hand rests on Robin's shoulder.

                    DEATH

          Now that I didn't see coming.

Robin drops to the ground. Susan screams.

                    SUSAN

          Baby, no... no.

She cries on her daughter's body, then jumps to her feet, furious at War.

                    SUSAN

          Look what you've done. I hate you.

She throws a rock at War. It bounces of his face. He raises his pipe length at her.

                    SUSAN

          I wish you were dead. I took you guys in
          when you had nothing, and this how you
          thank me? I hate you I hate you I hate
          you.

She throws all manner of rocks, metal, anything she can.

The pieces bounce off War, he drops the pipe, the anger drains from his face.

Susan is exhausted, she falls to her knees sobbing on the little body.

Death watches, he puts on his gloves.

Pestilence approaches Susan, she pulls away from him.

                    SUSAN

          Don't touch me. You're no better than he
          is. Just go away. Go away.

Pestilence looks back at War. War is near tears. He
looks back at Famine, who has tears streaming down his
face, over his jutting lower lip.

                    FAMINE

          Why War? What was so important about all
          this?

                    PESTILENCE

          I... we're sorry, Susan. I don't know
          what to...

He trails off. He looks to death

                    PESTILENCE

          What have we done?

                    DEATH

          What you have been trained to do, broth-
          er. There is no fault in you, or me.

                    PESTILENCE

          How can you be so...

                    DEATH

          Uncaring? Unfair?

                    WAR

          Fix it.

                    DEATH

          Me? "Fix it?"

EXT. STREET - DAY

In the small clearing amongst the destruction sits War
on a pile of debris. He holds his great axe in front of
him.

Pestilence and Famine hold the reins of the four
steeds, Death crouches near something SMALL moving on
the ground. It's a MOUSE, half covered by a brick.

Death takes The Book and scoots the brick off the mouse;
it scurries away under the debris.

The bodies from Death's grasp are covered in blankets
and coats, whatever is available.

Susan sits on the back of the ambulance, a blanket draped over her shoulders.

A semi-circle of people stand around staring at the Four Horsemen.

> DEATH
>
> I can not change what is written in the book, Brothers. You understand that?

Pestilence and Famine nod their heads solemnly. War just frowns looking at the body of Robin, Susan sitting behind.

> DEATH
>
> But if the book were not here, things might be different.

Pestilence and Famine look up at Death. War has a blank look on his face.

> PESTILENCE
>
> If The Book weren't here... War.

War looks to Pestilence, nothing going on in his head. Famine points at the book in Death's hand.

> FAMINE
>
> IF THE BOOK WERE NOT THERE.

> PESTILENCE
>
> Good grief, brother, use that squishy stuff between you ears for something other than filling space.

> WAR
>
> If... The Book...wasn't HERE.

A light goes on, he stands, grabs The Book from Death.

> WAR
>
> HA! If the book wasn't HERE.

War throws the book over a heap of debris.

> WAR
>
> I win. The Book is over THERE now!

War looks around the clearing. Nothing has changed. Pestilence rolls his eyes.

                    PESTILENCE

      It's not even really taking up THAT much
      space.

                      FAMINE

      That was pretty dense, even for you.

                      DEATH

      Would one of you please go get it before
      we all die of old age?

Famine scrambles over the heap.

EXT. BATTLE STREET - DAY

Death has the book again, War steps toward him.

                       WAR

        I need to throw if farther?

                    PESTILENCE

      Okay... even the book thinks you're
      stupid now.

                      DEATH

        Susan, take your daughter's hand.

Susan looks up slowly, slides down from the seat and
kneels next to Robin, taking her hand. She looks up at
Death and the other three, hope is in her eyes, she
smiles a little.

                      SUSAN

      I knew you couldn't be all bad.

                    PESTILENCE

      No, we're not bad. We just... are.

Death sets The Book on the ground. He raises the axe

                      SUSAN

      But, how will you know when it's time?

                      DEATH

      A new book is already being written.

Death swings down. The Book splits in half with a
deafening roar and flash of light.

Then all goes black.

EXT. CITY STREET - DAY

It's a sunny morning. Susan and Robin wait on the bus at a stop. Tom jogs up to them.

                    TOM

     You taking the 15? Mind if I ride with
     you?

Susan turns and smiles at Tom.

                    SUSAN

     Sure. Don't you work at night?

                    TOM

     Changed my shift. Nights were killing
     me.

The four brothers stand a few yards away. Famine, Pestilence and War sit atop their horses, who stamp at the ground. Death stands in front, he holds the reins to his steed.

Crazy Street Preacher can be heard.

                    PREACHER VO

     The end is near. Repent of your ways.

Robin turns in that direction - she sees the brothers. She looks at her mom, who is chatting away with Tom. She slips away and walks over to the brothers.

                    ROBIN

     I'll miss you guys.

                    DEATH

     Unfortunately we will always be here.

                    ROBIN

     See you at the End of the World, then?

                    PESTILENCE

     I can wait.

                    FAMINE

     I'm in no hurry.

                    WAR

     Waiting takes too long.

The other three give him dirty looks. He softens.

WAR

But I will do it.

FAMINE

We're taking back some things to keep us
busy.

He nods at the back of War's horse. Piles of video
games of all kinds are stacked and strapped to the
saddle, along with every type of game system. A wheeled
piece of ARTILLERY is tethered to his saddle.

Behind Pestilence's horse is a wheeled coat rack with a
few dozen suits hanging from it. He has the Terrarium
strapped to the back of the horse, and an espresso
machine.

Famine has stacks of cookbooks hanging from his horse.
He looks back at them, smiles. A frown jumps onto his
face.

FAMINE

The Book? Where's the Book? He pats
himself down.

ROBIN

I thought...

Famine produces a white book from under his robes. Gold
letters across the front read "The Joy of Cooking."

FAMINE

Whew, thought I'd lost it.

VOICE FROM BEHIND FAMINE'S HORSE

Can I see that?

Everyone turns to see Emeril Lagasse, hands bound and
sitting on a pony that is tethered to Famine's horse.

FAMINE

No.

Emeril pouts and slumps down in the saddle.

EMERIL

I just want to check...

FAMINE

I said no.

                    EMERIL

          What's it gonna hurt...

War leans back in his saddle

                      WAR

          He said No, Cooky Boy.

War maces Emeril square in the face. Emeril flails

                      WAR

          I love this stuff.

                    SUSAN

          Robin? Robin, where are you?

Susan and Tom look around the street, they spot Robin
standing ALONE by a lamp post.

                    SUSAN

          Honey, our bus is coming.

                    ROBIN

          I'll be right there, mom.

Robin pulls some change from her pocket, drops it in
a TIN CAN on the sidewalk next to a MAN in tattered
clothes; then she runs over to join her mother and Tom
as the BUS pulls up.

The man turns, it is Crazy Preacher.

                  PREACHER VO

          Bless you, child.

He holds up a BOOK he is reading. It is The Book. All
taped together with scraps of different kinds of tape:
duct, cellophane, painter's tape, masking.

He reads with wide eyes, moving his lips, flipping pages
quickly.

                   PREACHER

          Holy Shit...

His sign now reads "The end is really, REALLY near!"

FADE OUT

THE END